NONVIOLENCE

A CHRISTIAN INTERPRETATION

Nonviolence

A CHRISTIAN
INTERPRETATION

William Robert Miller

SCHOCKEN BOOKS · NEW YORK

First SCHOCKEN PAPERBACK *edition 1966*

Copyright © 1964 by
National Board of Young Men's Christian Associations

Library of Congress Catalog Card No. 66-14876

Manufactured in the United States of America

TO MY WIFE

EDITH LORRAINE MILLER

Contents

The Dynamics of Nonviolence

A Casebook of Nonviolence

Acknowledgments

This book and another, which is to follow it, had their nucleus in an article, "Notes on the Theory of Nonviolence," published in the October 1961 issue of *Gandhi Marg* (New Delhi). By that time the larger study embodied in the present book was well under way. I am first of all indebted to the publisher of this Gandhian quarterly, T. K. Mahadevan, and want to express my appreciation for his tolerance and generosity in giving space to my views, critical as they sometimes were of the orthodox Gandhian outlook.

I am also indebted to Richard B. Gregg, whose book *The Power of Nonviolence* has played such an important part in the United States, India and elsewhere. Although my own thinking has diverged from his, consultations and correspondence with him, especially in connection with the 1959 revision of his book, were extremely stimulating and fruitful. His book itself in its several editions was indispensable as a touchstone and point of departure.

During my years (1956-1962) as managing editor of *Fellowship* and of Fellowship Publications, I was saturated with reading and discussion of nonviolence. I must give thanks first of all to God for this rare opportunity, and secondly to the entire staff of the Fellowship of Reconciliation as well as to the editors of countless periodicals from all parts of the world which contributed immeasurably to my education during this period. I thank my former colleagues Brewster Kneen and the Rev. John C. Heidbrink for their comments and encouragement on portions of the manuscript in progress, and also Dr. John M. Swomley Jr., now professor of Christian social ethics at St. Paul's Theological Seminary in Kansas City. For my many talks with the Rev. Glenn E. Smiley, whose work as field secretary carried him into the heart of the nonviolent movement in the South, he deserves my gratitude; and the encouragement of the Rev. John Nevin Sayre of the International Fellowship of Reconciliation has consistently been a special blessing.

Space does not permit an elaborate accounting of the help given by many others who read the entire book or a single chapter, or simply were generous in answering a vital query. Among those who must be mentioned are Robert Brookins Gore of the Congress of Racial Equality, the Rev. Andrew J. Young of the Southern Christian Leadership Conference, Charles Jones of the Student Nonviolent Coordinating Committee, James E. Bristol of the American Friends Service Committee, Gene Sharp, Vincent Harding, Thomas Merton, Prof. A. J. P. Taylor of Cambridge University, Prof. Crane Brinton of Harvard, Prof. Roland H. Bainton of Yale Divinity School, Dr. Elemer Bako of the Library of Congress, Prof. Howard Zinn of Spelman College, Atlanta, Georgia, Prof. Nels F. S. Ferré of Andover Newton Theological School, and Prof. Magne Skodvin of the University of Oslo, Norway. It is hardly necessary to add that none of them can be saddled with blame for any defects the book may display, but in more than one instance their remarks supplemented what was inadequate or corrected what was inaccurate in the original manuscript.

Special thanks are due to Dr. John Oliver Nelson of Yale Divinity School for his long-time encouragement. He read the original draft version, almost wholly different from the final result. With characteristic generosity and Christian spirit, as chairman of Kirkridge, the Protestant retreat center near Bangor, Pennsylvania, he placed at my disposal during the summers of 1961 and 1962 the mountaintop lodge where a substantial segment of the writing was done. And finally, thanks to my wife, to whom this book is dedicated, for her love and long-suffering perseverence during those long stretches of time when the manuscript was her implacable rival.

WILLIAM ROBERT MILLER

Introduction

Nonviolence is an idea whose time has come. Since its dramatic advent in Mahatma Gandhi's campaigns for India's independence, which began in the 1920s, it has made its mark on the world. Though frequently seen in the struggle for racial justice in the United States in the 1960s, it has seldom been explored in any depth. Most of the studies that exist are imbedded in a context of pacifist propaganda or in the historical matrix of India and Gandhi's specific orientation.

The history of the idea of nonviolence as a religious or philosophical doctrine has been traced by some authors as far back as the Chhandogya Upanishad of ancient Hinduism, the Chinese Tao Te Ching (Sixth Century B.C.) and other ancient texts, not to mention the Bible and the fathers of the early Christian church. It has appeared in many forms, ranging from an exacting monastic discipline to a vague sort of advice, as in Plato, to overcome evil by good deeds. One implication, often erroneous, has been that this philosophy points to a search for quiet and repose. Certainly this bears no resemblance to the activities of such men as Gandhi or Martin Luther King. Nor, in most cases, have these counsels of gentleness served as a basis for movements of social change.

If we turn to the New Testament, we find a close identification between saintly purity and the practice of enduring attack without fighting back. Some individuals have gone so much farther in making what they consider nonviolence a way of life that they forbid killing poisonous insects. The majority of

Christians, on the other hand, have tampered with this principle until it has become little more than a caution against striking the first blow in all-out nuclear war. Our purpose is not to issue yet one more edition of the Sermon on the Mount with its hard counsels of perfection, nor to show that it does not mean what it says. Our aim is much more modest and limited: to show how contemporary man, without embracing nonviolence as a way of life, can nevertheless make effective use of it as a method of solving social problems. We shall make no sweeping claims for its efficacy. It is neither a miraculous cure-all nor a crackpot mirage. The choice it offers is not solely between saintliness and wallowing in evil. For those willing to take it seriously, there is a middle dimension and ample historical evidence to show that tangible results can be obtained —not only spiritual but down-to-earth results.

Much of the confusion about nonviolence arises from a tendency to trace its ancestry along an exclusively perfectionist route. One thinks almost automatically of Tolstoy, Thoreau, Francesco d'Assisi, the Friends, the Shakers, the German Baptists and Mennonites. These undoubtedly are important, but they represent only one side of the story. The other side is that of Christian protest and revolt, reflected in such figures as the radical priest, John Ball, who led the English peasants' rebellion; the men of the Boston Tea Party; the Chartists and many others. Often, in such men as Gerard Winstanley and Jan Hus, the two seemingly contradictory principles of nonresistance and revolt have been held together only to be wrenched apart by their followers, as with the two Hussites, Chelčický and Žižka, one a pacifist and the other a revolutionary general. What is relevant, however, is the recurrence of forms of protest which have mobilized masses of unarmed men. Seldom have they even thought about ruling out violence as a matter of principle, and in many cases they have gone on to armed insurrection or turned to conventional political means. Regardless of this they have also had an impact in a more or less nonviolent way. With due allowance for the riots and other disturbances that have punctuated it, the history of the labor movement is clearly in this tradition. Many of the actions led by Gandhi, King and other "apostles of nonviolence" more visibly reflect similarities to an industrial strike than to the traditional ways of religious nonresistance.

The fact is that nonviolence can be reduced neither to a moral philosophy nor a pragmatic method. It owes something to each and to the equilibrium that holds the two strands together. To an incalculable degree this blendedness has escaped the attention of the theorists. We owe much to the example of Gandhi, but it is noteworthy that in his writings he appears to take for granted much of the tactics and strategy adapted from a long tradition of protest and revolt and to place acute stress on his moral discoveries. As he saw it, practical nonviolence was an application of absolute moral truths in the realm of historical action. There is an element of cogency in such a view, but it has its pitfalls. Ultimately it makes the "one perfect act" a virtual substitute for social action. On the other side, however, the thrust of protest, uninformed of the possibilities of nonviolence, can have a destructive effect. How often a righteous cause has become perverted by a desperate resort to strong-arm tactics, rioting and terrorism! When it has worked effectively, both before, during and after the Gandhian era, nonviolence has proved to be an adaptation of the best features of both approaches.

Our intention is not merely to provide an ideological framework to make nonviolence palatable to the Christian mind, nor is it merely to find Christian equivalents for Hindu or other concepts such as those which figure in Gandhi's thinking. Least of all is it to proselytize for Christianity by giving a religious tone to secular ideas. Christianity, after all, is no occult wisdom. Both as a form of conduct and as a strategy of action, nonviolence is not only rooted in the history of the church—a striking fact in itself—but it stems from precisely those realities of human existence with which the Christian faith is vitally concerned. The man of good will who is not a Christian may be impatient with the theological dimension while still acting in accordance with an image of man and an ethic distilled from Christian doctrine. In any case it is not our purpose to promote the viewpoint of any particular sect. We have felt free to draw ecumenically from the thinking of Orthodox, Catholic, Protestant and Jewish writers, and to exclude nothing that is relevant.

If there is any narrow bias here, it is a bias of intent, of commitment to the Christian community of faith. Whatever this book may do for anyone else, we wish to demonstrate that contemporary Christians can find within their own tradition fully adequate resources for nonviolence. They need not, and in fact would be mistaken to, abandon their faith or their church—as Tolstoy, for example, argued—in order to use nonviolence. On the contrary, nonviolence is highly compatible with the church and can contribute to its renewal, making it more truly itself, while the church by its very nature and purpose has historically afforded the most congenial setting for nonviolence.

Although the reader may want to go on to further studies that would include the important legacy of Gandhi's campaigns in South Africa and India, we have chosen here to supplement rather than to rehash that legacy. There are surprisingly few studies of the many important nonviolent campaigns that have occurred outside the Gandhian orbit. Those that exist are often fragmentary or available only by burrowing through many books for scattered episodes, not all of which are reliable. Much of what is presented in the CASEBOOK section here is the product of new research, drawing upon hitherto untapped sources. Some of it simply makes available well-documented accounts that would otherwise be hard to find. Examples have been selected and treated for their instructive rather than their inspirational value. As much can be learned from representative failures as from successes, and we have attempted to assess these objectively to show both strengths and weaknesses, scope and limits. It is not just a matter of conjecture, it is a fact that "ordinary" Christians and others have been able to make non-violence relevant to their situation. The fact that Christian churches have played a part in these events without abandoning their historic traditions and without thereby becoming perfectionistic, universalistic, pacifist, Gandhian or Hindu, testifies to the undisclosed possibilities of Christian renewal that confront the church as a whole today. One need not be a Christian, however, to appreciate the fact that nonviolence is by no means limited to the special conditions of India or Alabama.

Similar considerations apply to our approach to theory. Insofar as it involves theology, it is a biblical one. We believe this is necessary to a full understanding. Aside from this, the discussion of organization, typology, and psychological and sociological dynamics is religiously neutral, equally compatible with Jewish, Christian or secular types of ethics. To the extent that there is a bias, it is again one of intent. The social structures we have in mind are those of a Western-style urban civilization rather than, say, of medieval serfs or preliterate primitives, and the psychological factors likewise. In short, without denying the essential unity of the human species or the range of application, we recognize the need for cultural adaptation and choose our orientation accordingly. The core of this book may have universal validity, but in its details it is addressed to characteristic Western conditions.

ordinary" Christians and others have been able to make nonviolence relevant to their situation. The fact that Christian
churches have played a part in these events without abandoning their historic traditions and without thereby becoming perfectionistic, universalist, pacifist, Gandhian or Hindu, testifies to the undisclosed possibilities of Christian renewal that
confront the church as a whole today. One need not be a
Christian, however, to appreciate the fact that nonviolence
is by no means limited to the special conditions of India or
Alabama.

Similar considerations apply to our approach to theory. Insofar as it involves theology, it is a biblical one. We believe
this is necessary to a full understanding. Aside from this, the
discussion of organization, typology, and psychological and
sociological dynamics is religiously neutral, equally compatible with Jewish, Christian or secular types of ethics. To the
extent that there is a bias, it is again one of intent. The social
structures we have in mind are those of a Western-style urban
civilization rather than, say, of medieval serfs or preliterate
primitives, and the psychological factors likewise. In short,
without denying the essential unity of the human species or the
range of application, we recognize the need for cultural adaptation and choose our orientation accordingly. The core of this
book may have universal validity, but in its details it is addressed to characteristic Western conditions.

The Dimensions
and Scope of Nonviolence

1

The Meaning of Violence and Nonviolence

What is nonviolence? Many of its critics and protagonists are readier to equate it with some other concept than to define it. Some equate it with love, others with cowardice. The word has been used interchangeably with simple inaction and with "direct action"; with "nonresistance" and with a resistance adorned with such adjectives as "bold" and "daring." It has been identified with "passive resistance" and set in opposition to "passive resistance."

The lack of clear and adequate definitions has not kept nonviolence from occurring and being recognizable in a general way. But if we are to understand how it works and what goes into it, we must have some idea of where it begins and ends, what its limitations and presuppositions are. To do this we shall find it useful to embark on a theoretical inquiry which will bring us into contact with a number of other concepts related to nonviolence but not identical with it. Like any exercise in theory concerning human relations and history, this takes us out of the actual and into the abstract, which is reality of a different order. If we were to search history for an exact model of theoretical nonviolence, we would be disappointed, for history does not work so neatly. It is infinitely more complex than even the most detailed theory could ever be.

At best our definitions can do no more than approximate the actualities they are designed to match—just as, for example, a theory of neurosis will inevitably differ from a psychiatrist's casebook. Yet the two are not unrelated. The actual cases provide the raw material from which the theory is constructed, and the theory in turn provides a framework on which the cases can be structured, organized and interpreted. When we come to examine historic episodes of nonviolence, we shall see how impossible it would be to make them fit our theory, but at the same time how valuable it is to have a theory as a guide to understanding these episodes. Theory does not get rid of ambiguity; it sheds light on it. Not full daylight, perhaps, but a torch without which we could only grope our way.

In the case of nonviolence, ideas are not lacking but they are often vague, imprecise and sentimentalized. A substantial part of our inquiry as we proceed involves simply a clarification of issues that are often confused. What do our central terms mean? What are they thought to mean but do not and cannot mean? The first step toward lucid discussion is to separate those ambiguities which are inherent from those imposed by faulty usage.

Hindu and Biblical Concepts

One area of confusion clusters around the words "love" and "nonviolence" and their relation to one another. To some extent the problem is one of translation and to some extent it is a problem arising from the dialog between Christian and Hindu ideas with their different emphases and contexts. The term "nonviolence" itself entered the English language as a translation of the Sanskrit "ahimsa," which Gandhi drew from the ancient texts of Hinduism to describe the pivotal principle of his philosophy. But as Pie Régamey has pointed out, in the French version of Gandhi's *From Yeravda Mandir,* we can translate *ahimsa* as *amour* (love). Lanza del Vasto identifies it with *charité* (charity—from *caritas,* the word for "love" in the Latin New Testament).[1] Gandhi himself wrote: *"Ahimsa* means love in the sense of St. Paul, and much more."[2]

Etymologically, however, the meaning of *ahimsa* is simple

[1] Reference notes appear at the end of each chapter.

enough: "nonharm" or "inoffensiveness." In the Upanishads, in the Yoga Sutra, in the Bhagavad Gita and in other sacred Hindu writings, as well as in the teachings of such recent Hindu sages as Vivekananda and Aurobindo, *ahimsa* is one of several duties or vows of discipline adhered to by anyone seeking saintly perfection. This is what the Mahabharata means when it calls *ahimsa* "the highest duty." But in none of the classic scriptures is it equated with love. In fact, the term has no positive content as such; it connotes only abstention. Although the religious philosophy of *karma yoga* has to do with good works, *ahimsa* figures in it as a purificatory vow, along with such others as celibacy, dietary restrictions and the like rather than as a way of doing good. The concept of love "in the sense of St. Paul" is not present at all.

But Gandhi at least believed that love was implicit in *ahimsa,* and professed to see profound similarities between the Bhagavad Gita and the Sermon on the Mount. In his reinterpretation of the Gita as "the gospel of selfless action" and in his blending of the Hindu concept of Brāhmān as impersonal cosmic truth with the biblical understanding of God as love, Gandhi achieved nothing less than a religious reformation within Hinduism. Thus the *ahimsa* which Gandhi identified with the love spoken of by Paul is no longer the unalloyed "nonharm" of the ancient or the orthodox Hinduism; it is already a Gandhian concept profoundly influenced by the New Testament.

In a later chapter we shall explore the meaning of love in greater depth. Here a basic definition will suffice. The English word "love," like its equivalent in most modern languages, encompasses a wide range of meanings. The Greek of the New Testament affords greater precision. In ordinary usage "love" may mean an emotion of affection, of carnal passion or of platonic affiliation. When we speak of "erotic" love, we are using one of several Greek words for "love"—*eros,* which is generally understood as having to do with sexuality but which in the New Testament means simply that kind of love which brings self-fulfillment. *Eros* may be expressed sexually or non-sexually. Its object may be a person or it may be the beauty of nature or of a work of art which we love and which thereby elevates us. There is also *philia*, the reciprocal, companionate form of love, as well as *philadelphia* (brotherliness) and *philanthropia* (humaneness or kindliness).

Overarching all of these kinds of love is *agapē*, signifying good *will* rather than good *feeling* toward a person, and carrying the connotation of *"showing* love by action." [3] When we speak of "agapaic" love it is this active, outgoing love that we have in mind, as did Paul. It is the ultimate love from which *eros* and the other kinds are all derived. *Agapē* is the love that "is God" and "is from God" (1 John 4:7-21)—freely given, active, affirming not on the basis of merit or attractiveness but encompassing all for whom God cares: not only self and friend but the stranger, the outsider, the enemy. Such a term as "altruism"—unselfish concern for others—points to *agapē*, but no other concept fully expresses its unique meaning. The theological implications are clear: to love agapaically means to love a person "in God"—to love him with the love that is of God's very essence. It is not something we are spontaneously impelled to do by our own nature; it is an act of faith that goes against the grain of ordinary human nature in a way that is parallel to *ahimsa*'s refusal to do harm.

It is not necessary to fuse the two concepts of *agapē* and *ahimsa,* nor to equate them. There are good reasons for keeping them distinct. In all its ramifications, *ahimsa* requires doing no harm at all to any living creature. Blind obedience to this principle has sometimes led, in India, to hordes of monkeys invading Hindu temples and endangering the safety of human worshipers. Gandhi was wise enough to modify the rule out of concern for the people, and in so doing he implicitly bowed to the higher, agapaic law. Although the two concepts may be highly compatible, it is obviously not the same thing to love someone and merely to abstain from harming him. Allowance must be made for those paradoxical cases in which *ahimsa* may be loveless or in which agapaic love may necessitate doing bodily harm. Granted that the most perfect expression of each includes the other, life nevertheless confronts us with painful dilemmas such as the classic one in which a psychopathic killer is about to shoot an innocent family. Ideally we should show our agapaic love for all by causing him to hand over his gun without hurting him. Or we may volunteer to be his first victim by thrusting ourselves into the line of fire, risking not only our own but the others' lives. Realistically we would have to choose between strict adherence to *ahimsa* toward the killer or a broad enough application of *agapē* to save the family with a minimum of harm to the killer.

The Hindu doctrine of *ahimsa* has its counterpart within Christianity, notably in such ascetics as Francesco d'Assisi and in such heretical sects as the Catharists and Bogomils, forming part of a pattern of bodily self-mortification that was believed to help men in freeing their spirits from the "prison of flesh" as part of a process of salvation. In contrast to this practice, in which *ahimsa* or nonresistance figures as an ascetic discipline for the sake of individual purity, denying the world in pursuit of an otherworldly destination, there is another tradition typified by the Mennonites and Quakers but shared by many other Christians from the earliest times of the apostolic church. In this tradition, the principle of doing no harm is seen as a way of redeeming the world rather than as a ladder for climbing out of it. More accurately, abstention from evil is thus seen as an accompaniment to the doing of good in human, this-worldly terms.

Gandhi may be criticized for failing to achieve the right equilibrium between the ascetic doctrines of ancient Hinduism and the agapaic emphasis of the New Testament. Throughout his life he was absorbed in a rigorous personal asceticism that perhaps had more to do with his own salvation than with the liberation of India. Yet in large measure his impact may be seen as an adaptation of *ahimsa,* modified by his own interpretation of *agapē* and biblical nonresistance, to the social struggle. Many writers have used "nonviolence" as the equivalent of a term which Gandhi himself coined—*satyagraha.* Much more than *ahimsa,* this is a word rich in ambiguities and carrying within it a host of implications. As Frank Moraes observes,

the Mahatma's conception of nonviolence or *ahimsa* was never passive. He certainly never compromised with evil, for he insisted that a wrong should not merely provoke protest but that it should be actively resisted. The practical expression of *ahimsa* was *satyagraha,* which literally means "the power of truth," but is generally described as "soul force." *Satyagraha,* which came to be known in its political form in India as civil disobedience, was described by Gandhi as the weapon of the strong, not the weak, its motive force arising from a feeling of inner strength and its practice calling for self-discipline. For *satyagraha* inflicted physical injury on none but the exponent who by enduring the maximum suffering without thought of counter-violence sought to shame or inspire the wrongdoer into doing right.[4]

There is much point in the alternative translation of *satyagraha* as "soul force," for "power of truth" alone does not capture the meaning. Behind both there are unsuspected implications. Nikhilananda, in his translation of the Upanishads, defines *"sat"* as "reality, existence." Hence the dual translations "soul" and "truth" involve a single idea around which revolves an elaborate philosophy. Perhaps the most accurate translation of *satyagraha* would have to be something like this: "power which comes through a tenacious devotion to the ultimate reality."

Like *ahimsa, satyagraha* is a serviceable enough term so long as we do not subject it to rigorous scrutiny. We are indebted to Gandhi for the general idea it represents, but we must also acknowledge that he never fully succeeded in freeing it from its Hindu context. This is a context that understands the soul or truth—*sat*—as an immutable spiritual principle set off against the instability of the actual world, which is ephemeral or illusory. In it, man's goal is to achieve *moksha* or salvation by liberating that within him which is likewise real so that it can be absorbed into the cosmic void of ultimate reality. The concepts of being, of the self, of human nature and all the rest that accord with such a philosophy are not very conducive to social action.

There is obvious merit, for example, in the consolation that one's own physical suffering is a small price to pay for the goal of salvation, but the underlying philosophy may be questioned when it also justifies a caste system which rationalizes the same fate for others. It is all too reminiscent of the feudalistic order of medieval Christendom, with its rationalizations of pomp and poverty, and its willingness to countenance physical cruelty on the grounds that it did not damage the soul. Gandhi, who considered himself a *"sanatanist"* Hindu, orthodox by his own standards, attempted to invest the many doctrines of Hinduism with new spiritual content largely derived from the New Testament. As a Hindu religious leader he could not help being preoccupied with such matters as "the service of the cow," the problem of untouchability and many other questions too exotic to warrant our attention. The point is that, whatever its indebtedness to or points of contact with either the gospel of Jesus Christ or Western culture, the warp and woof of Gandhi's thought was that of the Hindu religio-cultural setting. Unless we are Hindu missionaries, it is not our task to transplant these ideas but rather, as Gandhi himself suggested, to find the essential ones in relation to our own understanding of truth and reality. This may prove to be very different from what Gandhi had in mind.

The crux of the matter is that the biblical understanding of life has to do with persons and communities acting in history. The Hindu doctrine of *ahimsa* is based on a belief in the universal oneness of all created beings: the rat, the scorpion and the saint are each bearers of the same immortal soul in successive phases of its earthly migration. The biblical perspective affords scope for a sense of the "reverence for life" which this implies, and we see it vividly in Francesco d'Assisi's sense of kinship not only with animals but even with "Brother Fire." But it has a different ontological basis, and its primary focus is radically different because it sees man as a *person* in whom historical and biographical features are bound up with the transcendental to form a unique identity. To be sure, there may be inner conflicts and discrepancies, but they occur within an integral whole.

Moreover, as Surjit Singh has observed, "personality is created in relation—in relation between the human I and the divine Thou." [5] For Christians this relation is symbolized in Jesus Christ, but it is observable also in the Old Testament doctrines of creation and covenant, in which God is seen as the divine Person who creates man, breathing his spirit (*ruach* = breath) into him and molding him in his own image, and entering into an agreement with him that respects his freedom and integrity as a person. Interestingly, there is a tangential concept in Hinduism of *prana* as "vital breath" and as an aspect of Brāhmān, the ultimate reality. But in Hindu yoga it is the task of the self to control *prana* in all its forms, thereby subduing the body, while in the biblical view it is the task of the spirit to redeem and direct the self and its body. Through the spirit which makes him a person, biblical man is not given a ladder to climb out of history into the realm of the divine and eternal, but rather a link which binds history to God and gives it a meaning beyond itself.

Just as creation is a paradigm of the interpersonal relation of God and man, it is also a paradigm of the natural relation between human persons. But it must be noted that in each case this relation is flawed by human egotism, man's tendency to use his created freedom to defy God's will and to deny God's love. This is the meaning of sin—not some ineluctable evil implanted in man, but his willful rebellion against God, which is to say, against *agapē,* against spirit, against his own integrity as a person. To speak of sin is to speak of brokenness, both within the person and in relation between persons. And logically it is also to speak of conflict between man and man, and between groups of men. This is not only logical, it is an observable fact of human life.

Yet it is missing from Hinduism and, for that matter, from numerous forms of purported Christianity which overemphasize ritual, moral rules or other devices that attempt to substitute a method or formula for the "fear and trembling" of faith. These approaches see sin, if at all, as no more than a bad habit to be overcome by earnest tugging at one's own bootstraps or forcing oneself into a prescribed pattern of conduct. It is no argument against ritual or discipline, however, to say that they are not self-sufficient. A lifetime of yogic exercises or of upright "Christian" moral conduct is no substitute for an act of forgiveness or the acceptance of God's freely offered grace.

The biblical view not only recognizes the fact of sin, but shows that man can turn from it and be forgiven and healed, reconciled to God and thereby also enabled to exist in right relation to other men, since all share in the same actual and potential relation to God. The paradigm of this reconciliation is Jesus Christ, whose significance for the dimension of redemption is ably explained by Singh:

Thus the fullness of the measure of the stature of the Son of God is realized through reconciliation with God and then with man and the world. This inner reconciliation results in a coherent outlook by which man no more sees his life piecemeal but as a related whole. . . .

In Christ the primary relation is of person to person, and all other relations . . . follow after it. . . . The primacy of the person-to-person relation does not render it abstract. On the contrary, this relation is at once grounded in the divine-human dimension and the sociocultural dimension.[6]

This understanding of man's nature is both profoundly humanistic in the importance it attaches to man's choices and actions in history, and profoundly spiritual in showing that the measure and value of these historic choices and actions are anchored more deeply than in history—in fact, in the bedrock of ultimate reality.

In existential psychology the "coherent outlook" to which Singh refers is called the "centered self," a condition of existence in which a person's being is authenticated as an integrated whole capable of affirming itself in relation to other persons. It does not presuppose that the persons to whom it relates are centered selves. In fact, the basic principle of psychotherapy in these terms holds that the therapist as a centered self is capable of healing the self that is fragmented. He does so by establishing authentic relation with the patient, in whom he recognizes a potential for growth which can be guided in freedom to overcome the brokenness of neurosis.

The essential content of such authentic relation is agapaic love. In the therapeutic encounter it might be called "concern." In the divine-human dimension it is expressed as communion, and in the social it is experienced as community. Berdyaev uses a single term, *sobornost,* drawn from classical Orthodox theology, to signify the common character of both communion and community in this sense. Unlike the mystical notion of union with God, *sobornost* points to a meeting rather than a merging. Thus communion is an experience of fellowship in which God remains God and man remains man. Community in its truest sense is not something apart from God, for if agapaic love is truly present it is manifested as the Holy Spirit, which is the distinguishing mark of the church in the New Testament sense of *koinonia. Koinonia* means both "sharing" in the human sense of fellowship, bearing one another's burdens, and "having a share in" God's grace.[7] Hence we see how at every level the purposive thrust is the same, toward healing and integrating the solitary man within himself, in relation to God, in relation to another and in groups—all in relation to God and through God's active, unselfish, redeeming love. We shall have more to say about this process in a later chapter.

Force and Violence

What we are interested in at the moment is to note that the above discussion, sketchy as it is, affords some basis for an understanding of the essentials of violence, which we can now provisionally define in two ways: first, as the Oxford Universal Dictionary has it, "the exercise of physical force so as to inflict injury on or damage to persons or property"; and second, as a spiritual violation of the person or his relations. The Oxford definition of the verb "to violate" is also instructive: "to break, infringe or transgress unjustifiably; to fail to keep or observe duly."

Whether physical or spiritual, violence connotes destructiveness, which is intrinsically evil when it affects persons. Several things are left unspecified in the basic definition. Pure, unrestricted violence in its most extreme form is utter chaos—not simply an absolute negative but the negation of order, purpose and creativity: the antithesis of wholeness. If this is so, then in a relative sense we may conceive of a range of attenuation in which some acts are less violent than others. Without attempting to plot such a range in detail, we can distinguish between willful and accidental violence, between that which kills, cripples or mutilates and that which causes injuries that will heal or inflicts pain without damage. Also implicit is a range of psychological effects: some forms of violence may have no physical effects, though they have an impact ranging from momentary panic to severe trauma that produces incurable psychosis, or psychosomatic repercussions leading to death. Spiritually, an act may be called violent if it impairs a person's dignity or integrity, demeaning him or causing him to betray himself or his comrades. Physical violence inflicted on one person may take the form of psychological or spiritual violence in relation to another, either as a real or implied threat or in other ways. For example, self-inflicted violence made conditional upon the behavior of another may be highly violent in spirit.

We are concerned with violence primarily as a mode of conflict. Aside from any moral considerations, Kenneth Boulding has termed it "a chronic disease of society" because in situations of conflict "it frequently inhibits settlement; for it leaves no path to settlement open but conquest, and this may not be possible." [8] Short of complete annihilation, Boulding asserts, violence is able to end conflict by suppressing it, driving it underground, but it can do so only as long as it remains preponderant on the side of the victor. Such resolution as may occur must come from another quarter. Violence cannot effect it.

Physical force is a factor in violence, but not a determining one. There is an area of considerable ambiguity in which questions of proportion and legitimacy arise to distinguish between acts that are clearly violent but morally justified and those that are not justified, and between those that include physical force but not violence. It is clear that all the force present in a given society does not simply add up to a grand total of violence. Some acts of violence cancel each other. Some measures of force curb potential violence or eliminate actual violence, and some exceed their bounds and become violent or provoke violence. As a general observation, we may recognize lawful force as a restricted form of violence, controlled and used for a purpose which is ultimately redemptive. In saying this, we concede that there are circumstances in which a sub-Christian society must avail itself of sub-Christian modes of operation, even as efforts are made to render the latter obsolete. We are referring here to the processes of civilization in which violence yields to force and force to persuasion, not to a terrestrial utopia in which law becomes totally unneeded.

Persons who join together in a commitment of Christian fellowship have no need for sub-Christian means in their relation to one another, and they may choose for themselves a way of responding to violence from the outside which exposes them to harm. But they cannot choose this way for others, for to impose such vulnerability upon others would be to violate their personal integrity and freedom. Such a committed community, it must be added, will need to pray for grace and repent of lapses into resentment or anger among themselves. It takes more than pluck and grit, no matter how noble the aim.

There is a dilemma here which it is not our present purpose to attempt to resolve. It is sufficient to recognize it and to add that neither of the two choices is wholly satisfactory: the one eschewing any resort to force even at the cost of annihilation; the other seeking equilibrium by a redemptive minimum of force. Both warrant respect and a measure of suspicion. We must remember that we do not approach the question with a clean slate. Force and violence are present in the world as we confront it, and we cannot proceed as if they were absent. That is part of the legacy of sin and the task of redemption. Whatever the lines of demarcation, we cannot claim to be free of involvement in violence. Any attempt to extricate ourselves completely is a deception and a repudiation of history, a surrender rather than a redemption.

One further point must be made concerning the spiritual dimension of violence. Let us imagine that there are two men, one of whom chops his neighbor to bits with an ax in an excess of rage. Afterward, he experiences remorse and, through repentance, accepts his guilt and atones for it. The other man never actually injures anyone, but spends his life gleefully visualizing hideous tortures which he inflicts on persons in his imagination, although he treats those persons civilly when he meets them in actual life. Surely these two men cannot be evaluated solely on the basis of their actions, and surely the fantasy torturer is a worse specimen of mankind than the actual killer who has repented. This is just to suggest some of the many hidden complexities that may be present in a situation that appears very simple on the surface. Moreover, spiritual violence can have harmful results when it connects—possibly more damaging than a bullet wound in some cases.

Nonviolence

Absolute abstention from violence is chimerical, but we can within reasonable limits greatly restrict and control our involvement in violence to a point where we can begin to speak of nonviolence. It is not the general absence of violence which is decisive, however. Just as there is a difference between "unorganized" and "disorganized," or between "unreligious" and "nonreligious," we must introduce a purposive element to distinguish between "unviolent" and "nonviolent" conduct. We may take the former to mean conduct which simply happens to be more or less free of violence, and the latter to mean that which deliberately refrains from using violence or even lawful armed force in circumstances where such expedients could conceivably be applied.

We have insisted on maintaining a distinction between nonviolence and agapaic love. They are not the same, but there is a relation, for even when love may sanction violence it is never violent in spirit. Conversely, since nonviolence at its best is fulfilled by love it is not quite itself when it is loveless. But suppose it is reduced to a bare legalism and then harnessed to ends that are violent in spirit? What about people motivated by hate or ignorance attempting to obstruct justice by "nonviolent" means? An example would be a group of segregationists responding to integration by withdrawing their children from a previously all-white school, leaving it all-Negro. In doing so, they choose deliberately to refrain from overt violence, and therefore we must admit that their action is technically nonviolent.

This is a special case, but it is the kind that tests the rule and serves as a touchstone for the objectivity and ethical neutrality of the term. By saying that nonviolence can be merely technical we open up a wide range of other possible modifications that render it operational. We thus prohibit ourselves from inferring that a given case which meets the technical requirement also necessarily involves the motives and values we associate with nonviolence. In other words, we can see the difference between "mere" nonviolence and "true" nonviolence and understand that it is agapaic love which makes the difference. We may also see from such an example or others like it how effectively nonviolence may work as sheer technique, and how much it depends on other factors. Analysis in such terms will enable us to inquire, for instance, about the relative strategic importance of a moral purpose and of the means of exerting pressure or coercion in its behalf.

Strictly speaking, then, nonviolence as such "works" by omission, but in so doing it opens the way for forms of positive action of two kinds: personal conduct in relation to the immediate opponent, and tactical or strategic social action designed to coerce or to exert pressure. The positive action which occurs in personal conduct is the "soul force" that activates agapaic love in direct response to actual or threatened violence, but can the same be said of social action as such?

Coercion, Pressure and Persuasion

If we consider violence as essentially destructive, and lawful force as a civilized modification of violence, we may consider coercion as a further refinement of force characterized by virtual absence of any actual violence. In a sense, of course, both violence and force are means of coercion—that is, of securing someone's compliance against his will. A disabling blow or the threat of imprisonment can readily achieve this, but so can other means which, unlike laws that are backed up by the potential force of the state (or extralegal social rules sanctioned by mob violence and the like), are directly coercive without recourse to force or violence of any kind. The social snub, the cold shoulder, the silent treatment are powerful forms of psychological coercion which exploit man's need for social belonging and responsiveness, operating in terms of a simple Pavlovian stimulus-response operation which punishes disapproved behavior with ostracism and rewards approved behavior with social acceptance. It may even go on to reinforce approved behavior with tangible signs of acceptance in excess of the norm. Likewise, economic coercion in the form of boycott and other techniques forms a similar pattern. Withdrawal of patronage hurts the merchant's balance sheet and may ultimately force him out of business, while it is left to him to decide whether to let this happen or to regain lost patronage by meeting his customers' demands. Again, good behavior on his part may be reinforced afterward by an increase of patronage above the pre-boycott level. Much the same process occurs in the labor slowdown, strike and other tactics. In addition each of these methods may be used symbolically as a gesture of protest and of solidarity, implying a threat of coercion without actually exerting coercive power.

Coercion may occur without being intended. The early Christians and many later nonresistants did not employ nonviolence as a strategy in any sense, yet simply by witnessing to their faith and abstaining from abhorrent practices they often caused others to re-examine those practices. In some cases their witness may have been only persuasive, but in many others it inevitably took the tangible form of noncooperation which could not help being coercive. Gandhi on repeated occasions underwent fasts which he said were not intended to embarrass or coerce the British, but the circumstances were such that the British were forced to choose between making concessions or letting him die.

In each case, coercion interferes with the freedom of the person or group that is coerced. This poses an ethical problem not unlike that which arises in the case of violence. It would be specious to argue that a tactic which is intrinsically coercive becomes uncoercive when those who use it profess to be nonviolent. The use of such tactics must be acknowledged as inconsistent with an ethic of pure agapaic love. To the perfectionist it is not permissible. But the Christian realist may find in it a sub-Christian means that is relatively more acceptable than violence or force—a means, moreover, which more readily allows for redemptive modifications. This does not dispose of the ethical problem; it does not mean carte blanche to use coercion indiscriminately. Not only should it be used with a sense of proportion as to the magnitude of the conflict and its issues, but great care should be taken to affirm agapaic love in relation to the person who is the object of coercion. Only when such care is taken can we speak of coercion as "nonviolent." It is never truly nonviolent in itself and can never be fully transformed. It can, however, be conditioned and insulated.

Let us introduce here a somewhat more ambiguous, perhaps intermediate term: pressure. This is a term that seems to bridge both the more moderate forms of coercion and certain kinds of persuasion. It refers to actions that do not actually obstruct the opponent's freedom and yet go beyond the symbolic protest. One way of exerting pressure would be a limited boycott designed not to compel a merchant to change his policies or go bankrupt but only to make him tangibly aware of something amiss. Ethics aside, in many situations in which we seek to coerce, we may be unable to muster enough strength to do more than exert pressure. In others we may have the strength but choose for strategic reasons to exercise restraint. Depending on the circumstances it is of course ethically preferable to achieve as much as possible with the least amount of coercion.

On the other side of the bridge is persuasion, a category of action that is intrinsically more compatible with *agapē* than coercion is. In its purest form it shows a respect for the person which is in fact agapaic, requiring no further conditioning. For to persuade someone is to win him over, to help him to make a change of conduct that is based on an inner change of heart or will. Whether this is accomplished by appeal to reason or to moral sensibilities or religious feeling and conscience, the distinguishing fact is that it effects change from within and does not impose it from outside. Even persuasion, however, has its demonic side. It can be corrupted by auxiliary means that undermine integrity: not only bribery but cajolery, flattery, appeals to prejudice and the like. Even at this apparently far remove from actual violence there is room for the spirit of violence to operate, not in the form of physical injury but in ways that may be even more pernicious. To the extent that this is so, we may speak of "nonviolent" persuasion in a spiritual sense. Perhaps the best kind of persuasion is that exerted by the power of example. Whatever use is made of facts or moral arguments, the agapaic integrity of the nonviolent persuader can be counted on at least as a catalyst and perhaps more.

Complexities of Violence and Nonviolence

One thing emerges clearly from the foregoing. All forms of action that we have examined are relative and imperfect; none of them is intrinsically agapaic. Even those that are generally more open to *agapē* may not be so in specific instances. In addition, the actual situation in which one or another means of action is chosen will have its influence on the fitness of the choice. Moreover, it is clear that the choice of nonviolent means is only part of the process. A campaign of social action could be meticulously nonviolent in every detail but devoid of effective power. We have already noted that agapaic love "is God" and "is of God." It is not a moral principle or an inert abstraction of natural law which we can apply at will. It is power to which we have access not by reason or nature but by our faith and God's grace. It is not neutral but purposive power. We cannot channel it to serve a purpose of our own devising which is alien to it. It is not a power that we can generate. Only God is the generator; our role is that of a dependent transmitter.

Now this must not be interpreted in a moralistic way. God does not deny himself to sinners, and agapaic power is not reserved exclusively for the morally perfect or for those with full understanding of his purposes. When we discuss historic episodes, there is seldom any way in which we can determine how consciously Christian were the motives of the participants. In some cases we may search in vain for evidence of *agapē*. This does not mean we can afford to bypass God or that it will suffice to feign or fabricate *agapē* in our own nonviolent encounters. But it does evidently mean that history is not the simple product of human actions and that God's grace has its own logic that may baffle the morally upright. Biblical realism is humanistic, but it also relates to a living God who acts in history, sometimes presenting us with moments pregnant with opportunity—moments of potential *kairos,* the fullness of time —and sometimes with moments that are barren of such opportunity, in which we may nevertheless work and witness for God's purposes.

It is possible to compartmentalize the sacred and the secular instead of seeing that they intersect at every point in history. But such compartmentalization is a mistake leading to an arid simple moralism and an equally arid simple amoralism. The one is based on a one-dimensional moral scale in which nonviolence is always categorically right and violence always evil. The other hews to a brittle legalism of static justice. The biblical view is both more transcendental and more existential—it shows love in a fullness and ultimacy undreamed of by either moralist or amoralist, and it shows how relevant such love can be in every aspect of human affairs. But it also shows that man's destiny is not a smooth uphill path, and that God's purpose is worked out in history not solely by the redemptive acts of those who manifest the Holy Spirit, but also in often mysterious ways by the temptations and chastisements that befall them. The latter has frequently been tragically misunderstood and used as a justification by Christians to slaughter their fellow men. The confusion seems to arise from a human penchant for usurping God's prerogatives. "Vengeance is mine, I will repay, saith the Lord" (Romans 12:19) has too often been answered with "Never mind, Lord, I'll do it for you," which completely negates the injunction to leave it to God. To say that even such sin and stupidity somehow fit into God's ultimate purpose is not an endorsement for emulation.

We have to view history, including today and tomorrow,

in perspective. Though doing our utmost to act agapaically through nonviolence, we have to be attuned to the situation in which we find ourselves and not attempt to impose upon it rigid structures of abstraction that do not suit it. To do so is a denial of the dynamic of *agapē*. We must be prepared to retreat as well as to advance, and sometimes to halt and pray for strength and guidance. We must have a finely tempered realism about human nature, gauging how much we can endure and how much our comrades can endure. There is always the possibility of capitulation to violence, especially in the face of provocation, if we overreach our limits; and this can have disastrous consequences.

But it would be moralistic to assert that violence can have no other effects but disaster. As Berdyaev has observed of revolutions, even brutal and widespread violence can, in some situations, clear the air and reshuffle an existing balance of forces so as to open new channels for redemptive work. Ideally, nonviolence attempts to circumvent or forestall the tragic aspect of social change. Its task is never deliberately to provoke it, but there are times when we must accept such tragedy as part of history—and even as a burden of guilt that we must share—and go on with our work as best we can.

Violence does not merely erupt, though it may seem to. The way in which it occurs is important, as is the source from which it comes. The most serious acts of violence are those which are done by persons who are committed to nonviolence. These may indicate the need for increased discipline or better training before moving on. Acts of retaliatory violence by the opponent are, of course, to be expected. But their extent and severity may point to inadequacies in nonviolent conduct or tactics, and in each case it must be decided whether to attempt to overcome such retaliation by means of nonviolence alone or with the aid of police or other agents of lawful force. If the latter are available, only a perfectionist will refuse to call upon them when violence becomes unmanageable, or when it results in injury or death. Unless the entire community is pledged to vulnerability, those who are nonviolent have a clear responsibility to curb antisocial actions and to see that others are protected from those who commit them. Nonviolence alone can seldom do this. Another source of violence is rivals, allies or undisciplined masses related to the nonviolent movement itself but not actually a part of it. This poses a delicate problem. In a given case it may point up a discrepancy between the objectives of the movement and those of a segment of the community it seeks to represent. A typical example would be a middle-class movement that does not make room for the particular grievances of poorly paid workers or the unemployed against the same general opponent. The frustrations and resentments of these latter groups are likely to be keener and less easily disciplined, flaring up at a stage when those within the movement are able to maintain their own discipline. Maneuvering so as to allow for such factors, and seeking to broaden the social base and strengthen marginal allegiances, are perennial problems of any movement.

At the same time, it is biblical realism as well as sound psychology to observe that marginal outcroppings of violence may serve to underscore the urgency of a given situation and expedite its solution. It may do this or it may stiffen resistance and cause the whole campaign to deteriorate into rioting. Violence is unstable and risky—reason enough to avoid using it if possible. But the point is that its effects cannot be foreseen and provided for in the abstract. The specific lesson is an existential one, to be found in the situation itself. It should in any case be clear that a nonviolent movement has a responsibility to curb such outbursts, never to promote them. As a matter of policy they must be disavowed and should be atoned for by a gesture of penance and restitution within the context of the struggle in which they occur. But this does not preclude private evaluation of their objective historical or strategic effects, nor acting upon this evaluation.

Howard Zinn has argued that there are instances in which the use of a modicum of violence—such as the assassination of a dictator—can be more effective and actually reduce the sum total of violence that would occur if the outcome were produced in this way rather than through protracted conflict in which nonviolence is outmatched by ruthless armed force. Even in cases where such a simple alternative as a dead Hitler is not available, it is often true that nonviolence precipitates violence. Zinn says:

Nonviolence theorists will insist that the responsibility for the violence rests with those who committed it. But this dodges the question; the fact is that there was more violence in the world *after* the Freedom Riders began their rides than *before*. And for this there is only one justification: that the amount of violence was insignificant compared to the amount of justice won.[9]

The violence that nonviolence produces may not be directed solely at the nonviolent cadres, either. But this is not to say that nonviolence is just the same as other methods of conflict. It is only to caution against viewing it as a panacea or elevating as an absolute the relative truth that violence is evil and its absence is good. For the realist, at least, there are limits of possibility and usefulness within which any method or principle must be regarded, and nonviolence is no exception. Its distinctive merit is not that it keeps the incidence of violence on the level of the status quo, nor that it reduces it below that level; but that in most cases it produces less violence than would be the case if the struggle were waged by violent means. By the very fact of choosing to engage in nonviolent struggle instead of holding to an inert passivity in some quiet nook, we remove nonviolence from the category of the absolute and involve ourselves in existential risk, with all its consequences. It is not possible then to decide in advance what we will take responsibility for, and we must be prepared to share the blame for whatever happens.

The core of nonviolence is imbedded in personal conduct, specifically in the nonviolent person's capacity to absorb violence without retaliating. Without this, there can be no such thing as nonviolent tactics and strategy, which are only nonviolent to the extent that the leaders, cadres and masses make them so by their conduct. In a given situation, it may happen that suffering is not inflicted at all. What counts, however, is the possibility that it will and the readiness to bear it—and not only to bear it but to do so with dignity and a measure of agapaic resourcefulness. It requires not only courage but faith, and defiance freed of contempt or arrogance. Not every act of nonviolence can be expected to be perfect, but it must at least meet the minimum requirement of nonretaliation—and as much of the rest as the individual is capable of. For the aim is not merely to be a human punching bag but a witness testifying to the power of love by deeds of truth, and thereby fostering his just cause, inviting the opponent both singly and en masse to join him in it.

These in brief are the elements of nonviolence in Christian perspective and the realities with which they have to deal. In later chapters, after further examination of its theoretical scope, we shall describe in some detail how these elements function and what they require in order to do so.

REFERENCES IN CHAPTER 1

1   Pie Régamey: *Non-Violence et Conscience Chrétienne* (Paris: Cerf, 1958), p. 203n.
2   M. K. Gandhi in *Harijan*, March 14, 1936.
3   C. E. B. Cranfield: "Love" in Allan Richardson's *A Theological Word Book of the Bible* (New York: The Macmillan Co., 1958), p. 134.
4   Frank Moraes: "Gandhi Ten Years After" in *Foreign Affairs,* January 1958, p. 259f.
5   Surjit Singh: *Christology and Personality* (Copyright 1961, W. L. Jenkins, and used by permission. Philadelphia: The Westminster Press), p. 20.
6   *Ibid.,* p. 20f.
7   Cranfield: "Fellowship" in Richardson, *op. cit.,* p. 81ff.
8   Kenneth E. Boulding: *Conflict and Defense* (New York: Harper & Brothers, 1962), p. 323.
9   Howard Zinn: "The Force of Nonviolence" in *The Nation,* March 17, 1962, p. 229.

2

Three Types of Generic Nonviolence

When Gandhi began his campaign in South Africa in 1906, he called it "passive resistance." He was never happy about this phrase, however, and near the end of his life some four decades later, he wrote:

Europe mistook the bold and brave resistance full of wisdom by Jesus of Nazareth for passive resistance, as if it was of the weak. . . . Has not the West paid heavily in regarding Jesus as a Passive Resister? [1]

Even the term *satyagraha* came in for qualification: *"satyagraha* of the strong" and *"satyagraha* of the weak." Gandhi was no philologist, no semanticist. He used words loosely and, as the above example shows, he was more concerned with emotive connotations than with objective meanings. He was capable of using the same word in opposite ways because he was content to improvise. He was preoccupied with the immediate and with the ultimate, but little concerned with the historical. He was not the first man of action to leave so hectic a record of his thought—fragmentary, scattered, makeshift and often contradictory. The meanings assigned to the key words he used were often vague as he received them, and his interpreters have done little to correct this.

In the preceding chapter, we worked out a serviceable definition of "nonviolence" that enables us to use the term without requiring that in each case it must be found bold, brave or full of wisdom. Taking "nonviolence" as a generic term for all types of action which purposively abstain from force and violence in response to conflict, let us now examine the three principal terms which have historically been used to designate specific kinds of conduct that fit the meaning of the generic term. Once we are clear what the terms themselves mean, we can proceed to a further discussion, in the next chapter, of the modes or levels in which nonviolence functions. The three basic types under immediate scrutiny are: 1) nonresistance, 2) passive resistance, and 3) active nonviolent resistance or nonviolent direct action of an affirmative or aggressive kind.

Nonresistance and Resistance

It would be pointless to attempt a definition of any of these terms without first defining "resistance." The Latin components of the word are *re* (back or against) and *sistere,* the causative of *stare* (to stand). As commonly understood, to resist means to withstand, oppose, stand firm against something, to block its movement. All that the word contains in its etymology is "stand against." Whether with bravery or cowardice, armed or unarmed, knowingly or unknowingly are not indicated but remain to be supplied by usage and by adjectival or other explicit modifications. Taken by itself, unmodified, the word "resistance" says nothing about who started the fight, nor even that there is a fight, nor whether that which is resisted is then pushed back, pursued or reversed. All these and many other possible implications are external to the root meaning of the word itself.

By the same token, since the etymology of "nonresistance" simply negates the above, it would be most neatly defined as "not to stand against," hence to yield to something. Such a neat definition, however, would be misleading for our purposes. As is frequently the case with negations, this one comes into the language after the word which it negates has acquired certain connotations through common usage. In this particular case, "nonresistance" is a principle derived from a specific context: the Sermon on the Mount. Jesus says, "But I say unto you, that ye resist not evil: but whosoever shall smite thee on

thy right cheek, turn to him the other also." (Matt. 5:39) So
reads the King James text which was in use as the authorized
version when the word "nonresistance" entered the English language in 1643. The same verse in the New English Bible
(1961) reads: "But what I tell you is this: Do not set yourself
against the man who wrongs you. If someone slaps you on the
right cheek, turn and offer him your left."

The New Testament passage of which this is a part is called
by Robert Graves and Joshua Podro "a *midrash* on Proverbs
20:22 and 24:29, supported by a quotation from Lamenta-
tions 3:30. . . . Hillel stated this negatively (*Shabbath* 31a):
'Do not to others as thou wouldst not have them do unto
thee.'"[2] The passages which they cite are given in the Revised
Standard Version respectively as follows: "Do not say, 'I will
repay evil'; wait for the Lord, and he will help you." "Do not
say, 'I will do to him as he has done to me; I will pay him back
for what he has done.'" "Let him give his cheek to the smiter,
and be filled with insults." To these, Graves and Podro add
from the Apocrypha, "And what you hate, do not do to anyone" (Tobit 4:15a RSV).

In the Russian version of Matthew 5:39 (influential in
the philosophy of Tolstoy, who in turn influenced Gandhi) the
words corresponding to "resist not evil" are translatable as the
exact equivalent of the King James Version: *"Ne protivsya
zlomu."* The Russian root *protiv* functions as a word meaning
"against" or "opposite" and also as a suffix corresponding to
the English (from Latin) "anti-" and "contra-" as well as
"-proof" as in "foolproof." The words for "enemy" and "to
oppose" contain the same root. The word which Tolstoy uses
for "nonresistance" is *"neprotivleniya."* It is interesting to note
that Smirnitsky, the standard Russian-English dictionary, gives
the word only with the word for "evil" following it. Thus in
Russian, the concept is already narrowed down to "nonresistance to evil" rather than to force, violence or some other term.
In actual usage, this is also true of the English word. The con-

tent of the word is suggested by Tolstoy's interpretation of the biblical passage:

Never resist the evildoer by force, do not meet violence with violence. If they beat you, endure it; if they take your possessions, yield them up; if they compel you to work, work; and if they wish to take from you what you consider to be yours, give it up.[3]

Dietrich Bonhoeffer comments on the same passage:

The only way to overcome evil is to let it run itself to a standstill because it does not find the resistance it is looking for. Resistance merely creates further evil and adds fuel to the flames. But when evil meets no opposition and encounters no obstacle but only patient endurance, its sting is drawn, and at last it meets an opponent which is more than its match.[4]

From the foregoing it should be clear that what is meant is not a craven acquiescence in evil, but a yielding on one level of conduct which on another level at the same time is some kind of action to overcome the same evil. The Apostle Paul, in his letter to the Roman Christians, recapitulates in his own words the gist of Matthew 5:38ff and adds: "Do not let evil conquer you, but use good to defeat evil." (Rom. 12:21 NEB) Bonhoeffer comments further:

We are concerned not with evil in the abstract but with the evil *person*. . . . Patient endurance of evil does not mean a recognition of its rights. That is sheer sentimentality, and Jesus will have nothing to do with it. The shameful assault, the deed of violence and the act of exploitation are still evil.[5]

The point is that Christian conduct, without resisting, is stronger than evil. It should be remembered that nonresistance is only one facet in a many-faceted structure of faith and ethics. By itself it is of no intrinsic value, but it is a way of maintaining righteousness in the face of danger that is not only physical but also moral in that it invites the possibility of evil in the act of resistance. This is clearly a perfectionist view that leaves no room for relativities. But even on its own terms there remains a degree of ambiguity: does pure nonresistance consist in going about one's business despite persecution or can it also mean engaging in redemptive activity? That is, when confronted with evil does one assume that one's ordinary conduct is sufficient witness for good or does one take the evil as a challenge to extraordinary deeds specifically designed to have a redemptive effect on the evildoer?

André Trocmé makes the point that Jesus rejected not only the temptation of Zealot violence but also that of quietistic withdrawal. He rejects the view of Jesus as

a kind of sublime yogi, a refugee outside the world on the shores of eternity, an ascetic who bade his disciples to follow him into solitude in order to teach them an ideal without relevance to the concrete problems of this world.[6]

This meant, for the early Christians—as for the Jesus who did good deeds on the Sabbath and drove the money-changers out of the temple—carrying out a divinely ordained mission in the world and accepting the consequences in hardship, suffering and death without trying to save themselves by resistance or by flight. Far from being models of sweet reasonableness, however, those who acted in this way more often exhibited scorn than love for their enemies, even while conforming to the rule of nonresistance. Cadoux tells of numerous instances like these from the third century:

One Christian tore down the first edict of persecution posted up by Diocletianus; another fearlessly seized the governor's hand as he was in the act of sacrificing, and exhorted him to abandon his error; another strode forward in open court and rebuked a judge for his ruthless sentences.[7]

At the same time, Cadoux states that "it was quite unusual for Christians to attempt any physical resistance to the violence of the pagans"[8] and

there were those who, stimulated by an extraordinary zeal, exposed themselves on their own initiative to the notice and severity of the government officials, and rushed eagerly to meet the extreme penalty. In the persecution of Valerianus, three Christians at first avoided martyrdom, but then, repenting, hastened to Caesarea, gave themselves up to the judges, and were sentenced to death.[9]

Throughout history, even during the early centuries of the church's vigor, the Christian witness in all its fullness has been a rarity. Nonresistance has not always been loveless and unkind, but it has often been so, and those who have practiced it have often been emboldened by a bloodthirsty desire for their enemies' destruction, which they have counted upon God to provide.

To summarize briefly the teaching and witness of Jesus on this point, "pure Christianity" consists in doing good for the enemy in a spirit of love and not resisting the enemy but trying to redeem him. If there is any vengeance to be done, that is up to God and it is not for Christians even to wish it. Pure nonresistance remains pure only while it remains part of the context of redemptive activity. In this context, which is perfectionistic, it is validated in terms of the intrinsic goodness of such faith and conduct in immediate relation to God, heedless of worldly consequences. Although the adherent of pure nonresistance shares in the human hope that his actions will be effective here and now, his decision is not conditional upon any expectation of success. Such an absolute commitment promises no tangible results and is not primarily concerned with survival. It offers a way of life that is fundamentally a way to die pure—so far as men can be pure, at any rate— which may in the process purify the world by its meaningful sacrifice. Wrenched from its New Testament setting and erected as a separate principle, it offers the temptation of a way to die with clean hands and a dirty soul.

As we have seen in the preceding chapter, nonresistance figures as a monastic discipline in Hinduism, Buddhism, Catharism and other religions that have as their objective the voluntary annihilation of the self. In each of these and in perfectionist Christianity, nonresistance is seen as a way of absorbing unearned suffering, which has redemptive effect, and not as a way of minimizing or averting suffering. As Trocmé points out above, Christians address themselves to the problems of this world, and it is by virtue of this fact that their nonresistance is concerned with the world as well as with their personal purity: through their nonresistant conduct and the suffering it entails they hope to redeem the evil person, not merely to use their response to him as a means to their own salvation.

Entirely absent from the concept of nonresistance is any notion of its use as a tactic or strategem. By definition it does not impede the evil person's actions, although of course it may have a psychological or moral effect of causing him to hesitate, to halt, to be ashamed of himself and to repent. Only in this oblique sense can it be at all coercive, and indeed by itself it is static—a vacuum to be filled with the power of redemptive love. There is in nonresistance per se a straightforward simplicity that presupposes courage, implying a whole constellation of refusals to obey orders that are sacrilegious or morally wrong, regardless of whether these refusals are spurred by love or scorn. The true nonresistant, whatever his motive, will die sooner than permit the impermissible. He may perhaps not act to prevent it but offers his life as a sanction. The aggressor may be deterred by unwillingness to shed innocent blood, or he may be brutal enough to attain his aim "over the dead body" of the nonresistant.

Historically, nonresistance has been almost invariably of a religious character, the expression of a conviction heedless of cost. There are true martyrs and there is also the "martyr complex," which is in an altogether different category, but always a temptation. The nonresistant martyr witnesses to his faith and takes whatever punishment may be meted out to him. It is the act of witness that counts. The foolhardy pseudo-martyr is vainly concerned with displaying his suffering, mistaking this alone for witness and courting it as a good in itself.

On the fringes of authentic nonresistance there is a tendency to fanaticism that ranges beyond those who court persecution to those who, like the Russian Bezmolitovtsy, set themselves on fire as a means of protest. Somewhere this side of fanaticism are such cases as the Catholic nuns who protected their chastity by disfiguring their faces, or the Hindu women who hurled themselves into a well, committing suicide to escape being raped. It may well be asked whether chastity is so precious as to be equated with life and its redemptive possibilities, and under what circumstances, if any, self-injury is justifiable.

These questions arise on the periphery, but they are latent within the sphere of nonresistance as such. It is impossible to say how much of apparently authentic nonresistance might be motivated by pathological factors such as masochism, for example; and indeed the question need not be an important one for us, except that a sect or movement which embraces nonresistance is likely to attract a certain number of unstable personalities as well as healthy stalwarts.

In the broader context, nonresistance serves as the substance of nonviolent personal conduct. It can also serve as a form of group or mass protest on a temporary and expedient basis, and need not be the expression of a distinct way of life based on permanent commitment, although it is from the latter that it takes its example.

Passive Resistance

If nonresistance is a feature of perfectionism, Christian or otherwise, passive resistance is essentially rooted in a very different tradition, that of pragmatic resistance as conducted by those who were unarmed or poorly armed. We shall later discuss the implications of resistance as a possible prelude to revolution. Here we will only observe that passive resistance has no necessary intrinsic kinship to nonresistance. Historically its appeal has been to justice rather than to love; it has functioned as a means of defending rights and asserting claims rather than of conserving spiritual integrity as such. Sabotage and the "scorched earth" policy, both destructive, have sometimes been classified under this heading. Hence the term can be used to identify a number of types of direct action—that is, action engaged in directly by the populace rather than through political representatives, military formations or other "indirect" means.

Rioting and assassination are forms of direct action manifesting resistance. A well-disciplined strike is another, and it may come within that sector which we call "passive." Externally, passive resistance differs sharply from nonresistance. If the latter means "going the second mile," passive resistance means refusing to go the first mile. Its characteristic ways of resisting are noncooperation and withdrawal: the walkout, the boycott, which seek to coerce the opponent by a deliberate refusal to fulfill a role which the opponent depends upon the resisters to perform.

The American theorist of nonresistance, Adin Ballou, whose study, *Christian Non-Resistance,* shaped Tolstoy's thinking and through it Gandhi's, asserted the idea of "moral resistance" as an internal link between the two externally dissimilar forms, in effect extending the moral boundary of nonresistance into this new area. In its inception, Gandhi's concept of *satyagraha* is an adaptation of this insight to a Hindu philosophical perspective. We would prefer not to fuse morality with this form of resistance, since it is not innately more moral, but Ballou's essential insight may be preserved in the observation that passive resistance forms an extension of the field of moral possibility embodied in nonresistance—the resolve to avoid bodily injury to the opponent. In other words, we can claim passive resistance as a type of direct action which is more or less clearly nonviolent, and which can be made explicitly so through disciplined nonviolent personal conduct.

Its connotative use as a broad term covering everything from a silent attitudinal protest to the full sweep of defiance verging on revolt has left "passive resistance" often simply a vague synonym for nonviolence, but it has a more precise meaning that deserves to be reclaimed. Specifically, it has a tactical application in the various forms of nonviolent action that work by disengagement, refusal to perform, etc. It may indeed form a whole strategy of withdrawal, or it may serve to implement a more complex strategy. The point is that technically there is a range of nonviolent action which is tactically passive, and this fact has nothing to do with passivity of the will or emotions.

The boycott is a case in point. Withdrawal of patronage is a passive gesture. It does not actively assert a claim, but makes the claim known and felt economically through the loss that results. If the opponent has depended heavily upon the resisters' support, its withdrawal can have a powerful impact.

Nonviolent Direct Action

The basic nonviolent alternative to the boycott is the sit-in or some other form of action which tactically takes the offensive and moves into the problem area rather than withdrawing from it. It means inaugurating de facto change rather than creating pressure to induce change. It places the opponent in a position in which he must either accept the fact of change as it confronts him, or resist it. Thus, although in a general sense this type of nonviolence may be a form of resistance, its specific characteristics are assertive. It has variously been called "active nonviolent resistance," "affirmative nonviolence," "positive action" and, perhaps most commonly, "nonviolent direct action." None of these terms is fully satisfactory, largely because none of them makes clearly explicit the distinction between itself and passive resistance, which as a result is often lumped with it.

The distinction we wish to observe in this concept is a meaningful one, especially in its implications. For it is usually in nonviolent direct action that we must confront civil disobedience and the complex of legal and moral problems that it entails. Also, this form of action places more exacting demands upon nonviolent personal conduct, since it involves meeting the opponent on his own or disputed territory. Conflict is likely to be more acute here and the threat or reality of force or violence more direct.

In addition to these distinct types of nonviolence there are two categories of action that fit into nonviolent campaigns. First, there are actions which presuppose nonviolence but are mobile in their applicability. The act of standing or sitting as a human obstacle is an example, such as sitting on railroad tracks or on a roadway to block the movement of the opponent's vehicles. Another is the practice of "going limp" when arrested. The nonviolent cadre thus compels the opponent to lift him bodily. Such tactics lend themselves to all three types of nonviolence and defy easy classification, combining elements of passivity and of direct action. This fact raises a problem of interpretation that cannot be resolved theoretically but must be referred to the situation in which such conduct is used. In essence the problem is an ethical one that applies also to the whole spectrum of nonviolence.

It is hard to conceive of any situation in which nonresistance would be ethically prohibited, but the closer we get to direct action the more we have to justify our actions from an ethical perspective and also perhaps from a legal one. As we have already said, extreme measures require extreme compensation by acts and gestures of love. But even granting this, we must ask whether the situation itself justifies the use of direct action at all. We do not arbitrarily move from boycott to sit-in unless the conflict and the issues are so urgent and the boycott so unproductive by itself that a sit-in is ethically defensible. In general, extreme measures are to be reserved until moderate ones have been tried and fail. Given an extreme situation, of course, a type of nonviolence that is equally extreme is justly proportioned and not excessive at all.

But such tactics as bodily obstruction and going limp are psychologically volatile, offering a high level of expressive gratification that must be judiciously weighed not only against their ethical but their psychological appropriateness. Will they register an effective protest or will they stiffen the opponent's hostility and perhaps offend neutrals? The same questions may be asked of self-imposed suffering in the fast or hunger strike. Although obviously passive as social action, they may be strongly coercive psychologically and interpreted as blackmail of a very reprehensible kind.

Second, there are types of action which form an important part of many nonviolent campaigns but which are outside the scope of nonviolence as such. The poster walk, the march, picketing and other forms of public demonstration can be conducted "unviolently" by persons who are quite unprepared for nonviolence, so long as they occur in a situation where they are accepted as a legitimate form of extralegal protest. Unlike more conventional activities such as voting, petitioning, writing letters to editors and the like, they are nevertheless a form of action which may have to confront force or violence in situations that do not provide the stability of acceptance. And frequently this is the case where social conflict exists on a level that makes any of the types of nonviolence applicable. In such a context these otherwise "unviolent" actions may be entrusted only to those trained and prepared to act nonviolently. They become nonviolent by implication.

Also in this category are certain actions that have historically arisen in the context of nonviolent campaigns and have seldom been used otherwise: the public prayer vigil, both silent and vocal, and the prayer pilgrimage. These have been criticized as a perversion of worship and defended as a religiously purified kind of demonstration that witnesses to explicitly religious motives. Its defenders argue further that, because it is rooted in love, this kind of witness is intrinsically nonviolent. In terms of our analysis and typology, this claim misses the point by confusing love with nonviolence. The two are not identical and from a tactical standpoint these actions resemble public demonstrations in that they can be performed independently of a nonviolent campaign and, whatever their intrinsic merit, require an effective discipline of nonviolent response to attack if they are to be considered part of a nonviolent campaign. Given the occasion, however, these actions may well play a vital part in such a campaign.

Alternative Classifications

The above classification of types owes much to study and analysis of the work of others who have offered typologies in this area. Gene Sharp arranges nine categories along a "horizontal" spectrum that mixes those we have used above with a separate dimension that we shall consider as levels of conduct, strategy and tactics. Sharp's categories are ranged from conservative to revolutionary in the following order: 1) nonresistance, 2) active reconciliation, 3) moral resistance, 4) selective nonviolence, 5) passive resistance, 6) peaceful resistance, 7) nonviolent direct action, 8) *satyagraha* and 9) nonviolent revolution. One of the difficulties of such a system is the apparent fluidity of its criteria and the consequent arbitrariness of distinctions. *Satyagraha,* for instance, is so generic a term that it encompasses most if not all of the types listed before it, while active reconciliation can be more accurately viewed not as a type of nonviolent action but as a separate process related to any of these types. Also, additional intermediate categories might readily be inserted among those types that do form a consistent spectrum, e.g., "selective nonresistance" or "selective passive resistance." [10]

Along somewhat similar lines, C. J. Cadoux [11] has diagramed a much more elaborate spectrum that is useful in locating conventionally "unviolent" and specifically nonviolent actions within a broad range that includes gradations of these and also of force and violence. This is reproduced on the opposite page with minor modifications:

NONCOERCIVE
- Personal example
- Intercessory prayer
- Conciliatory discussion
- Direct acts of love
- Nonresistance
- Unmerited suffering
- Self-imposed penance
- Arguments and appeals
- Mediation
- Arbitration
- Promises
- Rewards
- Bribes

COERCIVE   *Examples*

NONINJURIOUS

Psychological { Noncooperation   Active resistance
                Civil Disobedience   Strike, boycott
                Threats }
                Anger   } show of force "War of nerves"

Physical { Restraint by manual force
            Bodily obstruction

INJURIOUS

Temporarily incapacitating action   Judo
Disablement with recoverable
   damage   Broken bone
Pain without permanent harm   Wrestling hold
Damage to personality (psycho-
   logical)   Neurosis
Permanent physical disablement   Crippling
Permanent damage to personality   Psychosis
Incidental or accidental homicide
Willful murder
Posthumous desecration or muti-
   lation
Torture
Mutilation

As elaborate as it is, this scheme could be elaborated still further as a bare list or refined into comprehensive structural detail. For our purposes it affords an instructive background that is, however, too unwieldy to serve as a tool of analysis.

Closer to our approach is the system devised by the sociologist Clarence Marsh Case, whose pioneer work [12] still commands respect and warrants study. His typology is more sharply focused along functional lines and is less complicated by moral evaluations than either Cadoux or Sharp:

PERSUASION

1. By argument.
2. By suffering: a) nonresistant martyrdom when suffering is inflicted by the opponent; b) self-inflicted, e.g., a hunger strike.

NONVIOLENT COERCION

1. Indirect action: strike, boycott, noncooperation (withdrawal from voluntary cooperation with opponent).
2. Political action through institutions and culture—combining partisan persuasion and impersonal coercion of law and established traditions. This involves the threat or use of force or "legitimated violence" by police, courts and prisons.
3. Social coercion: a) ostracism, b) collective pressure through passive resistance.

VIOLENT COERCION

1. Threat of violence or force.
2. Use of violence or force.

In general, our departure from Case's system derives from our basic concept of nonviolence as it has developed since Case wrote, and as it is related to our theological and ethical perspective. We would set aside his category of political action as being distinct from nonviolence. Our use of the term "passive resistance" corresponds roughly to his "indirect action" and "nonviolent direct action" to his "social coercion."

As is true of any theoretical formulation, any set of types or definitions must be general enough to withstand contact with the actualities from which it is derived. Those that we have selected are not sacrosanct. It is hoped that they have both sufficient precision and resilience to be serviceable in all cases. But there may well be situations in which the terminology of Case, Sharp, Cadoux or some other theorist can give added guidance. In any event our theoretical equipment is not yet complete until we augment our basic typology of horizontal range with a further typology of vertical levels on which they operate.

REFERENCES IN CHAPTER 2

1 M. K. Gandhi in *Harijan*, December 7, 1947.

2 Graves and Podro: *The Nazarene Gospel Restored* (Garden City, N. Y.: Doubleday & Co., Inc., 1954), p. 238.

3 L. N. Tolstoy: "What I Believe" in *The Tolstoy Centennial Edition* (London: Oxford Univ. Press, 1928-1937), Vol. 11, p. 398.

4 Dietrich Bonhoeffer: *The Cost of Discipleship* (New York: The Macmillan Co., second edition, 1960), p. 127.

5 *Ibid.*, p. 128.

6 André Trocmé: *Jésus-Christ et la Révolution Non Violente* (Geneva: Labor et Fides, 1961), p. 165.

7 C. J. Cadoux: *The Early Church and the World* (Edinburgh: Clark, 1925), p. 531f.

8 *Ibid.*, p. 532.

9 *Ibid.*, p. 529f.

10 See Gene Sharp: "A Study of the Meanings of Nonviolence" in *Gandhi Marg* (New Delhi), October 1959, p. 270.

11 C. J. Cadoux: *Christian Pacifism Re-examined* (Oxford: Basil Blackwell, 1940), p. 45.

12 C. M. Case: *Non-Violent Coercion* (New York: The Century Co., 1923), p. 397, *et seq.*

3

Levels of Generic Nonviolence

In addition to the three basic types of generic nonviolence there are different levels of motivation and organization on which each type can operate. In terms of motivation, the Quaker pamphlet *A Perspective on Nonviolence* [1] distinguishes between: 1) technique adopted as an expedient; 2) policy based on commitment and 3) spiritual discipline as "an act of trust in God and obedience to his will." These three categories may, however, be regarded as basically two: the expedient and the absolutist or holistic, with "policy based on commitment" comprising an area of overlap between these two. Historically the absolutist has usually been typified by nonresistance, though not always; and in more recent times it has often been the absolutists who have taken the lead in developing passive resistance and active nonviolence as a means of achieving relevance without abandoning their absolute commitment.

In a sense, this "absolutism" is of the essence of nonviolence. Nonviolent conduct as such—the act of refraining from violence even under direct provocation or attack—is either completely nonviolent or not so at all, and this fact is decisive in distinguishing between nonviolent action and conventional action. The distinction between expediency and absolutism comes into play in another way, however, in that the former relates nonviolent conduct to a given situation and certain limits, not necessarily excluding armed force or other means in another situation or under conditions that exceed the immediate commitment, while the thoroughgoing absolutist does not contemplate any departure from his holistic discipline and is prepared to find his justification outside the realm of historical results.

The levels that are of chief interest to us are accessible to the absolutist, but they are related primarily to the practical structuring of activity as an expedient technique. There are three such levels: 1) the spontaneous or subtactical, 2) the tactical and 3) the strategic. The first of these is in one sense the diametrical opposite of the holistic and in another it may be an expression of it. In the first sense—spontaneous—it is an unstable expression of good will arising from little or no forethought and having no prior, agreed-upon commitment, no idea of developing nonviolence in a systematic or sustained way. A more or less random crowd of unarmed demonstrators which resists provocation but has no plan for further nonviolent action would come under this heading. The other—subtactical—is an action that may be based on a limited commitment of expediency but is more likely to be associated with absolutism. Its chief characteristic is not that it is unplanned but that it is unrelated to a strategy of nonviolence. It is an isolated act or a "witness." It is possible to have a series of such subtactical actions or a variety of them simultaneously without any thought of strategy or of general policy.

This brings us to the all-important levels of tactics and strategy. Cadets of the U.S. Military Academy are taught that strategy is the art and science of developing and using the political, economic, psychological and military forces of a nation, during peace and during war, to afford the maximum support to national policies, in order to increase the probabilities and favorable consequences of victory and to lessen the chances of defeat. Specifically military strategy is the art and science of employing the armed forces of a nation to secure the objectives of national policy by the application of force or the threat of force. The fundamental law of strategy is to be stronger at the decisive point.

Cadets are taught that tactics are the employment of units

in combat, the ordered arrangement and maneuver of units in relation to each other and/or in relation to the enemy.

These definitions sum up the best thinking of military commanders from Sun Tzu and Alexander the Great to modern generals, and perhaps the pithiest definition is Clausewitz's: "Tactics is the art of using troops in battle; strategy is the art of using battles to win the war."

These definitions can be readily adapted from military conflict to social conflict involving nonviolence rather than armed force. Analogous to the West Point definitions we may say that over-all strategy would mean the use of nonviolence along with political action, conventional social action, publicity techniques and other methods in order to achieve an objective and to lessen the chances of defeat. A specifically nonviolent strategy would be an orchestration of a variety of tactics involving strategic leadership analogous to a military general staff. It is the task of the leadership to deploy their units of nonviolent cadres—persons disciplined in nonviolent conduct —in a manner most calculated to exert maximum strength at the decisive point rather than to allow them to undertake uncoordinated or sporadic actions of a subtactical kind.

Pursuing the analogy, nonviolent tactics are those actions undertaken by disciplined nonviolent cadres in direct confrontation with the opponent—in other words, the way in which organized groups of persons trained in nonviolent conduct act within their given sector of action in the furtherance of the larger objectives of nonviolent strategy.

It is the bearing on the objective that is tactical. In the case of a group of nonviolent cadres conducting a sit-in at a store, for example, the act of sitting in is the tactic. It is not all that the cadres are called upon to do; they also have to respond nonviolently to jeering, harassment and the like. These responses form another category as nonviolent conduct. If there are many coordinated sit-in actions, they form a sit-in strategy. But this may not be the case. The strategy may consist largely of economic boycott, and then we would speak of a boycott strategy supported by sit-in tactics. The distinctions between these levels are flexible and relative, and for greater fluency we might want to refer to minor and major strategies, and to tactics that have a delaying or holding purpose in contrast to those that move toward a strategic objective.

Sit-ins, stand-ins, walk-ins and the like are typical tactics of direct action. Forms of nonresistance such as allowing oneself to be arrested may be used tactically. Walkouts, boycotts and the like are typical passive resistance tactics. In a somewhat distinctive category are a number of bodily obstruction tactics that may be technically passive but carry a strong element of active interference, as exemplified by Indians in the independence struggles who lay down on railroad tracks to prevent trains from moving. Cadres sitting or standing in a doorway or road, singly or in groups interlocking their arms, are likewise using this type of tactic. Perhaps its most common manifestation in the United States has been the practice of "going limp" when arrested, or of pairs of cadres sitting back-to-back and linking arms to make it harder for police to carry them away.

In each specific case, little can be said of the intrinsic merit of any tactic. The questions to be asked are: what purpose does it serve in relation to strategy, what conduct does it demand, what other tactics may be needed to augment it, what further problems does it cause, how effective is it likely to be and is it nonviolent in content and in spirit?

In contrast with the undifferentiated use of nonviolence either holistically or spontaneously, we begin to see a spectrum of consistent levels that begins with nonviolent conduct and discipline as the basic individual resource and advances upward organizationally from subtactical actions by an individual or group to tactical actions by many groups as part of a concerted nonviolent campaign supported by legislative and judicial measures, by radio, television and press appeals, by conventional mass demonstrations and the like, together forming an over-all strategy which expresses a general policy.

Nonviolence in a Supporting Role

Just as troops may be tactically deployed for policing purposes in an internal emergency without a war strategy, nonviolent tactics may be used in the service of a campaign built around conventional political or social action. That is, they may function to support strategies other than nonviolent ones. A sit-in or withdrawal of patronage, for example, may be used tactically to add pressure in a situation where the main effort toward a solution is proceeding through the courts. Such a strategy is judicial rather than nonviolent, even though nonviolent cadres are deployed and may have to withstand harsh treatment just as in a campaign of strategic nonviolence.

Acts of nonviolence, when serving as tactics in a conventional campaign, do not thereby make it a "nonviolent" campaign, though they may give it a nonviolent coloration. There is an understandable tendency among some enthusiasts to claim even ordinary conventional action as nonviolent and to capitalize on the presence of authentically nonviolent elements for propaganda purposes, but as a simple matter of fact it is misleading to describe such campaigns in this way, even if every participant in a conventional action is wholeheartedly committed to nonviolence.

The campaign which has conventional action as its backbone is only one type, perhaps the most prevalent. In others, tactical or subtactical nonviolence may occur as an adjunct to insurrectionary violence. We are not arguing for their compatibility, but historically this has happened: nonviolence in one sector, with sabotage, terrorism and guerrilla warfare in others forming the strategic backbone. Finally, there is a type of campaign in which the strategic burden is carried primarily by nonviolence, supported tactically or subtactically by conventional and even violent actions of some kinds.

There are clear historical examples of social-action campaigns restricted to conventional methods, but every other kind is a mixture involving various proportions of conventional action and violence, or conventional action and nonviolence, or all three together. Particularly when resistance occurs on a large scale it becomes a problem to control or coordinate the different kinds of action that may arise—to move people from the conventional to the nonviolent, as well as to curb outbreaks of violence, and to orchestrate the activities of different organizations in the pursuit of the same objective.

As in political or military operations, nonviolent tactics and strategy are arts that require talent and imagination to be effective. The good tactician or strategist not only must understand the principles of nonviolence but also needs a good sense of timing. He must be able to appraise the facts of the situation and decide whether to exercise restraint or daring at the crucial moment. He must be able to conceive the right symbolic act or gesture to dramatize the campaign in a forceful and striking way, and for this he may turn to a number of actions that have no tactical or strategic value as such. Public fasting, silent vigils and the like, though not inherently nonviolent, may serve to underline the spiritual dimension and the nonviolent intent of tactics which are themselves somewhat ambiguous. Poster walks and picketing, though conventional, can be so designed as to point up the nonviolent emphasis. The strategist must know, too, how to sustain reverses and losses and regroup his followers; and, sometimes lacking strategic avenues for their energies, he must devise outlets to enable them to express themselves as much for the sake of releasing charged-up emotions as for communicating with others. Above all, he must be able to coordinate a variety of tactics so that they augment one another.

Broadly speaking, the classic pattern of a nonviolent strategy begins with conventional action: investigating the facts that comprise the issue or grievance; formation of a leadership committee; the building of organized mass support; presentation of the facts to the authorities. (In a later chapter on the dynamics of the campaign, we shall discuss these and subsequent steps in detail.) The committee at this point is presumably able to make a clear case on the basis of the facts and will be ready with a petition, mass rally or other suitable tactic to show that it has adequate backing. If the prestige of a number of distinguished persons or community organizations can be enlisted in support of the cause, this too may be helpful. In some few cases where the issue is a clearly moral one, respected by the opponent, the support of a few key persons of acknowledged moral integrity may be enough to settle the issue.

Means of Winning Support

If negotiations fail, additional tactical measures may be employed: publicity through newspapers, magazines, radio and television in a variety of forms—news releases, advertisements, letters to the editors, etc.—to gain public support beyond the immediate constituency and thus to create additional leverage. The strategic question will arise now whether to embark on a campaign to secure local or national legislation, to press for enforcement of existing laws, to carry the struggle through the courts, to engage in electoral action, etc. A choice of this kind is most likely of strategic significance and must be weighed carefully because it will determine the major allocations of time and effort. A very large campaign may involve two or more parallel strategies, but even here one or another is likely to receive primary emphasis throughout the campaign, or else it may be desirable that the emphasis shift from one to another strategy. The point here is simply that in considering political action, for example, a decision must be made whether to engage in it as a tactical project to which a limited number of people are assigned, while the main effort is channeled elsewhere; to channel the main effort into political actions; or to omit it. Once the main lines of strategy are marked out, they cannot easily be changed without seriously disrupting the campaign, and while a maximum of flexibility and maneuverability is desirable it is inevitably limited by this fact.

Assuming that circumstances warrant a strategy of non-violence, we may also assume that a number of types of conventional action are simultaneously being used in a tactical capacity. Now we move into a phase of public protest activity: distributing leaflets, picketing, poster-walking, silent vigils. From these tactics on the threshold of nonviolent action, we move into passive resistance focused on the issue, and finally to active nonviolence, likewise focused on the issue.

At no point in the campaign is the door closed on negotiations. They may conceivably be going on throughout, though more likely they are suspended and resumed on the opponent's initiative. At no point does it cease to be vitally important to keep the committee going, to activate interest and rapport with the community, to continue to get wide and favorable publicity. The campaign proceeds by augmenting these tactics with stronger ones, holding the strongest and most difficult tactics in reserve till the final stages, as support for nonviolent direct action.

Circumstances will dictate the departures from the above pattern. It would obviously be foolish to begin with attempts to negotiate if the opponent had already ruled this out. In a police state the would-be negotiators might be shot or imprisoned. Gandhi made it a rule of his strategy that actions were announced in advance, but in such a way that the British were not enabled to nip them in the bud. In this he showed adroitness in managing two things—the act itself and the moral image associated with the manner in which it was performed. Both are important, but sometimes it may be necessary to choose between them. The gesture of openness is an excellent way of enhancing the latter, but it is not the only way and if it forestalls the act itself it had better be foregone. The important thing from the strategic viewpoint is to keep the moral image clear—that is, to make sure that the omission of this or that step is not interpreted as trickery or deviousness. Whatever extenuations there may be for any misconduct, they are not likely to offset the objective outcome. Ways must be found, not to create an illusion of moral uprightness, but to communicate tangible moral intent without fraud and without surrender.

The general pattern moves by stages from moderate to extreme forms of conventional action and then from moderate to extreme forms of nonviolent action. This movement carries with it a quickening of pace and tempo. As it goes toward the extreme it becomes riskier, harder to sustain. Greater demands are placed upon morale, courage, physical energy and discipline. At the farthest extreme, nonviolent action takes the form of outright breaches of law and if these are on a wide scale we are in the midst of a revolutionary situation in which it may be difficult to maintain order and to curb outbursts of violence. Hence the choice of tactics and their orchestration into a strategy is relatively easy when the means are conventional, but increasingly difficult and delicate as they become more extreme. It is the task of the strategist to map out the campaign as far ahead as possible, to foresee the choices that will be confronted, to devise alternative plans in advance of a rapidly changing situation, and finally to be equipped to make pivotal decisions at crucial moments.

Obviously it would be very unwise to begin a campaign with mass civil disobedience or others forms of direct action. The chances of quick defeat and of riot would be too high. But it is not inconceivable that in certain circumstances, as in a totalitarian state, secret and underground substitutes might be developed in place of what we have called conventional action. In every circumstance, however, the understanding and application of strategy and tactics are essential to the effective use of nonviolence.

REFERENCE IN CHAPTER 3

1   Philadelphia: Friends Peace Committee, 1957.

4

Civil Disobedience

Civil disobedience or civil resistance is a form of nonviolent direct action that involves breaking the law. Because of this fact, it requires detailed consideration by the student of non-violence.

The term "civil disobedience" is often associated with an essay by Henry David Thoreau, *The Duty of Civil Disobedience*. It is a curious fact, however, that the phrase does not appear in Thoreau's essay at all, which originally appeared in 1849 with the title *Resistance to Civil Government*, as a retort to Paley's *Duty of Submission to Civil Government*.

In law the word "civil" originally pertained to the members of a *civitas* or free political community, and is thus used in modern times to distinguish the rights of the free citizen against the claims of public policy. The term "civil" is also used in contradistinction to "military," "ecclesiastical," "natural" or "foreign." [1]

The question posed by Thoreau is an ancient one. Civil government, whether by democratic or other presumably just means, is a way of maintaining order and justice within a community. Unlike military regulations or church ordinances, which may be arbitrary, and unlike "natural" laws, which are not of man's making, civil law presupposes consent by the whole citizenry for the sake of harmoniously managing their common affairs. Each person tacitly agrees to abide by the will of the civil community even if it does not in every detail correspond to his own will. The same general principle applies in a monarchy, a dictatorship or a democracy. And so does the counter-principle stated by Thoreau, which is that occasions may arise when a member of the community must withdraw his support. Even in a democracy based on the will of the majority, the minority, whether large or small, Thoreau argues, has rights that it can and must assert whether the majority recognizes them or not.

Lactantius, writing in 304 A.D., addressed this question in terms of Christian civil resistance to the laws of an un-Christian state:

Constancy is a virtue, not in order that we may resist those who injure [us] . . . but that, when [men] bid us act contrary to the Law of God and contrary to justice, we may be frightened away by no threats or punishments from preferring the bidding of God to the bidding of man.[2]

It is worth noting that, like other fathers of the early church, Lactantius here simultaneously affirms nonresistance to the evildoer and stubborn resistance to evil laws. In the third century, according to Cadoux, "Christians reserved to themselves the right of deliberately and avowedly disobeying the laws and orders of the State, whenever those laws and orders came into conflict with what they felt to be the Law of God." [3] In other matters not involving such conflict, they were scrupulously law-abiding.

Thoreau's Application

Thoreau, who was more strongly influenced by William Godwin's libertarian *Political Justice* and by the philosophy of Emerson than by the Christian tradition, appealed to the rights of conscience rather than to the laws of God. The kernel of his political outlook is expressed in the following extracts from his often cited but seldom quoted essay:

Must the citizen ever for a moment, or in the least degree, resign his conscience to the legislator? Why has every man a conscience, then? . . . It is not desirable to cultivate a respect for the law, so much as for the right. . . . Law never made men a whit more just; and, by means of their respect for it, even the well-disposed are daily made the agents of injustice.[4]

Unjust laws exist: shall we be content to obey them, or shall we endeavor to amend them, and obey them until we have succeeded, or shall we transgress them at once? . . . If the injustice is part of the necessary friction of government, let it go, let it go . . . but if it is of such a nature that it requires you to be the agent of injustice to another, then, I say, break the law. Let your life be a counter friction to stop the machine. What I have to do is to see, at any rate, that I do not lend myself to the wrong which I condemn.[5]

Cast your whole vote, not a strip of paper merely, but your whole influence. A minority is powerless while it conforms to the majority; it is not even a minority then; but it is irresistible when it clogs by its whole weight. If the alternative is to keep all just men in prison or to give up war and slavery, the State will not hesitate to choose. . . . When the subject has refused allegiance, and the officer has resigned his office, then the revolution is accomplished.[6]

There is a discrepancy between civil and moral law, and it is the latter which is of utmost importance. Because men respect the former they are sometimes misled into betraying the latter. If they discover the discrepancy, should they trust to the gradual and orderly processes of the law to resolve it? If it is an incidental sort of injustice, occasioned by the inevitable clumsiness of government, we ought to bear with it. But if, as Thoreau elsewhere states, it is a law such as the Fugitive Slave Law, which was unjust to the fugitive slave, we must break the civil law if we are to obey the moral law which demands justice for the slave. As a matter of individual conscience we must do this, but by so doing our breach of the civil law serves as a vote more powerful than the electoral ballot to repeal that law. If enough men who believe in the moral law will exert their weight in this way, even though they are a numerical minority, they may succeed in clogging the processes of government to such an extent that the government will reconsider its actions. If enough men will break the law and go to jail, if office-holders will resign in protest, the government will find that the only way to restore order is to accede to their just demands.

In addition to the Fugitive Slave Law, Thoreau protested against the Mexican War and refused to pay taxes for it. His protest was a distinguished one, but it was isolated and ineffective. Although he stated the general principle of disobedience and projected its revolutionary possibility, he offered no strategy for a mass movement.

Thoreau was a man of acute moral righteousness. He was an "individual anarchist" in the sense that he felt that he could live justly without the benefit of the civil law. By obeying the laws of conscience he was sure to obey those of the civil laws that were worth obeying. He was willing to acquiesce in incidental injustices to himself but highly sensitive when the civil law sought to conscript his conscience in behalf of injustice to others. In this his outlook corresponded closely to that of Lactantius. It did also in a further respect: he took it for granted that the just man accepts whatever punishment is meted out to him for his breach of the civil law.

Such a philosophy applied on a social scale must, to be viable, presuppose a society of men who all possess a similar moral righteousness. It is not our concern here to enter into an argument with the proponents of social anarchism on this point. But whether or not an anarchic society is possible on a large and permanent scale, given certain conditions, the historical fact up to the present has been that actual communities of this type have been both small and short-lived. This fact indicates two things—both that it *is* possible for a group of committed and disciplined people to live as Thoreau did (and perhaps better), and that this cannot be expected of the whole population of any community. Even in an emergency when a community makes its best showing there are likely to be individuals who take advantage of the absence of order to commit crimes.

The Churches Take a Stand

Emil Brunner has pointed out the difficulties inherent in the medieval philosophy of "natural law" developed by the Roman Catholic Church, when it entered into competition with the civil law or, as he calls it, "the positive law of the state." The outlook of the men of the Reformation on this question represented a radical departure. "They took their stand clearly on the side of positive law," Brunner says, "granting to the law of nature the function of a criterion." [7] That is, the reformers had the wisdom to acknowledge the existence of a higher moral law to which moral men might aspire and in light of which they might refashion the civil law. But only the civil law could be made to serve as the normative basis for regulating human affairs. Thus an individual has the right and duty to appeal from laws he deems unjust, and to try to change them in accordance with the higher criterion which is the law of God as his conscience sees it. But if there is to be both civil order and liberty of conscience, men must give common allegiance to the civil law and relinquish their pretensions to a monopoly of moral truth.

The point may seem to be a fine one, but it is crucial to an understanding of civil disobedience: the truly conscientious civil resister not only appeals to a higher moral law but he also shows respect for the principle of civil law. Moreover, he recognizes the binding force of the very law which he deems unjust and does not try to evade its consequences. He balances his subjective moral right of disobedience against society's objective legal right to punish him. Though he chooses deliberately to act in defiance of the law, his act is not an act of lawlessness. And this is true, it is important to note, not merely with reference to a higher moral law but precisely with reference to the laws of a society whose basic legitimacy he may question. Thoreau spoke of the rights of a minority, but in many cases in which civil resistance has been invoked it has been a disfranchised *majority* that has done so.

The question of disfranchisement is a pertinent one. Speaking of the resort to nonviolence by Negroes in the Southern states, Paul Ramsey says:

The duty to observe the law, we have said, has full force only where people of any race in our society effectively have the vote, and can participate politically at the state and local levels in the changing of undesirable local ordinances or discriminatory state statutes.[8]

Invoking Jean Calvin's doctrine of the right of civil resistance against tyranny or grave injustice in which a "lesser magistrate" may have recourse to the natural law to correct an erring "higher magistrate," Ramsey continues:

Every man must have political initiative as a "minor magistrate." His magisterial capacity as a citizen should make it possible for him to participate democratically in making the laws, applying in his own right the "criterion" of natural justice to help determine the legal requirements. Anyone who would cast out the members of any race from exercising the franchise . . . cannot then with clean hands and a clean heart insist that they should still be law-abiding people.[9]

Under the terms of Calvin's doctrine not only civil disobedience but armed resistance is morally permissible, says Ramsey, "where states have become wholly totalitarian, where the means for changing laws have become clogged and men wholly frustrated in their search for legal justice."[10] It is prudence alone, he argues, that dictates nonviolence rather than recourse to armed revolution.

Which Conscience to Follow?

However conscientious it may be, civil disobedience is a serious matter that is not justified simply by the willingness of the civil resister to take the consequences. As Ramsey points out, the truly conscientious man will respect the conscience of the law as well as his own. That is, he will consider carefully whether the issue is of such a nature that he is justified in overriding and thwarting the conscience of his opponents who are upholding the law. Is he challenging a vested minority that has obtained the acquiescence of a misled majority, or is he contesting against a whole society that has had the impudence to disagree with him? Even if it is clear that society is wrong, does he have the moral right to impede its actions when he is free to use methods short of civil disobedience to persuade society to his views?

Alan Lovell has made a useful distinction between the tactical and the strategic significance of civil resistance. In its tactical aspect it serves as a stimulus to a faltering democratic system. "In this case you affect people . . . by an emotional challenge, which eventually affects political parties and eventually governments." Or, like the general strike, it can be seen as "a complete method of politics; that is, if you want to get nuclear disarmament you get it by the fact that so many people refuse to work on armaments that it would be impossible to go on with the arms program." [11]

In the former instance it is a matter of resorting to extralegal tactics in support of a strategy carried on within the legal framework of a democracy, exerting pressure for changes within the system. "If you do an act of civil disobedience, are prepared to go to jail or take some kind of personal risk," Lovell says, "you show that there is something more serious to the business than being just out for your own ends. . . . It adds a quality of seriousness to your action." [12] Here the act of civil disobedience functions as a symbolic gesture; it is not intended to disrupt or thwart the opponent's course of action.

But in the latter case, what is intended is the short-circuiting of democratic processes and the imposition of rule by a self-constituted oligarchy—a strategy with clearly revolutionary implications. We are not here asking whether such a revolutionary step may be warranted or not. It may be that in a specific situation democratic institutions have so decayed or atrophied that revolution by such means is justified. But certainly it is a grave matter calling for the utmost objectivity in assessing the situation, lest we find proponents of nonviolence in the bizarre position of staging a minority *putsch* against a free society.

In the context of the same campaign for nuclear disarmament in Britain which furnished the context for Lovell's remarks, Canon L. John Collins discusses the question illuminatingly:

First, a distinction must be drawn, I think, between a refusal to obey a law which is repugnant to conscience and a deliberate breaking of laws, which in themselves cause no offense to conscience, in order to gain publicity and to bring pressure to bear upon governments. . . . If a citizen is asked by his government to do something which is repugnant to his conscience then, I believe, he should refuse—and, of course, accept the consequences.

Secondly, I am not in principle and in all circumstances opposed to civil disobedience as a technique whether against tyranny or against a government which, though enjoying the support of the majority, insists upon policies which are seen as a threat to peace and justice. . . .

But when and when not to indulge in nonviolent civil disobedience are matters for the most careful consideration. It is a question of weighing up expedience and consequences. . . .

. . . It is possible [in Britain today] to change policies by legal methods of persuasion. Some may feel that the democratic processes are slow, limited and often ineffective . . . but will the technique of civil disobedience be more likely to produce quick results? . . .

I have much sympathy with those who argue for civil disobedience as a shock treatment to be administered to a lunatic body politic. . . . But I am inclined to believe that the publicity obtained by "sit down" and other such demonstrations does not in the long run prosper our cause but, rather, tends to destroy the effectiveness of our democratic efforts.[13]

Canon Collins goes on to say that "demonstrations based on civil disobedience as an expedient technique open the way for some of the more ugly forms of mob hysteria and violence," and cites an instance in which such elements were present.

A technique of what must be described as "blackmail" of a minority against the majority must inevitably strain the police (who are forced to try to uphold the law) and give opportunity for "toughs" and "agents provocateurs" to provoke violence.[14]

Finally he notes the presence of anarchists seeking to make use of the civil-disobedience campaign "to destroy the British Constitution and to bring all administration to a standstill." He believes that if they succeeded the government would be taken over "not by noble devotees of nonviolence but by some ugly and dangerous form of dictatorship." [15]

Gandhi's Views

Gandhi had some idea of the volatility of civil disobedience when he contemplated his first nationwide use of it in 1921. "Those only can take up civil disobedience," he wrote, "who believe in willing obedience even to irksome laws imposed by the state so long as they do not hurt their conscience or religion, and are prepared equally willingly to suffer the penalty of civil disobedience." [16] Twenty-three years later in a speech to congressmen from Maharashtra, June 29, 1944, he reaffirmed this view in even stronger terms: "Civil disobedience is a very potent weapon. But everyone cannot wield it. For that one needs training and inner strength. It requires occasions for its use." [17]

To this we may add that it requires wisdom and restraint on the part of the strategist of nonviolence in choosing the occasions for its use. Maintenance of firm nonviolent discipline and the exclusion of unreliable elements—a difficult task—appear to be of prime importance. As the comments of Ramsey and Collins both suggest, the presence or absence of legal channels for desired change is a key factor in the situation.

Assuming that the situation is one that justifies and demands civil resistance, we must now confront the possibility that if it succeeds it may in some circumstances precipitate a revolutionary situation. We shall turn to this question in the next chapter.

The character of civil disobedience, the manner in which it is asserted and the context in which it arises all hinge on this question, which implies a failure of the existing civil order. So long as the existing order is a stable one, and perhaps even if it is not, certain specific types of purported civil disobedience may be seriously questioned. Is it compatible with the spirit of nonviolence to run from the police, to use bodily force to break through a police cordon, to refuse to obey or resist arrest by physical noncooperation, compelling the police to push or carry the noncooperator? Such actions seem closer to the insurrectionary anarchism of Sorel and Bakunin than to anything envisaged by Thoreau, despite his talk of clogging the machinery of the state. When such methods are invoked in the name of nonviolence without a context of broad popular sympathy as a cushion, the psychological repercussions can be very damaging. Gandhi advised great care and prudence to avoid inciting or needlessly antagonizing the authorities, and for the same reasons such acts can also alienate both moderate sympathizers and the neutral public or, given a revolutionary situation, undermine respect for lawful order in general and promote irresponsible, inflammatory responses leading to chaos. In the case of an isolated individual it may be written off as fanaticism, but when contemplated as part of a campaign, mass civil disobedience is dynamite.

Not every instance of nonviolent direct action constitutes civil disobedience. It may be used, for example, against customs and practices that have no legal basis or expression, or where local and national laws are at variance. Civil disobedience means specifically a breach of the law without recourse to other legality except in a moral sense. We must also bear in mind the important distinctions among selective, symbolic breaches of law to gain publicity or to establish a course of legal action, strategic mass disobedience of one particularly onerous statute, an across-the-board defiance of all unjust laws and, finally, refusal to submit to any laws of an unjust government. Within the range of this spectrum are the extremes of moral protest and the verge of revolution.

REFERENCES IN CHAPTER 4

1 See *Black's Law Dictionary* (St. Paul, Minn.: West Publishing Co., third edition, 1933), p. 331.
2 Lactantius: *Divinae Institutiones,* VI, xvii, 24.
3 C. J. Cadoux: *The Early Church and the World* (Edinburgh: Clark, 1925), p. 528.
4 Henry David Thoreau: "Civil Disobedience" in *Walden and Other Writings* (New York: Modern Library, Inc., 1937), p. 636f.
5 *Ibid.,* p. 644.
6 *Ibid.,* p. 647.
7 Emil Brunner: *Justice and the Social Order* (New York: Harper & Brothers, 1945), p. 93.
8 Paul Ramsey: *Christian Ethics and the Sit-In* (New York: Association Press, 1961), p. 96f.
9 *Ibid.,* p. 97.
10 *Ibid.,* p. 92.
11 Alan Lovell: "Direct Action" in *New Left Review* (London), March-April 1961, p. 16.
12 *Ibid.,* p. 18.
13 L. John Collins: "Civil Disobedience" in *Christian Action* (London), Autumn 1961, p. 12ff.
14 *Ibid.,* p. 14.
15 *Ibid.*
16 M. K. Gandhi in *Young India,* November 3, 1921.
17 Quoted in Pyarelal: *Mahatma Gandhi: The Last Phase* (Ahmedabad: Navajivan, 1956), Vol. 1, p. 25.

5

Resistance and Revolution

In Gene Sharp's typology of nonviolence, the final category was "nonviolent revolution." The phrase has an exciting ring and has often been used with oratorical flourish to describe almost any kind of change effected through the use of non-violence. But properly speaking, in the sense in which Sharp uses it, it means nothing less than the unseating of one political regime in a society and its replacement by another. For the Gandhian it implies much more as well: the establishment of a new, revolutionary type of nonviolent society: *sarvodaya* or nonviolent socialism, a society of federated local units as envisaged by Vinoba Bhave and Jayaprakash Narayan, based on voluntary cooperation and substituting nonviolent sanctions for armed force in the regulation of its affairs.

In this chapter, however, we are not so much concerned with the nature of such a society, nor even necessarily with the question of whether it would be the outcome of revolution. Our primary concern is to inquire how nonviolence can move from active civil resistance that challenges and changes the superstructure of society to full-scale revolution that alters the basic power structure.

The revolutionary potential of nonviolence is already evident in the fact that civil disobedience on a wide and protracted scale is capable of undermining an existing power structure. This may precipitate a crisis that sets the stage for revolution. Is it then possible by nonviolent means to effect a transition to a new society, placing the nonviolent leaders in power and keeping them there?

James M. Lawson Jr., speaking at the 1961 annual meeting of the Southern Christian Leadership Conference, declared: "The emerging nonviolent movement is a revolutionary enterprise moving toward real revolution and total revolution." As a concrete way of effecting this, he proposed the recruitment and training of a nonviolent army of from 2,000 to 8,000 volunteers.

Let us work out with them a private discipline, reconciliation in personal life. Let us establish work camps for training, study, reading, meditation and constructive work in voting, repairing neighborhood slums, community centers.

Let us prepare these people for mass nonviolent action in the Deep South. Let us recruit people who will be willing to go at a given moment and stay in jail indefinitely. . . .

A campaign with such an army would cause world-wide crisis, on a scale unknown in the Western world except for actual war.

The sit-ins and freedom rides won concessions within the existing system. These constitute only "the prelude to revolution"; the nonviolent army would exert such pressure as to cause "structural changes":

There will be no revolution until we see Negro faces in all positions that help to mold public opinion, help to shape policy for America.

Lawson does not go into further detail than this, but it is clear from the above that he envisages the complete wresting of political power from the hands of white supremacists in the states of the Deep South and its transfer to state, county and local governments representing the whole population, including the substantial and largely disfranchised Negro population.

The states in which this would occur have a limited sovereignty within the United States. This fact immediately attenuates the scope of revolution in this context. Granting this reservation, is it conceivable that Lawson's revolution would be wholly nonviolent or would his proposed nonviolent army simply provide leverage to activate the machinery of Federal power, backed up, ultimately, by the legitimate and constitutional use of armed force? In any event, the nonviolent movement in the South has seldom hesitated to invoke the police powers of the Federal Government or to avail itself of Federal justice through the courts. Even if it developed preponderant numerical strength it is apparent not only that it would make maximum use of legal avenues rather than attempt a seizure of power through nonviolent direct action, but that it would appeal to Federal power to aid in opening and safeguarding those avenues.

One student of nonviolence and of revolution, Michael Walzer, has argued that nonviolent methods are inherently defensive, suited to resistance but not to revolution in the proper sense.

The boycott and the strike are forms of resistance, though the passive immobility of the sit-down is perhaps its best symbol. All these were first used in the fight against economic injustice, and socialists once hoped that the worker would carry on from these activities to revolution. But the refusal to work, the refusal to buy, the refusal to move are not, in fact, revolutionary. They are acts of stoppage and withdrawal, expressions of discontent, requiring physical presence, self-control and solidarity. But they do not point to transformation and often enough [they appeal to] threatened standards and ancient liberties, the good society that once had been. The general strike in Budapest in 1956 seems to me an act of resistance: a public and demonstrative repudiation of an oppressive ruling party. But in the absence of any group comparable to the Puritans, Jacobins or Bolsheviks, it would be difficult to argue that there was a Hungarian revolution, in the full sense of that term.[1]

If the Hungarian events did not comprise a revolution in the full sense, however, there is no gainsaying the fact that movement occurred from resistance to active revolt and incipient revolution. And if the presence of a group such as the Puritans, Jacobins or Bolsheviks is the hallmark of a bona fide revolution, is it not a fact that each of these groups had its origins in a tradition of resistance? Turning Walzer's analysis around, it may be said that nonviolent methods are not inherently revolutionary but they can serve as a springboard to revolution, given certain additional factors, of which a revolutionary organization may be one. To the extent that the independence campaigns of India and Ghana may be described as movements of this kind, it may be worth examining the classic pattern of the modern revolution and observing points of similarity with these examples of nonviolent revolutionary change.

Crane Brinton, in his authoritative study, *The Anatomy of Revolution,* has provided us with the basic framework from which we have derived the following outline. Brinton analyzes the stages through which the Cromwellian, French, American and Russian revolutions moved, finding certain uniformities among them that enable us to speak of a classical sequence of events.

Sequence for a Revolution

Revolutions are not begun by people who are starving and miserable; they spring from hope rather than despair. They arise where the antagonisms of social classes are complex rather than simple, and where there are no wide gaps in their stratification. A factor of key importance, illustrated in India by the roots of the independence movement in the Hindu Renaissance, is the intellectuals' desertion of the status quo, inaugurating a revolutionary cultural climate in advance of the political manifestations of revolution. The final factors which Brinton observes are the inefficiency of the government machinery in adjusting to new pressures and the political ineptitude of the ruling class.

What triggers revolution in the classical case is the resistance of the people to the collection of taxes, an act of civil resistance as we have already defined it. In both India and Ghana the initial events were more closely related to the ultimate objective of independence.

Next comes further civil disobedience in the form of overt

illegal acts that challenge constituted authority. A perfect example is the march of workers in Petrograd in February 1917. "At the critical moment the soldiers refused to march against the people, but regiment by regiment came over instead to join them." [2] Brinton advances the tentative generalization that

no government has ever fallen before revolutionists until it has lost control over its armed forces or lost the ability to use them effectively; and conversely that no revolutionists have ever succeeded until they have got a predominance of effective armed force on their side.[3]

Ghana is an exception in that no armed forces were involved. In India the situation was somewhat complicated by the fact that both British and Indian troops were in the service of the British raj; but the defections of the latter into Bose's Azad Hind Fauz, the naval mutiny of 1948 and the demobilization of some 2,500,000 Indian troops at the end of World War II all undoubtedly comprise loss of their effective control by the British. It is not so clear whether they met Brinton's converse condition, though probably they did in a latent sense, and if the British had not moved out in time there might have been military clashes.

We now come to the seizure of power by a broad coalition of revolutionary forces and the establishment of a moderate legal government. In India, this was the Congress Party; in Ghana, the Convention People's Party. The actual accession to power is relatively easy, so little support does the old regime have. Brinton calls this the "honeymoon stage" of coexistence among moderates and radicals who comprise the revolutionary forces.

After the honeymoon, said the French moderate P. V. Vergniaud, "the revolution, like Saturn, devours its children." [4]

In all our revolutions there is a tendency for power to go from Right to Center to Left, from the conservatives of the old regime to the moderates to the radicals or extremists. As power moves along this line, it gets more and more concentrated, more and more narrows its base in the country and among the people.[5]

It is perhaps premature to evaluate a development of this kind in India or Ghana, but in each, apparently radical moves have been successfully undercut by a popular chief of state pursuing a left-of-center policy, jettisoning dissident former colleagues and silencing extreme opponents by arbitrary police methods. It is difficult to say whether this represents a bypassing of the subsequent stages of the classical revolution or a kind of encapsulation of them in sublimated form. Or it may be that the fact of nonviolence, though failing to produce a nonviolent society, has indeed produced a new sequence of postrevolutionary developments. But all of this is sheer conjecture.

A key development in the classic pattern that effectuates the drive toward the left is the rise of what Trotsky called *dvoevlastie*—dual power or dual sovereignty. As Brinton puts it,

the legal government finds opposed to it, once the first steps in actual revolution have been taken, not merely hostile individuals and parties—this any government finds—but a rival government, better organized, better staffed, better obeyed. This rival government is of course illegal, but not all of its leaders and followers are from the beginning consciously aiming to supplant the legal government. . . .

Once the first stage in revolution is over, the struggle that arises between moderates and extremists comes to be a struggle between two rival government machines.[6]

In the Russian Revolution, the moderate provisional government faced the more radical and popular soviets, or councils of workers', soldiers' and peasants' deputies. The radical turn of the October Revolution hinged on the cry, "All power to the soviets," and it was through them that the Bolsheviks achieved power. In the French Revolution, Jacobin societies sprang up throughout the country to challenge the authority of the legal

Assembly. In America, deviating from the pattern somewhat, town meetings were controlled by illegalists who developed the Continental Congress parallel to the colonial regimes.

It is interesting to note that although they had precedents in the past the soviets and Jacobin societies arose directly from the revolutionary situation. In the American colonies it was a matter of adapting rooted native institutions to a revolutionary purpose. In India the principle embraced a broad variety of institutions consciously and carefully set up in conjunction with the resistance movement over a period of decades and in large part related to the projected needs of the postrevolutionary society. Hannah Arendt has observed that the springing up of such institutions is a universal feature of revolutions, pointing to a popular instinct for federalism based on the "direct regeneration of democracy" which has consistently been overridden in each revolution by the party system. This is true not only of the four revolutions which Brinton studied, but of the Paris Commune of 1870, the Chinese Revolution, the Cuban Revolution of 1960 and others.[7]

The final phases of the classic revolution are the accession of the extremists, the reign of terror and the Thermidorean reaction. We need not go into great detail here, but let us note that Brinton calls the second of these "the reign of terror and virtue" in which persecution extends not only to counterrevolutionaries but to anyone exhibiting indifference to the revolution. In this situation the extremists set out puritanically to stamp out even minor vices in "heroic attempts to close once for all the gap between human nature and human aspirations."[8] Among the reasons Brinton gives for the terror are the habit of violence, the inexperience of the extremist administrators and the newness of the government machinery, and the recklessness and drive of the leaders. ("They are not formed for compromise, for the dull expedients of politics in unexcited, relatively stable societies.") Arendt would add, as would Martin Buber and others, that this phase also signals the triumph of the state over the federative councils, which now are either smashed or emasculated and kept as appendages of party government.[9] The reign of terror and "virtue" is imposed by cliques substituting state control for these popular institutions.

In the end there is a reaction against the hectic factionalism and intolerance—or as Brinton puts it, "a convalescence from the fever of revolution"—with the advent of the strong man as ruler: Washington, Cromwell, Napoleon, Lenin. The highest hopes of the revolution recede, revolts by the extreme left (Shays, Winstanley, Babeuf, the Kronstadt garrison) are crushed, the people are tired, and crime, corruption, extravagance and relaxation of discipline all toll the knell of the Republic of Virtue. We shall leave it an open question whether India and Ghana have passed through this stage yet and whether Nehru and Nkrumah fill the role of the strong man. In the French and Russian revolutions the leadership passed from, roughly speaking, Lafayette to Danton to Robespierre to Napoleon, and from Mirsky to Kerensky to Lenin. In the English and American revolutions the shift in the locus of power is not so readily identified with individuals. To the extent that America had a Robespierre it was Samuel Adams or Thomas Paine, but neither of these men decisively held the reins of government at any time. In England, Cromwell himself rode out the transitions much as Nehru did in India.

The Roots of Revolutions

The Russian Revolution was preceded by a century or more of sporadic peasant revolts growing out of direct resistance, which was often bloody. For a time, in some areas, under such leaders as Emilian Pugachov and Stepan Razin, these revolts reached the proportions of protracted guerrilla warfare. When the revolution broke out it reignited these fires of revolt throughout Russia, sweeping the countryside into civil war. This fact brings us back to Walzer's statement about the "unrevolutionary" character of resistance—and to Brinton's observation that the revolutionization of the intellectuals is a prerequisite to revolution and, indeed, the first real harbinger of it. Mass discontent may express itself for a long time through violent or nonviolent acts of resistance without any hope of producing a revolution. Once the discontent of the intellectuals has matured to a certain point, however, a chance occurrence of mass protest offers a kairotic moment for the intellectuals to step in and provide articulate leadership. In February 1917 all of the revolutionary parties and leaders, who had long been advocating revolution, were taken by surprise when one day they found themselves with a revolution on their hands. As Trotsky tells us in his *History of the Russian Revolution,* this did not fit in with the plans of any of the revolutionists, who immediately scrambled to place themselves at the head of the spontaneous mass movement. Had this not occurred, the February events would have been just one more revolt, not the doorsill of revolution.

A frustrating fact which the would-be revolutionist usually cannot face is that revolutions are born, not made. No amount of revolutionary agitation by a "vanguard" group, be it nonviolent or violently insurrectionary, can produce a revolution. Such a group would be well advised to invest its efforts in constructive work compatible with the revolutionary goals until the conditions arise that can produce a revolutionary situation.

The strategic importance of the constructive program of nonviolence will be mentioned in a later chapter. In the context of revolution we need only to point out its importance in providing a stable, rooted and broad base for the government of dual power, capable of withstanding attacks both from the old regime and from internal factions. There must be time for the instrumentalities of the constructive program to acquire the status of institutions that transcend political allegiances and hence command the loyalties of all who in the moment of crisis may fall prey to factionalism. Probably it is not possible to avoid factionalism, but it is important to devise ways to moderate it and keep it from breaking out into an overt struggle for power.

Nonviolence in the Transfer of Power

To return for a moment to the idea of revolution in Lawson's sense—the transfer of power within states having only a limited sovereignty—there is a point at which the constructive program becomes subrevolutionary in relation to the political and social structure. This is evident in the Southern states of the United States, where the objective is not the overthrow of the whites by the Negroes but a change of customs and laws on the basis of equality. Neither Trotsky's nor Gandhi's concept of dual power quite fits the case. Although there is scope for Negro community self-improvement organizations, they would be self-defeating if they only engaged in constructive work within their segregated confines. A distinctive dimension in this struggle is shown precisely in the rise of interracial organizations, both of a semiofficial consultative type such as mayors' committees and of a voluntary character such as the various human-relations councils. In addition, the racial openness of the predominantly Negro civil-rights organizations contributes to the same process, setting a pattern for the racially integrated society toward which these groups are working. In another dimension the effort to increase the Negro vote through lawsuits and voter-education activities has a clearly subrevolutionary function, paving the way for political action to unseat segregationist state and local governments without smashing the machinery but with crucial power changes in view. In the classical pattern of revolution involving a sovereign state, however, such possibilities do not exist.

In both India and Ghana the British withdrew and turned the government over to the indigenous leaders. Had they not done so, could the nonviolent revolution have been consummated in the face of British armed resistance? Bose's success in organizing his Azad Hind Fauz, taken together with the widespread resort to sabotage in the Quit India campaign, suggest the likelihood that the British would have been ousted by armed force. But supposing a much broader movement firmly committed to nonviolence and geared to a functioning system of dual power, could the British have been forced out by nonviolent methods?

This would have meant appealing directly to each British soldier to recognize and respect the government of independent India and to refuse to obey orders from his superiors to violate India's laws. In principle this is the kind of appeal the workers of Petrograd made to the troops of the tsarist regime with considerable though not complete success. In the Russian Revolution, as in others, the preponderance of the troops of the old regime became troops of the new regime and, augmented by armed civilians, engaged in combat with those troops that remained loyal to the old regime. That is the initial violence of the revolution, which sets in motion the vicious cycle that culminates in the reign of terror.

How is this violence to be averted and the revolution kept on a nonviolent footing? It seems unrealistic to expect that every last soldier can be won over to the side of the new society or even relied upon to remain neutral, so long as his superiors have the power to punish him for failing to obey orders.

Gandhi's solution would have called for a million Indians to let themselves be killed in order gradually to convert the British by the sheer moral weight of their conduct. Maybe this would have worked, and maybe this course would be the only thoroughly nonviolent one, but it presupposes a degree of self-sacrifice far in excess of the human possibilities evident in the history of India or any other country up to now. Nor does this proposal take account of the vast capacities of men to rationalize and divest themselves of guilt. Indeed, such a move might well have inured the British soldier to wanton slaughter of unarmed people by confirming him in his belief that Indian life was cheap. A healthy assertion of the integrity and value of a life risked in the encounter of nonviolence with armed force is part of the dynamic by which such an appeal works. Even if Gandhi's million *satyagrahis* had stepped forward, the sacrifice of their lives would have been a blind gamble.

If the revolution has passed into the stage of dual power, in which the legality of the revolutionary institutions is affirmed and that of the old regime's is denied, then in a juridical sense the latter are outlaws from the viewpoint of the revolution. This fact provides a legal justification for depriving the old regime of its weapons. It would seem to be compatible with the ethics of nonviolence in such a situation to seize and destroy these weapons by nonviolent raids on arsenals and ordnance depots, and to use adequate manual force (not striking but holding so as to render harmless) to restrain would-be attackers, and even to take them into custody.

Some such measures must be devised to meet contingencies of hard-core resistance at this stage, though it would be inadvisable and perhaps disastrous to apply such extreme tactics in any phase of nonviolent strategy short of actual revolution. If such practical measures are not developed and made a part of nonviolent training well in advance of the need for their use, persons who are not committed to nonviolence will almost certainly seize the initiative at this point and resort to arms.

Those who, by engaging in civil disobedience, help to bring about the revolutionary crisis that places this question on the agenda have a moral obligation to face the problems that ensue. If they have assumed leadership in the struggle, they owe it to their followers to see them through and not to hand over their destinies to desperate extremists at a crucial moment that finds them unprepared. The fully nonviolent revolution, triumphing over all obstacles without counting on the prudent withdrawal of the opponent, has yet to be made, and it is not at all certain that it is a historical possibility.

Revolution has a deeply tragic side, nowhere more evident than in the rise and fall of what Brinton called "the reign of virtue" accompanying the extremist terror. Because the revolutionary aims of the holistic believer in nonviolence tend to resemble those of the extremists, it is worth noting what happens to the idealism of the latter when means are (temporarily, it is thought) divorced from ends. As Arendt puts it, "Wherever knowing and doing have parted company, the space of freedom is lost." [10]

The Problem of Means and Ends

Albert Camus says that what so often contaminates revolution is its readiness to substitute abstract virtue for love. When human beings are reduced to statistics as masses to be manipulated, expediency is enthroned and the door is flung open to terrorism. Or as Nikolai Berdyaev expresses it:

Revolution seeks triumph at all costs and whatever may happen. Triumph is achieved by force. This force inevitably turns into violence. There is a fateful mistake of the makers of revolution which is connected with their relation to time. The present is regarded exclusively as a means, the future as an end. . . . But the future in which the exalted end was to be realized never comes. In it there will again be those same repulsive means. Violence never leads to freedom. Hatred never leads to brotherhood. [11]

Yet, possessing destructive power, the utopian visionary is subject to a colossal temptation to use it to eliminate the obstacles he sees standing in the way of the realization of his vision. Robespierre and St.-Just, not bloodthirsty villains but moralists of high purpose, sent to the guillotine those men who, in their judgment, stood in the way of establishing a society in which the death penalty would be abolished forever. If, as they earnestly believed, the hope of such a society rested upon them, did they not have a sacred obligation to remain in power and dispose of anyone who sought to smash this hope? It was only for the immediate present, for the duration of the emergency. Tomorrow, after the storm, they would implement their dream. "Revolution without honor," wrote Camus, "calculated revolution which, in preferring an abstract concept of man to a man of flesh and blood, denies existence as many times as necessary, puts resentment in the place of love." [12] Brotherhood is not established by destroying the enemies of brotherhood, but only by affirming itself. Resistance may spring from brotherhood but it can be corrupted when it acquires power and passes beyond rebellion into revolution. Then, "contaminated by resentment, it denies life, dashes toward destruction" and leads to "rancor, malice and tyranny" which call forth new resistance. Camus' plea is that rebellion set limits for itself, resolving not to sacrifice the present for the future, no matter how great the temptation to think that tomorrow's children can build utopia upon today's injustices.

One solution, of course, would be to avoid the temptation by doing nothing. For many people throughout the world this would mean continuing to endure the unendurable. We live in a revolutionary age and if revolutions are not led by good men they will nevertheless occur. But no man is so good that he can easily resist the temptation either to take the short cut of Robespierre or to retire from the scene, leaving matters to those whom the Robespierres would guillotine. For it is not only a temptation but a dilemma and a challenge. In the end, it must be recognized that the nonviolent method itself is not enough. Its special merit is that it allows scope for love, but it is no substitute for it. In the end, the nonviolent revolutionist must care more about constructive action to build the good society *now*, about effecting a revolution of the spirit *now*, than about attacking evil. The demolition of the old order is necessary but in the end the revolution can only triumph in defense of what is under construction. In Martin Buber's apt phrase, if a revolution is to give birth to a new society there must first be conception and gestation. You don't get a new society from an empty womb. Moreover, the greater likelihood is that nonviolence's major contribution will always be either that of a spur to legal change, as Walzer suggests, or that of a precursor of violent upheaval in which its goals may be sabotaged or perverted.

REFERENCES IN CHAPTER 5

1 Michael Walzer: "The Idea of Resistance" in *Dissent* (New York), Autumn 1960, p. 372f.
2 Crane Brinton: *The Anatomy of Revolution* (New York: Prentice-Hall, Inc., 1952), p. 96.
3 *Ibid.*, p. 98f.
4 Quoted in *ibid.*, p. 134.
5 *Ibid.*, p. 136.
6 *Ibid.*, pp. 147-148.
7 See Hannah Arendt: *On Revolution* (New York: The Viking Press, 1963), p. 265ff.
8 Brinton: *op. cit.*, p. 223.
9 See Arendt, *op. cit.*, p. 269. Also Martin Buber: *Paths in Utopia* (Boston: Beacon Press, Inc., 1958).
10 *Ibid.*, p. 268.
11 Nikolai Berdyaev: *Slavery and Freedom* (New York: Charles Scribner's Sons, 1944), p. 195.
12 Albert Camus: *The Rebel* (original title, *L'Homme Révolté*) (New York: Alfred A. Knopf, 1954), p. 272f.

6

Nonviolent National Defense

George Orwell, whose name has become virtually synonymous with political pessimism, wrote not long before he died: "It seems doubtful whether civilization can stand another major war, and it is at least thinkable that the way out lies through nonviolence." [1]

Orwell wrote these words on the threshold of the nuclear age. Since then, the development of megaton nuclear weapons, supersonic missiles and other devices has increased the catastrophic dimension of modern warfare to an extent that defies comprehension. Estimates vary concerning the possibilities of survival, let alone victory, in a war using such weapons, and it is not the purpose of this book to take a position on this vital issue. There is general agreement, however, that the issue is a grave one, and it is surprising that so little thinking has been done to explore the possibilities of nonviolence as an alternative.

In a discussion of fourteen alternative national policies ranging all the way from a national "act of renunciation" to preventive war, the military analyst Herman Kahn omits any reference to a strategy of nonviolence. After accounting for the distinctive nonresistant witness of the Religious Society of Friends, quoting from their manifesto of 1660 to King Charles, Kahn devotes a paragraph or so to "moral pacifism" and adds the following remarks about "nuclear pacifism":

Many of these nuclear pacifists are willing to use such low levels of force as local guerrilla warfare, or even conventional high explosive military weapons to resist a nuclear attack. Some hope that, by a single dramatic gesture, or a series of them, we can "reform"

97

the Soviets (and the Chinese?) and then the rest of the world. . . .
This argument often concludes that at the worst the United States
and Europe, and possibly the world, would suffer a relatively peaceful takeover, and the resultant tyranny would mellow with time.[2]

Kahn does refer vaguely to "volunteer nonviolent groups
that could interpose themselves in various situations and risk
their lives for the principles of peace and progress," [3] but this
and the above are far from a serious discussion of the problem,
and it is characteristic of many writers to confuse seventeenth-
century Quaker nonresistance with twentieth-century pragmatic nonviolence. Often enough they are encouraged in this
by the Quakers and other pacifists, but it is no excuse for
responsible thinkers who are capable of detailed and acute
analysis to indulge in blurry-eyed fantasy when confronting
nonviolence. As a result of this apparent unwillingness to examine the idea seriously and in detail and to speculate about it
theoretically, it is relegated to a shadowy and largely propagandistic existence. Slowly, however, the idea has intruded itself into the minds of a few capable nonpacifist thinkers, and it
is with their views that we shall be chiefly concerned in this
chapter.

The conjunction of thought about nonviolence and nuclear
war is largely accidental. India received its independence
within a couple of years of the first military use of the atomic
bomb. In a broader sense it is also true that the era of Gandhian
nonviolence coincides with the era of total war, whether we
date the latter from the advent of the Gatling gun, of high ex-
plosives or the bombing of civilian populations inaugurated at
Guernica, Spain, in 1937. The spread of devastation has a long
history that has greatly accelerated the problem of justice in
warfare during the past century or more. The advent of the
nuclear era has only provided a final, devastating jolt, introducing the possibility of instantaneous annihilation for entire
civilizations.

There is no such thing as a nonviolent defense against modern war, and for our present purposes this is as true of the long-

range cannon of World War I as it is of the twenty-megaton nuclear missiles of World War III. There is nothing that passive resistance or civil resistance can do to ward off such an attack if it comes. For that matter, there is little or nothing that can be done by any known available means, military or otherwise, to prevent the damage inflicted by such an attack, and meaningful discussion of the problem usually turns to the question of preventing the attack itself, or of steps to be taken afterward. In speaking of nonviolence in relation to modern war, what Orwell had in mind, in common with others who have thought about it, depends upon face-to-face confrontation with enemy troops equipped for garrison duty: nonviolence as a way of meeting invasion or, more likely, of resisting and repulsing a military occupation force.

A variety of proposals for such action have been advanced. Some of them are rather fanciful and far-fetched, in one case for example presupposing the prior dismantling of the entire military establishment and the virtual conversion of everybody to pacifism. To such views as these we would say, with C. J. Cadoux (himself a distinguished pacifist):

Pacifists would be well advised not to argue as if the State could be expected now in every case to turn the other cheek and to overcome the evil in neighbor-states solely with good. The demand that the State shall act fully up to the highest ethical level which the citizens *as a whole* will approve is perfectly reasonable; the belief that this level can and ought to be progressively raised with the lapse of time is also reasonable: what is not reasonable is to demand, under threat or implication of censure, that the State shall *now* act as if it could share to the full the exacting ethical ideal which is, as a matter of fact, held by only a tiny fraction of its constituents.[4]

Kennan's Approach

The views that we shall consider in this chapter are predicated on the belief that national defense is a necessity of national existence, that communism is not an enviable political system, that the threat of Soviet aggression is real and not imaginary, and that we do not wish to be ruled by a foreign power or its agents, be it draconically totalitarian or otherwise. Our objective is peace and freedom, by which is meant both civil and international order and a way of life featuring civil rights and liberties for all people, as expressed in our Constitution. We recognize further, with Arne Naess, that the majority of people in our country, as indeed in any country, believe in the present system of defense by military means. "If one takes away the only means of defense a person believes to be truly effective," writes Naess, "he certainly has every reason to feel frustrated. Thus a reduction of reliance on the military must be preceded by the development of increased confidence in and the gradual adoption of alternative means of defense." [5] We are assuming, in other words, that nonviolent means are to be developed to such a point as to warrant public confidence before implementing any significant reduction of armaments. The reader who challenges any of these assumptions may, of course, set them aside in favor of a sunnier view.

George F. Kennan has made an approach to the problem that is worth quoting at length. In 1958 he proposed that Western Europe could be defended not by exclusively nonviolent methods but by means that give wide scope to such methods along with others. His views carry particular weight because of his expert knowledge of international affairs. It was Kennan who, as a member of the policy planning staff on the U.S. State Department, developed the earlier policy of containment which has been credited with holding the USSR's territorial ambitions in check since 1946.

If the armed forces of the United States and Britain were not present on the continent, the problem of defense for the continental nations would be primarily one of the internal health and discipline of the respective national societies and of the manner in which they were organized to prevent the conquest and subjugation of their national life by unscrupulous and foreign-inspired minorities in their midst. What they need is a strategic doctrine addressed to this reality. Under such a doctrine, armed forces would indeed be needed; but I would suggest that as a general rule these forces might better be paramilitary ones, of a territorial-militia type, somewhat on the Swiss example, rather than regular military units on the World War II pattern. . . . The training of such forces ought to be such as to prepare them not only to offer whatever overt resistance might be possible to a foreign invader but also to constitute the core of a civil resistance movement on any territory that might be overrun by the enemy; and every forethought should be exercised to facilitate their assumption and execution of this role in the case of necessity. For this reason they need not, and should not, be burdened with heavy equipment or elaborate supply requirements, and this means—and it is no small advantage—that they could be maintained at a small fraction of the cost per unit of the present conventional [military] establishments.[6]

The characteristic features of this strategy are such as to localize the structure of defense. For the concept of the ring of steel at the frontier, Kennan substitutes that of the citizen army honeycombing the entire country.

The purpose would be to place the country in a position where it could face the Kremlin and say to it: "Look here, you may be able to overrun us, if you are unwise enough to attempt it, but you will have small profit from it; we are in a position to assure that not a single Communist or other person likely to perform your political business will be available to you for this purpose. . . . Your stay among us will not be a happy one . . ."[7]

Kennan believes that any nation that can say this "will have little need for foreign garrisons to assure its immunity from Soviet attack." Such preparations would serve as a powerful non-nuclear and indeed only partially military deterrent.

We need not concern ourselves here with the paramilitary side of Kennan's proposal. What is of interest to us is his insistence that this citizen army be prepared to function as the core of a civil resistance movement. Need such a movement be headed by citizen-army forces? Might it not equally or better be built within the primary institutions of society—in local churches, labor unions, public schools, YMCAs and the like? The Federal, state and local governments might aid in coordinating such a movement in its initial stages, but these, together with their armed forces, would bear the initial brunt if invasion actually took place. It would seem wise, therefore, to be sure that other institutions were well seeded for resistance too. In the Basque area of Spain, republican resistance to the Franco regime was carried on through football associations long after the capitulation of the government structures—and this was in a situation in which resistance was improvised only after military defeat.

Loosening the Enemy's Grip

One of the first prerequisites of a nonmilitary defense, according to Arne Naess, is a firm and articulate sense of common purpose. What do we stand for as a nation? What do we have that is worth defending, worth sacrificing for? What are the terms on which we can unite for our common defense? These are questions of vital importance. A decadent, moribund society wallowing in random pleasures with every man out for his own private ends can purchase a nuclear deterrent, but it cannot build a system of defense that requires active community participation.

This does not mean uniformity of thought and certainly not a highly centralized leadership. Diffusion of leadership at the grass-roots level and the habit of making decisions without relying upon commands from "top people"—a maximum of this provides needed resilience for determined action in face-to-face encounters with enemy forces, when normal lines of communication may be broken. This need clearly implies that we will be in a better position to respond to such an emergency (and perhaps more ordinary emergencies as well) if we unglue our eyes from our television screens more often and spend some time working in a church social-action project or similar small-group activities with linkages to the community.

In Kennan's proposal, civil resistance is characterized as "the united and organized hostility of an entire nation" which will make an invader "pay bitterly for every day" of occupation. Naess, however, argues cogently against anything resembling terrorism or a scorched-earth policy, or even "psychological warfare, which may resort to all types of threats and deception in verbal propaganda." [8] This is not simply a matter of moral puritanism, which could hardly be expected from a large population, but of prudent tactics compatible with a strategy of nonviolence. Consider the situation from the viewpoint of the participants. Our aim is not to make the enemy soldiers trigger-happy, but on the contrary to establish rapport with them as persons and thereby to make them feel incongruous to the situation in which their leaders have placed them. We want to be able to say to each enemy soldier: "What is a nice boy like you doing here? Look at the dirty mess they've got you into, pestering decent folk like your own." Such resistance would manifest hostility not to the man but to the role he has been called upon to play, and we must at all times carefully distinguish between the two in our actions and in the way we verbally and symbolically interpret our actions. Rather than making the actual invader, the person who happens to confront us as a soldier, "pay bitterly," we want to enlist his inner sympathy and move him in the direction of neutrality, ultimately undermining his confidence in his superiors and leading him to mutiny or to desert. As in revolution, so also in war.

Thorough training would be necessary to assure effectiveness. To expect a population of 180,000,000—or a single county for that matter—even to begin to apply such methods spontaneously, without training, would be fatuous indeed. Even after months of the most rigorous training that might be expected, without an imminent threat of war hanging over their heads to impress its seriousness upon them, large numbers of people would still remain unprepared. This is to be expected.

The primary need is not to train every citizen in advance, but first to honeycomb the nation with small groups of trained people capable of organizing and leading resistance in time of crisis, and second to create, as far as possible, a favorable public opinion that would overcome the strangeness of the method.

Great care would have to be taken, of course, to avoid any sentimentalizing. People must not be led to believe that effects will be instantaneous, irreversible or universal. Also, the kind of "fraternizing" with enemy troops envisioned above may lead to a temptation to collaborationism, which must be guarded against. Only full and free discussion during the training period will make it possible to prepare for every imaginable contingency, making full use of the resources of psychologists and social scientists, who will have an important part to play at this stage. Full advantage would also be taken of every available technique of publicity and education by both governmental and voluntary agencies to facilitate the training program. And since it would be impossible to carry this out secretly, it would also be necessary to develop effective means of propaganda to inform the enemy population of our intentions, and especially to counter the enemy's propaganda by which he will try to inoculate his population against our strategy.

The strategy of nonviolent defense does not end with the sole tactic of establishing rapport with the enemy soldiers. Coupled with this would be a variety of measures. It cannot be too strongly stressed, however, that in all of these it is important to maintain rapport with the occupation troops as persons. Our ultimate hope lies in neutralizing those troops or, if possible, activating them against their leaders.

At the same time that we, with manifest personal friendliness, make it clear to the soldier that he is unwelcome as a soldier in our country, we shall be engaging in actions on a social scale that confirm this and make it difficult or impossible for the invader's administration to function. As Johan Galtung has well said, "a desire for freedom cannot be symbolized by passivity." [9]

Galtung, a colleague of Naess at the Institute for Social Research of the University of Oslo, has made a number of concrete suggestions concerning specific kinds of nonviolent action in such a situation.

Nonviolent resistance must be such that the form of resistance itself clearly indicates the goal which the group has set itself. If one is fighting for democratic rights like freedom of speech, an excellent form of resistance will be to break the prohibitions of the occupying forces on this point, e.g. arrange illegal meetings all over the country . . . and in a speech explain the goals of the resistance. Such a form will make it much clearer to the opponent what the goal is than, for example, a strike of milk delivery men. But the resistance must be made collective, at the same time showing the individual opponent that one is not against him as a person. . . .[10]

Nonviolent resistance operates by refusing cooperation with the opponent in order to prevent him from achieving his goals. How can we prevent the opponent from achieving his goals when we cannot stop him by physical means? . . . We take it for granted that he is interested in exploiting for his own ends the land he has conquered, or in introducing another form of government. . . . In any event he will need a certain amount of cooperation from the inhabitants. . . . Exactly this cooperation or this access to the country's riches can be denied the opponent.[11]

Galtung, who is a pacifist and one who generally adheres closely to Gandhian ideas, considers sabotage to be within the scope of nonviolent action so long as it does not injure persons. For example a train could be wrecked while untended and motionless, but not while manned or in motion. He continues:

The population of the occupied country may choose to lower its standard of living by voluntarily making factories inoperable by removing parts of machines and destroying means of communication rather than cooperate in the opponent's unjust use of them.[12]

Although Galtung also includes an all-industry general

strike, Naess cautions against the use of blanket, all-out resistance:

The weakness of a policy of general nonviolent resistance is that it cannot be upheld at all costs; if repression gradually stiffens it is impossible to continue defending, for instance, the major organizations of a democratic government. Automatic refusal to cooperate in food distribution may result in a famine. Self-inflicted hardships of this sort cannot easily be asked or expected of a populace except in critical periods of very short duration.[13]

Other tactics cited by Galtung are: a concerted boycott against all goods imported from the invader nation, refusal to pay taxes levied by the invader, systematic disobedience of laws promulgated by the invader. (For a classic example of the latter, see page 230.) Preparations will have been made for an "underground government" that will function secretly once the regular government is suppressed or taken over. Depending upon circumstances, government officials might demonstratively resign their posts en masse to inconvenience the enemy administrators. To do this would not be merely a symbolic gesture, however, if it became the signal for a transfer of effective administration to the underground. It would be impossible for the invader to know in detail the names of each person in every neighborhood who held this or that responsibility for education, justice, etc. In a complex society such as ours, important decisions would require the judgment of experts: how, for example, could an underground government maintain control over water supply, electricity and other public utilities and services? Certainly it would be technically feasible for a disciplined underground to inform the people to store water in their homes and then cut off the general water supply for a day or two. Similarly, with adequate and careful planning it might be possible for the people to prepare themselves for a symbolic cut-off of electric power. Numerous tactical strategems of this sort could be devised and planned for. In many cases particular strategems would be one-shot affairs, unrepeatable because of measures the enemy would take in light of them. In many others undoubtedly the resisters could maintain continuous control.

The resisters would have to expect reprisals and be prepared to endure them nonviolently, avoiding panic that could result in resorting to terroristic methods of resistance. For many of the resisters, terrorism would be a highly prevalent temptation because of its value as a release for pent-up emotional stresses. But the instantaneous satisfactions afforded by stabbing enemy soldiers in the back must be carefully weighed against the long-term strategic emphasis on neutralizing them as enemies. No study has been made—at least this side of the Iron Curtain—of the possibilities of abducting key enemy officials by manual force and attempting, while holding them prisoner, to treat them so kindly as to plant in them seeds of discontent with the regime they uphold. If this idea seems wildly impractical, however, consider the amazing successes of the Chinese Communists in "brainwashing" American prisoners of war during the Korean conflict. If a totalitarian regime can succeed in converting naïve American soldiers into Communist sympathizers, surely there must be ways in which American defenders of democracy could produce real conversions among Communists or other ideologues, even if the latter are well indoctrinated, because of the inner contradictions in their ideology. This is only one of numerous avenues of psycho-social research that would have to be explored.

Problems of Organization

Among the lessons of recent history, however, Naess discusses the successful resistance of Norwegian school teachers against Nazi rule. (See page 253 for a detailed account.) To this he then contrasts the situation in Nazi-occupied Poland, where

the pressure on school teachers was in part so heavy that direct resistance at the schools and within the school organizations was impossible. But teaching was conducted "privately" in tiny groups, a form of micro-resistance.[14]

Naess defines micro-resistance as "resistance by individuals and tiny, temporary groups." These would function in a subtactical way, isolated from larger underground organizational structures, and would not be directly affected in the event of the exposure of the latter.

Most of the significant examples of resistance on a national scale which has succeeded in some degree exhibit a number of common characteristics: the resisting country is relatively small and compact and the population is homogeneous in ethnic culture; resistance was improvised after the collapse of military defense and was conducted as an expedient, stopgap measure without long-range strategy; and the invader had a larger population and a sizable occupation force.

In devising a nonviolent defense strategy these facts should be taken into account. A large, ethnically heterogeneous country such as the United States might be handicapped by existing internal divisions. An obvious initial problem in the planning stage would be posed by the prevalence of Negro-white segregation in a large part of the country. This problem must be squarely faced and solved. We are not attempting to prejudge it here on the merits of the case for or against desegregation, but simply to state that it constitutes a problem in relation to foreign invasion. The Norwegians and the Poles did not have this problem.

On the other hand, the size of the country, in both land area and population, would be a distinct advantage. Both China and the USSR combined would find it a vexing problem to deploy the number of troops and administrative personnel to manage a nation as large as the United States, even with a halfhearted program of resistance to cope with. And as we have indicated repeatedly, full-scale advance preparation and planning would introduce an entirely new dimension.

Who would undertake the training of a nonviolent leadership cadre? George Kennan, as we saw, proposed that the members of his paramilitary citizen army would themselves comprise this cadre. For reasons already given, we have indicated the advisability of a separate nonviolent organizational structure. The psychologist Jerome D. Frank, however, has well stated the role the military could perform:

A nonviolent campaign against a Communist occupation would . . . require a tight, highly disciplined organization with diffusion of leadership, carefully worked-out clandestine methods of communication, and other measures very similar to those which would be required to survive a nuclear attack. In fact, if a country ever committed itself to an exclusive policy of nonviolence, it would probably have to rely on the military, as the only group with sufficient knowledge of organization and discipline, to train and lead the civilian population in this type of combat.[15]

While taking advantage of the special skills provided by the military—it is inconceivable that a program of nonviolent defense could be launched without their cooperation—these skills would, in our view, become the property of the churchmen, unionists, school teachers and other civilians after their training. Although liaison with the military and with civil government would be maintained, it would be of such a nature that the nonviolent clandestine groups could carry on independently at a moment's notice if liaison were broken by enemy actions of any kind. Moreover, it is essential that nonviolent organization be predicated on the inner strength of the local community rather than on any overarching authoritarian structure, such as that of even the most democratic of armies. The more inextricably the nonviolent organization is enmeshed in the stable and permanent structures of the society itself, the harder it will be for the enemy to smoke it out and isolate it. The entire congregation of every parish church, for example, must be capable of being suspected as a unit of the nonviolent resistance—though in fact there will exist within it a handful of leaders who have received expert training and, around them, a nucleus of people whom these leaders have trained, with the balance of the congregation informed but not fully trained. This is not a question of holding back training from anyone who wants it, but of realistically facing the fact that it is impossible to expect the requisite degree of interest and involvement from everyone. Nonetheless, what this adds up to is a church that is organized for nonviolence, and its natural linkages in the over-all scheme will follow the existing contours of ecclesiastical structure and community relationships rather than direct ties with military or governmental districts. By this means, the enemy would have to smash the church as a whole in all its ramifications to get at the agents of resistance. Such a pattern multiplied throughout the fabric of society would make for great resilience.

Given such an organization, asks one Roman Catholic exponent of nonviolence, Kaspar Mayr,

> Wouldn't the united action of a people against injustice powerfully heighten their inner defensive strength, build unity and so cause the opposite of what the usurper intends: not submission but life in freedom based on inner strength? Wouldn't nonviolent defense also preserve cultural properties, even if it undoubtedly demanded hard sacrifice . . . ? [16]

That these are more than merely pious hopes founded on a perfectionist ethic is strongly indicated in Frank's observation of the psychology of this "inner strength" when he says that

> persons who as individuals might use violence to defend themselves or their families against attack . . . can commit themselves to nonviolent methods when they are in the service of a well-worked-out program and have strong group support. Only about 100 of Gandhi's followers were fully committed to his philosophy.[17]

Undoubtedly it would require a widespread sense of imminent crisis to weld together this kind of unity from which to draw inner strength. Contrasting the demands of a nonviolent resistance with those of a military defense policy, Norman K. Gottwald of Andover Newton Theological School observes that "it necessitates a stronger sense of national purpose and a greater willingness on the part of citizens to be informed politically and to subordinate personal interests to state interests." [18] He goes on to weigh the dangers of a "monolithic statism" connected with such a policy as compared with similar dangers "inherent in our present over-militarized society with its con-centration of power and national destiny in the hands of a few political and military leaders." [19] An important difference, as we have already noted, is that a well-constructed movement would be rooted in community institutions outside the power structure of the state as such. But Gottwald's point has rele-vance if we find government exceeding its role as initiator and coordinator.

The Supranational View

As a cadre-building bulwark of the program, some form of constructive organization has been recommended, oriented in the direction of international relations, to promote cultural con-tacts and perform work that would strengthen the world image of the resisting nation as peace-loving. Naess lays great stress on such activity.

International service should be undertaken for its own sake, to relieve suffering and meet human needs. It is also important as a means of expressing and implementing our nation's way of life and principles.[20]

In addition to its intrinsic merits, which should form the pri-mary focus rather than any ulterior design simply to *use* such service to undergird our defenses,

international service can contribute to the creation of a more sym-pathetic attitude toward our country and way of life which would reduce the chances of aggressive action against us. . . . It will help create a positive sense of purpose and mission comparable to that which often accompanies military efforts, but without certain of the disadvantages of such measures, and in giving our citizens experi-ence in working cooperatively in a common altruistic cause it will enhance their ability to practice this cooperation in other tasks in time of crisis.

[Finally,] knowledge of international service conveyed to the troops and population of a potential enemy might reduce their motivation to take aggressive action against us, cause them to carry out repressive orders inefficiently and increase the chances of their deserting or mutinying in support of freedom.[21]

Gottwald comes to a similar conclusion, though neither had access to the other's writing on the matter. Rather than a strictly national service organization, however, the one Gottwald envisions would be based on the North Atlantic Treaty Organization. Gottwald's "freedom youth corps" would be set up

to carry out cultural and economic projects in all the NATO countries and wherever invited, hopefully, within Communist countries as part of cultural exchange programs. Simultaneously they would be trained in methods of resistance to enemy occupation. They would serve as the cadres for a large-scale civil resistance plan whose aim it would be to make enemy occupation of NATO countries a distinct political and military liability.[22]

The reference to NATO is apt, for the principle of nonviolent national defense is relevant to multinational defense as well. Many of the smaller nations might be capable of making a brave gesture of resistance, but this would almost certainly have a negligible impact on a large and powerful conqueror. It is apparent that geographical size and interior diversifications of social organization, technology and other features would be of strategic importance. The invasion of a single small country unaided by any allies poses complex problems that we are not prepared to discuss in any detail here. By "small" here we are thinking of a Denmark, a Latvia or a Belgium. And by "single" we imply that the conqueror is prepared to concentrate his military power on that sole country and rotate his troops sufficiently to forestall any establishment of rapport. Such a case would probably be rare, but we might conjecture that substantial evacuations of refugees and the establishment of resistance bases in adjacent countries might provide a means of using nonviolence for a protracted period. Studies should be made to discover whether some type of nonviolent intervention by countries not under attack would be feasible. If the armed invasion were countered by a well-prepared nonviolent counterinvasion by international-service cadres of the type suggested by Gottwald, would it result in nipping the armed invasion in the bud, or in the liquidation of the resistance forces of the allies? Such questions as these need to be fully explored by men accustomed to the complexities of military strategy as well as by those in the behavioral sciences.

One highly esteemed military strategist has made a beginning, not on the defense of a single small nation, but of larger nations and of the NATO bloc. Sir Stephen King-Hall, a retired British naval commander with a distinguished war record, is the author of such books as *Imperial Defense* and *Total Victory*. His 1958 book, *Defense in the Nuclear Age,* however, marks Commander King-Hall's entry into a new dimension of strategy. In it, he advances the view that war can no longer be waged by military means. He rejects alike the idea that it can be limited to non-nuclear weapons and that a war with nuclear weapons could result in anything approximating victory.

What is remarkable is that King-Hall emerges as an exponent of nonviolent resistance—on grounds of military necessity! His thorough knowledge of military operations and the fact that he does not regard himself as a convert to pacifism give weight to his assessment of the possibilities of such resistance.

In his discussion of defense plans, King-Hall begins with the assumption that the United States will not go along with his strategy. Hence he speaks of a European Treaty Organization rather than NATO. He proposes that the ETO countries would have no nuclear arms at all, and that their total armed strength would consist of "about ten divisions and corresponding air and sea forces" which "would gradually be reduced to a frontier guard" capable of offering token military resistance.[23]

In the event of attack, after the frontier guards were overcome (their existence would be primarily a safeguard against infiltration of border areas), the ETO nations would resort to nonviolence. Echoing a caution we have voiced above from various sources, he says:

To be effective this resistance must be organized in advance and not expected to spring out of the occupation in an *ad hoc* manner, any more than armed forces are expected to be created when military operations begin. A soldier of sorts can be trained in three months; to train a fairly competent nonviolent resister might require three years.[24]

Commander King-Hall examines one pacifist program (outlined in the pamphlet *Pacifism and Invasion* by Jessie Wallace Hughan) and finds its proposals unconvincing. Among his objections are the human impracticability of a nationwide hunger strike or sit-down strike and the limitation of the pacifist vision to "making the occupation difficult for the enemy."

The object of nonviolent resistance must be to *make the occupation dangerous for the enemy*. It cannot be "dangerous" to him from a military point of view, it must therefore be made dangerous to him from a political warfare angle, for this is the battlefield on which, if victory can be achieved, it will be total.[25]

The primary focus of the struggle, in King-Hall's view, is ideological and psychological rather than military. He discounts as unrealistic the possibility that the Soviet Union (whom he sees as the enemy) would embark on a massacre of the inhabitants, and also regards it as unreasonable to believe the invasion troops would be ready to terrorize the civilian population. On the latter point, he attributes the horrors of the Russian occupation of Berlin in 1945 to the fact that it came as the climax to a long and bitter military struggle—one in which, moreover, the government which the Soviet troops identified with the people of Berlin had been responsible for savage atrocities against the Russians.

The distinction between an occupation as the climax of a military battle and one as the beginning of a psychological struggle is of the utmost importance.[26]

As a broad outline of resistance conduct, King-Hall offers five suggestions, the first two having to do with the material aspects of the national life of the ETO states and the last three with "ideas and attitudes of mind":

1. The economic life of the country to be maintained, that is to say, transport services, industrial production, agriculture, distribution and all activities concerned with the body-keeping business of the nation should proceed so far as possible in a normal manner or in accordance with directions issued by the occupying power.

2. As regards government, the attitude toward the enemy should be: "We have our well-established administrative arrangements and if you do not like them we await to hear from you what alternatives you have in mind."

3. To refuse *at all costs* to say or write anything contrary to the principles of our way of life or to accept denial of freedom of speech and association.

4. To use every opportunity in personal contact with the occupying forces to expose the fallacies of communism and advantages of democracy.

5. In general to behave *vis-à-vis* the occupying forces with dignity and moral superiority. This is the key rule.[27]

Among the specific applications of the above principles, under point 3 he proposes that the task of a newspaper editor "should be to cause differences of opinion in the enemy administration as to whether or not his paper should be closed down," meanwhile functioning as a "subtle weapon" of resistance. If closed down, "illegal and clandestine news sheets and bulletins and radio transmissions might come into operation." [28]

King-Hall acknowledges the tentative and preliminary character of his proposals. They constitute suggestions rather than a detailed strategy, which would have to be worked out by an authorized body of strategists. A large part of his study is devoted to convincing the reader of the need for rethinking defense policy. The primary need, King-Hall believes, is the establishment in his country of a royal commission ready to embark on a detailed factual and theoretical exploration of the possibilities.

One of King-Hall's colleagues in the British military establishment, Captain B. H. Liddell Hart, who enjoys a wider reputation than King-Hall as a strategist, has discussed the latter's thinking in his book, *Deterrent or Defense*.

While the practicability of his proposals can be questioned, his argument presents a challenge which deserves the fullest consideration—and cannot be ignored. . . .

Even on practical grounds there is a stronger case for nonviolence than is generally realized. Its power has been demonstrated at various times, and it has achieved some notable successes.[29]

Liddell Hart observes that the sporadic nonviolence against Nazi Germany in Denmark, Norway and the Netherlands impressed Hitler as "contemptible weakness—although there is evidence that it did embarrass many of his generals, brought up in a better code, and baffled them more than the violent resistance movements in occupied countries." [30] Much depends on a fundamental similarity of the moral code of the invaders and the resisters. Nonviolence requires more strict and widespread discipline than an army, and its effectiveness "is undermined if even a small proportion of the community play into the opponent's hand—through weakness, self-interest or pugnacity." [31]

Without closing the door on it, Liddell Hart on balance remains skeptical of the applicability of nonviolence as national policy on two counts. First, he doubts that any government "could be persuaded to embark on such a revolutionary experiment"; and second, he remains unconvinced that it could be practiced effectively on a national scale, for the reasons given above.

His first point is well taken. It is hard to imagine how a government, or any nongovernmental institution of national scope, could have the imagination to allocate funds and personnel to study the question, not to mention embarking on the experiment as a policy. Until this is done, the validity of Liddell Hart's second point will remain obscure. He may be proved right. Meanwhile, the need for competent research and informed speculation on this question will not slacken in its urgency so long as weapons of massive destructiveness continue to be piled up.

REFERENCES IN CHAPTER 6

1   George Orwell: "Reflections on Gandhi" in *Shooting an Elephant and Other Essays* (London: Secker and Warburg, 1950), p. 111.
2   Herman Kahn: *Thinking About the Unthinkable* (New York: Horizon Press, Inc., 1962), p. 236. Reprinted by permission of the publisher.
3   *Ibid.*, p. 237.
4   C. J. Cadoux: *Christian Pacifism Re-examined* (Oxford: Basil Blackwell, 1940), p. 131.
5   Arne Naess: "Non-Military Defense" in a book edited by Quincy Wright, William M. Evan and Morton Deutsch: *How to Prevent World War III* (New York: Simon and Schuster, Inc., 1962), p. 125.
6   George F. Kennan: *Russia, the Atom and the West* (New York: Harper and Brothers, 1958), p. 63.
7   *Ibid.*
8   Naess, *op. cit.*, p. 131.
9   Johan Galtung: *Forsvar Uten Militærwesen* (Oslo: Folkereisning Mot Krig, c. 1959), p. 73. The author is greatly indebted to Mrs. Berit M. Lakey for translating the chapter from which this and the following quotations are taken.
10 *Ibid.*, p. 80f.
11 *Ibid.*, p. 81.
12 *Ibid.*
13 Naess, *op. cit.*, p. 131f.
14 *Ibid.*
15 Jerome D. Frank: *Sanity and World Peace* (Des Moines: World Peace Broadcasting Foundation, 1961. Mimeographed), p. 7.
16 Kaspar Mayr: *Der Andere Weg* (Nürnberg, Germany: Glock und Lutz, 1957), p. 256.
17 Jerome D. Frank: *Sanity and Survival: The Nonviolent Alternative* (Berkeley, Calif.: Acts for Peace, 1960), p. 12.
18 Norman K. Gottwald: "Some Strategies of Nonviolence" in *Worldview* (New York), April 1961, p. 5.
19 *Ibid.*
20 Naess, *op. cit.*, p. 127.
21 *Ibid.*, p. 127f.
22 Gottwald, *op. cit.*
23 Stephen King-Hall: *Defense in the Nuclear Age* (Nyack, N.Y.: Fellowship Publications, 1959), p. 147n.

24 *Ibid.*, p. 192.
25 *Ibid.*, p. 199.
26 *Ibid.*, p. 200.
27 *Ibid.*
28 *Ibid.*, p. 205.
29 B. H. Liddell Hart: *Deterrent or Defense* (New York: Frederick A. Praeger, Inc., 1960), p. 220f.
30 *Ibid.*, p. 221.
31 *Ibid.*

7

An International Nonviolent
Peace Force

In the late 1930s Mahatma Gandhi proposed the idea of a *shanti dal* or nonviolent peace brigade to deal with communal strife between Hindus and Muslims in the struggle for Indian independence. Of the members of such a locally based organization, Gandhi wrote:

Theirs will be the duty of seeking occasions for bringing warring communities together, carrying on peace propaganda, engaging in activities that would bring and keep them in touch with every single person, male and female, adult and child, in their parish or division.[1]

Gandhi referred to the idea again a few times, but nothing was ever done during his lifetime to implement it. Who knows how many lives it might have saved when the hideous massacres began in 1947?

As he conceived it, *shanti dal* was a nonviolent method of riot control involving individuals or small teams wearing distinctive dress but engaged in constructive work within the local community until moments of conflict arose, when they would be ready to do rescue and first-aid work. Later he projected a similar scheme to deal with international conflict, and shortly before his assassination he called a conference to discuss it. When it met without his leadership in 1949 an international corresponding committee was set up, but it soon lapsed into silence and inaction.

It remained for his spiritual heir, Vinoba Bhave, and his associates in the *sarvodaya* movement of the 1950s to revive the concept of *shanti dal* and then later to introduce the idea of *shanti sena,* the nonviolent peace army moving out of the local setting to act on the world scene.

The idea of an international armed force such as the United Nations Emergency Force that was used to resolve the Suez and Congo crises in 1957 and 1961 is a product of fairly recent thinking. It has, in turn, given impetus in pacifist circles to the idea of a nonviolent counterpart or alternative to UNEF. Indeed, to the extent that any thinking has been done it has tended to take the form of a specific adaptation of nonviolence to the situations that UNEF or a more permanent "world army" is designed to deal with. Roy Finch articulates this viewpoint when he observes:

The arms of the UNEF troops in the Near East are only a token; the 2,000-man force could easily be crushed by either side. It is effective only because it is backed up by "world opinion" and by the big powers.[2]

Finch then proceeds to argue from this basis that the United Nations would be ill-advised to expand the "token" arms of UNEF, since its effectiveness lies elsewhere.

Certain aspects of the police-force proposal might make sense— if they were transposed fully into a nonviolent key. A *Peace Service* of unarmed volunteers (men and women also, *not* recruited from regular armies) wearing a special uniform or other symbol and ready to leave at a moment's notice to interpose themselves in conflict situations on behalf of the United Nations might be an effective way of waging peace. . . . It would be an entirely new *kind* of army, as different from the old kinds as the United Nations itself purports to be from old kinds of national sovereignty.[3]

It is fitting that this concept is advanced by an absolute pacifist and that most of the support it has received has also come from pacifists—and no less surprising that, in contrast with the idea of a nonviolent national defense, it has barely begun to receive attention from nonpacifists. For it is precisely here that the moral scruples and the vision of international peace which are the twin hallmarks of pacifism compel the pacifist to take his most principled stand. And conversely it is precisely here that, from a nonpacifist point of view, the means of implementing this vision without clearly operable moral imperatives are most nebulous. Novel as the idea of a nonviolent national defense may be, it is basically an adaptation of the techniques of passive resistance and civil disobedience—which have occurred in history on a national scale—to ideas of military strategy and national solidarity that are generally accepted. The idea of the use of nonviolence in the way Finch suggests, or as a projection from Gandhi's sketch of *shanti dal,* is an adaptation of nonviolent methods that remain to be developed, to an international ethos which itself has barely begun to take shape.

An International Conference

Consequently there has been little concrete theorizing and much tentative groping, almost exclusively by persons representing a holistic view of nonviolence, whether of Gandhian or of Western pacifist origin. In 1960 this groping, however, began to seek tangible form when the Triennial Conference of the War Resisters International met in India at Gandhigram. Chiefly three tributary forces were impelling both *sarvodayists* and pacifists toward such a step. Two of these we have already noted: the pressure of international events, with the pacifist desire to convert the United Nations to nonviolence, and Vinoba's pursuit of the Gandhian concept, which had by now resulted in the enrollment of 2,000 "peace soldiers" in India. The third and highly catalytic factor was the rise, during the preceding few years, of pacifist action groups such as the Committee for Nonviolent Action in the United States and the Direct Action Committee Against Nuclear War in England.

Both the American and the English groups (the latter gave way to the Committee of One Hundred) arose against the background of larger movements that embraced an ideology of nonviolence. Although there was nothing that could be called a mass peace movement in the United States, such peace organizations as existed linked themselves with the nonviolent struggle for racial integration, which did have something of the scope of a mass movement. A pacifist direct-actionist could gain experience and whet his morale by joining in a sit-in. And however separate the sit-ins and the peace actions in which he engaged, he had some basis to speculate on the possibilities of mass support for the latter, since the former had already received such support. In England, the mass movement of the Campaign for Nuclear Disarmament provided an even more congenial context for the direct-actionist as a kind of vanguard element of an already pacifist-tinged body. Elsewhere, too, such groups as Action Civique Non Violente in France, though lacking a mass base at home, could find moral support in the British and American movements.

Conditions were such that direct-action groups were able, in this period, to carry out such actions as the boarding of Polaris submarines in both New London and Holy Loch, the sailing of the ketch *Golden Rule* toward the U.S. nuclear test zone in the South Pacific, the San Francisco–Moscow peace march, and other such actions. Although they did not enjoy spectacular growth, these organizations held together, gained experience and began to envision types of action that might have direct and decisive impact on the international scene. Americans and Britons who had engaged in direct action against their own governments made so bold as to hoist banners in Moscow calling for an end to Soviet nuclear tests, and to form a team to invade the French Sahara to protest against a nuclear explosion conducted by the French Government. In 1960 these direct-actionists were very warm to the idea of an international team that would take "the next step" in a direction in which they were already headed.

A Variety of Approaches

As there were diverse origins, so there were diverse conceptions of the route to be taken. One proposal, advanced in a joint statement by the Indian *sarvodaya* leader, Jayaprakash Narayan, and the distinguished Spanish republican, Salvador de Madariaga, pursues the line of reasoning advanced above by Roy Finch. It would call for a body of unarmed World Peace Guards acting under United Nations auspices, to intervene and halt hostilities chiefly by interposing themselves between the armed combat troops of the parties to a given dispute. Following is an extract from the Madariaga-Narayan statement that summarizes this position better than any paraphrase:

The presence of a body of regular Peace Guards intervening with no weapons whatsoever between two forces combating or about to combat might have considerable effect. They would not be there as a fanciful improvisation, but as the positive and practical application of a previously negotiated and ratified Charter binding all UN members. This Charter should insure:

1. Inviolability of the Peace Guards.
2. Their right to go anywhere at any time from the day they had been given an assignment by the UN.
3. Their right to intervene in any conflict of any nature when asked by one or both of the parties involved, or by a third party.

The Peace Guard would be parachutists. They would be able to stop advancing armies by refusing to move from roads, railways or airfields. They would be empowered to act in any capacity their chiefs might think adequate for the situation, though they would never use force. They would be endowed with a complete system for recording and transmitting facts, such as TV cameras and broadcasting material. Their uniform should be simple, clear and appealing.[4]

The authors of this statement recognize the difficulty that would face their proposal before it was even adopted. Their stress, however, is on the recognized international status of their nonviolent peace guard. Given this condition, their tactics then would be drawn chiefly from the arsenal of Gandhian civil disobedience, with emphasis on bodily obstruction. The condition of legal status under an international charter demarcates this approach from the other two.

A second approach is essentially that of *shanti sena*, projected on an international scale—an autonomous voluntary organization which would not wait for United Nations authorization but would establish itself and make its services available independently, undoubtedly hoping for eventual recognition by all governments. Aside from its unofficial status, its functions resemble closely those of the Madariaga-Narayan peace guard. The following is excerpted from a proposal made by Arlo Tatum, secretary of the War Resisters International:

The World Peace Brigade should aim for becoming an instrument to be used in international agreements and disagreements. In this area would fall:

1. Border patrol and the reporting of violations, as on the Israel-Arab borders and the 38th Parallel in Korea. In such instances there would be a policy of outgoing fraternization, unlike armed patrols. Service to persons in the area would be an integral part of Brigade activities.

2. It should offer volunteers to any nation prepared to disarm.

3. It should be prepared to accept responsibility for inspection and control of any disarmament agreement, as an utterly impartial body.

4. It should stand ready to enter any area where the facts are in dispute as to the cause of disturbances, and report back, but continue to work in the area.

5. The Brigade should develop its own information network, so that such difficulties are discovered when possible *before* a crisis situation develops.[5]

As in the domestic concept of *shanti dal*, Tatum's version of *shanti sena* is coupled with a program of constructive service work, and training in nonviolence would be rooted in domestic depressed areas. "Volunteers would be sought and trained for Brigade activity in their own community, rather than simply for service in far-off places." [6]

Among the many questions which this proposal suggests are the basic problems of legal status, financing and efficient administration. If, for example, the World Council of Churches and its constituent members, or the International Confederation of Free Trade Unions, were to take so radical a step on their own, it is not difficult to visualize the complex problems of staff and budget that would instantly arise. Assuming that neither of these organizations could be persuaded to take such a step (or, what is the same thing for our purposes, that they could not be persuaded more easily than the United Nations), is it conceivable that the general public in any countries would support a wholly new organizational structure devised expressly to serve as a base for an International Peace Brigade?

This consideration leads us to the third approach to the question of nonviolence on the international scene. It is largely a permutation of the second proposal above. At Brummana, Lebanon, in December 1961, an international conference was held to establish a World Peace Brigade along much the same lines as those Tatum sketches above. The sponsors included a number of distinguished nonpacifists such as Josue de Castro of Brazil, Martin Buber of Israel, Leopold Infeld of Poland, Kenneth Kaunda of Northern Rhodesia, Julius Nyerere of Tanganyika and Alan Paton of South Africa, as well as distinguished pacifists such as Martin Niemöller, Danilo Dolci, Abbé Pierre and others. Very few of the sponsors actually attended the meeting. Virtually without exception the fifty participants are identifiable as Gandhians, Quakers, nuclear disarmers and pacifist direct-actionists.

The final report of the Brummana Conference, written by Bradford Lyttle of the Committee for Nonviolent Action (USA) states: "There has been created an international framework for carrying out and interpreting nonviolent direct-action projects and programs. What is needed now is someone who possesses that strange power of moral and political imagination and perception which will lead him to see the action which history demands"—in short, a new incarnation of Gandhi. The conference also adopted a Statement of Principles and Aims which leaves the reader in no doubt concerning the nobility of the Brigade's intentions—basically "to bring the liberating and transforming power of nonviolence to bear more effectively on our world." But it says no more about how this is to be done than Arlo Tatum's above-quoted outline.

Practical exigencies made the World Peace Brigade's beginnings much humbler than its envisioned tasks. The first major project was a scheme to stage a march of nonviolent volunteers across the border from Tanganyika into Northern Rhodesia in support of the independence of the latter country, with the encouragement of nationalist leaders Julius Nyerere of Tanganyika and Kenneth Kaunda of Northern Rhodesia and including direct action by Africans in the latter country. In Dar es Salaam, Tanganyika, the World Peace Brigade set up a training center in mid-1962 to train cadres for struggle in nonviolent campaigns for freedom from colonial rule. This idea is interesting as an alternative to the centers operating in the Congo and elsewhere to train saboteurs, assassins and commandos for the freedom movements, but after much fanfare nothing came of this scheme. Another early project of the World Peace Brigade was the sponsoring of a number of small ocean-going vessels on voyages of protest against nuclear weapons. Their impact, however, was negligible.

Both of these ventures are a far cry from the specific purposes envisioned in the idea of *shanti sena,* commendable as they may be as ways of promoting colonial freedom or nuclear disarmament. The World Peace Brigade is little more than an expansion of pacifist direct-action programs from the activities of separate national groups to a coordinated international effort by the same groups, pooling the resources and techniques they formerly used singly. It remains to be seen whether this development can serve as a springboard to a genuine international nonviolent group capable of intervening in disputes between nations. The latter concept, though only in its infancy, has fired the imagination of a number of people. Among them has been Bertrand Russell, who set up a foundation in 1963 for the express purpose of sending nonviolent cadres on missions in the field of international conflict. It will require further exploration and perhaps relevant experimentation and research by nonpacifists, however, before any meaningful evaluation can be made. Perhaps the key to any further steps must be the chartering of such a group by the United Nations or some other international agency laying claim to both legality and impartiality. The odds against a poorly equipped, under-financed organization without any recognized credentials except its own avowed good intentions would seem to be overwhelming.

REFERENCES IN CHAPTER 7

1   M. K. Gandhi in *Harijan*, March 26, 1938.
2   Roy Finch: "There Is a Better Way" in *Fellowship*, March 1, 1958, p. 24.
3   *Ibid.*
4   Salvador de Madariaga and Jayaprakash Narayan: "A World Peace Guard" in *Fellowship*, May 1, 1961.
5   Arlo Tatum: "The World Peace Brigade" in *The War Resister* (London), Fourth Quarter 1961, pp. 4-5.
6   *Ibid.*, p. 4.

The Dynamics of
Nonviolence

8

Phases of Action in
a Nonviolent Strategy

How does nonviolence work? Where do we begin and what is required to carry out a campaign based on a nonviolent strategy? So far we have attempted to define nonviolence and to delineate its range of applications, and we have also made some preliminary observations about a possible sequence beginning with conventional action and progressing to the brink of revolution. Not every campaign would begin at the same point, nor would it necessarily go so far. Each campaign, in fact, requires its own strategy based on the distinctive features of the situation it must confront. Tactics that are successful in one situation may or may not be applicable to another. As Kaspar Mayr has well said, "There are no infallibly valid methods applicable to all cases. They must be as various as life itself and at any given time growing out of the situation in which they are to be used." [1]

Mayr's caution is aimed specifically at the temptation to resort to Gandhi's *satyagraha* campaigns as master plans to be imposed on any occasion. So much of the available literature has been based on these campaigns and the Gandhian philosophy on which they were based that the temptation is an understandable one. Nonviolent cadres can benefit greatly from a study of this literature, but it must be placed in proper perspective. By far the best source for this purpose is Joan V. Bondurant's analysis of five *satyagraha* campaigns in her excellent book, *Conquest of Violence* (Princeton University Press

1958, pp. 45-102). Without this and many other studies, our present chapter could not have been written.

Our purpose here, however, is not merely to translate Gandhi's Hindu concepts into Western terminology, and certainly not to offer a master plan of any sort, but to stake out the major considerations that are likely to apply in most campaigns waged in a context of European, American and perhaps some other Western-type society and culture. This will necessitate a degree of simplification which may be overcome through study of actual historical examples, as in the CASE-BOOK of this volume. Also, for the sake of brevity and clarity we shall in this chapter skimp a number of important questions that can be dealt with more fully in the remaining chapters of this section. Taken together, they are intended to enable a group of people to organize and prepare themselves to conduct a nonviolent campaign. As we shall see, the campaign cannot adequately be understood without studying these questions, but they will not become meaningful until we have the broad setting to which they apply.

Preliminary Considerations

The background to any strategy of nonviolence is a recognition of the fact that we are considering nonviolence as a form of social action, and this requires at least an elementary understanding of society as a structure of social forces. Nonviolence on the level of tactics and strategy is not the pure expression of love or good will, not a device for avoiding or patching up conflicts, not a magic remedy for injustice. It is a means of action for waging social conflict, which may or may not achieve its objectives. This is not to say, of course, that it cannot also be seen as a way of life, as we have observed elsewhere.

When we speak of agapaic love in relations between persons, we are dealing with another dimension, relevant to but not identical with social action. In the latter, we must recognize that societies are made up not merely of an aggregate of individual persons, each a child of God with unique possibilities, nor of a conglomeration of interpersonal encounters, but that in any village, city, state, county or nation there are distinct groupings which function socially. They may be grouped as church members, as golfers, as baseball fans or in many other ways, some of which may be relevant and others less so. The same individual is a part of several social realities, including "the general public," "the electorate," etc. He may be seen as a newspaper reader, a television viewer, a consumer, a worker.

Some of these social roles are more or less random, some are conditioned by habit and custom, and still others are expressed and regulated through institutions. The latter point to the effective centers of social control—broadly speaking, the "power structure" with its leadership or "power elite." This category includes government and its policy-makers, those who wield power through armed force (e.g., a nation's general staff, a city's police commissioner or chief), those who make economic policy (merchants, bankers, industrialists) and those who maintain social norms, class distinctions and the like in a broader sense. Often the same "power elite" members act as a social class.

Admittedly sketchy, some such approach to social structure is indispensable in waging a social struggle. Later on, when we refer to "the opponent," it will not always be possible to specify whether we mean the proprietor of a store, the business community as a whole or perhaps a large segment of the population functioning as a general public, a consumer group or something else. For simplicity, we shall speak of "the opponent" as the ruling group or individual, and any sizable group of non-policy-making people as "the opponent's masses." We may also have occasion to refer to functionaries such as policemen, who form an instrumental part of the power structure below the policy level. Only with such an approach can we begin to distinguish between actions that may be socially relevant and those that are not.

This is only a beginning, and we can do little more than suggest some of the problems that may arise in any social structure. In a given case, is our strategic opponent the whole power elite or only some segment of it? Can we count on the neutrality of some segments of it if we concentrate on others? For example, will pressure directed at merchants have positive or negative repercussions on the business community as a whole? Will it have political effects? Conversely, will pressure directed toward city hall produce desired changes in stores? Again, is the general public reachable through organizations that might be receptive to our point of view? Is it organized in such a way as to facilitate systematic retaliation against us? Is it perhaps unorganized but likely to act as a mob? And if so, is the power structure likely to impede or augment mob action? Finally, are there levels of power such as local and national that are committed to different policies, one of which can aid us against the other? These are a few of the many questions for the nonviolent strategist to consider before launching a campaign, and to keep under review at all times.

Any effort to organize effectively for nonviolent mass action must also confront questions about its own structure that can only be answered fully in relation to its distinctive situation. Basically, however, it will consist of three tiers: the leadership group, disciplined cadres and mass base. These tiers are somewhat analogous to the military categories of staff officers, combat troops and garrison or support troops; but social conflict is not the same as military conflict, and the analogy should not be pressed too closely. There is also a resemblance to the elite-functionary-mass arrangement of the social structure itself, but there are important differences, as there must be between a movement and a stable order. A nonviolent movement has greater fluidity and more overlap. In Gandhian terms, the three tiers consist of fully dedicated *satyagrahis,* constructive workers who are in training to become *satyagrahis,* and masses that may be activated to take part in mass actions led by *satyagrahis.* If we combine the two conceptions it will illuminate the distinctive character of nonviolent organization. The leadership functions not only as "general staff" but also takes to the field with the cadres. The cadres who function below the leadership level (as well as those who function at that level) alternate between "combat" and "garrison" duty. And in much of the latter they are engaged in constructive work that involves the masses and provides a maximum of fluidity from top to bottom.

Another important sociological consideration is the innately democratic character of nonviolent organization. This is not to say that it is immune to corruption, that it cannot become petrified in an authoritarian way, but that it usually arises without the existence of a rigid structure and that it depends heavily upon the active support of the masses. Whether the latter formally vote or not, there is little the leaders can do without consulting their wishes; they can be persuaded but not forced.

Overt social conflict, as contrasted with scattered antagonisms, does not spring from abstract principles of injustice or evil. A large number of people may live for a long time in a situation that makes them victims of injustice, and each in his own way feels this injustice as what C. Wright Mills called a "personal trouble." Many may recognize that other people as well as themselves are afflicted by the same trouble, and even recognize that it has the same source, but they still experience it as a "personal trouble" until something happens that reveals it as a social issue. To be sure, there are troubles that remain personal, and not every personal trouble has potential social impact. The point here is that social conflict occurs when a substantial number of people experience a common grievance that is then articulated as a problem which requires not merely individual adjustments but changes in the social structure.

It is out of this process of maturation, which may be very slow or extremely rapid, that the makings of a mass movement are produced—and not by a group of theorists going out to drum up a following. Whether the leaders of such a movement are already there or come in from the outside, they become the leaders by virtue of the fact that they offer an answer to questions which people in the situation are impelled by their own experience to ask. The nature of the asking is not an intellectual act, however. The masses speak in question marks and exclamation marks, looking for someone to write out the words, which they will then recognize as their own questions and exclamations. The first task of the leader is to serve as a spokesman. Second to this he offers solutions and organizes their implementation. The presence of conflict also brings with it a closing of ranks by the masses. As Lewis Coser has observed,

Conflict with another group leads to the mobilization of the energies of group members and hence to increased cohesion of the group. Whether increase in centralization accompanies this increase in cohesion depends upon both the character of the conflict and the type of group.[2]

If the conflict is an acute one, we may expect that, for the duration of the campaign, community organizations and other institutions of our group will both focus their attention on the conflict and respond favorably to attempts by our leaders to coordinate them, and that with the termination of conflict they will tend to pull apart once more, perhaps even in an exaggerated way. It is the common response to the conflict which initially creates solidarity, not some magical power of nonviolence or of inspired leaders, and a letdown is virtually certain to come if conflict is suspended, unless viable means are devised to assure permanent cooperation in the absence of actual conflict.

The point at which a social conflict recognizably begins is a moment of crisis which may occur dramatically and unexpectedly or may be the result of agitation. Whether spontaneous or induced, however, it is not an artificial event. A social issue has been in the making and it is now precipitated into the consciousness of the masses. The crisis usually comes in conjunction with some event which otherwise would not call forth a decisive response but which now serves as a pivotal issue, symbolizing the larger social issue. For example, the arrest of Rosa Parks (see page 299) on a bus in Montgomery, Alabama, in itself constituted a minor grievance by comparison with the shooting of a man some time earlier, but it came as a culmination of a series of such "troubles" that added up to an important immediate issue reflecting a social reality: the lack of decent treatment of Negroes on the city buses in a general context of racial discrimination. This issue in turn was expanded from "decent treatment" to "desegregation," and linked with the generic issue of racial equality in other forms of public accommodation. The water was there all the time, but it was the stone marked "Rosa Parks" that made the splash with its circles rippling out from that event.

Given the underlying causes, a group of potential leaders could have been in existence, waiting for such a pivotal event and ready with trained cadres to go into action. They might even take action calculated to cause such an event and thus hasten the process. But it is not the content of the event which makes it pivotal; it is the response of the community to it.

Preparing for the Campaign

It is only with the moment of crisis that leadership becomes effective, social conflict is being waged and a campaign is under way. In many cases there may have been no advance preparation of any kind, and everything has to be quickly improvised, with untrained people getting their basic training in the midst of the conflict itself. There is much that can and should be done well in advance, however, if it is possible to do so. In the following pages we shall discuss the entire course of a campaign, from the preparatory stages through to the farthest-reaching conclusions, even though in many cases the scope of an actual campaign would be less ambitious.

Let us start with the assumption that we are an assortment

of individuals who have decided to meet together in order to discuss what we think is a social issue. We might be a church social-action committee, a ministerial association, a trade-union group or some other such pre-existing body, or we might be individuals who are meeting for the first time. In the former case, we shall have to decide whether we can use our existing organizational apparatus or devise a new one. Here we shall assume that we are starting from scratch.

Our very first task will be to check our several impressions of the situation. Are we all talking about the same problem? Is each of us acquainted with all the relevant facts? What are our respective sources of information? If there are differences of emphasis or interpretation, these should be disposed of and common agreement reached concerning the real issue and the facts that concern it.

Now, granted that we know the facts, one of us must take the responsibility to state them carefully in writing, adding the necessary documentation. It will probably be advisable to set up a file and gather reliable information. Time and facilities will have to be allocated for this purpose. Although each of us should keep informed, one of us should take the responsibility for preparing reports for eventual publication.

Next, how do we propose that the issue be resolved? We discuss the solution and put it into written form, estimating the minimum and maximum demands we are prepared to make, and we decide which of the opponent's representatives may be most effectively approached. When the time comes, we shall have ready a brief and clear statement of grievances and a concise list of maximum demands concerning a tangible issue, supported by documentation—all of this in a form ready to hand to the opponent and to the press and, with abbreviated documentation, to be distributed to the masses we seek to lead. In addition to this, we should draft a detailed statement of the maximum demands we are making, for use in negotiations. We may share this with the opponent, while reserving for our own private use an outline of the minimum we are willing to settle for. The latter will be disclosed to the opponent in due course if settlement is unobtainable on better terms. It would be poor strategy to make concessions beforehand or to indicate what we are prepared to forego until required to.

Gandhi, despite his insistence on strict, even ascetic discipline for the "true *satyagrahi,*" recognized that it was not possible in practice to secure perfect adherence to nonviolence by all members of a mass movement. "It is enough," he said, "for one person only to possess it even as one general is enough to regulate and dispense of the energy of millions of soldiers." [8] Referring to the highly effective and well-organized Salt March, in which thousands took part who were not free of hate or anger in their daily conduct, Gandhi later added: "Their belief in nonviolence was unintelligent. . . . But their belief in their leaders was genuine." [4]

A heavy responsibility therefore rests upon the leadership to be well trained and capable of marshaling the activities and holding the allegiance of masses whom we will be unable to train fully. Recognizing the potentialities and limitations that this implies, we begin to discuss possible strategy and allocate leadership roles. Decisions must be made to bring into the leadership group persons with needed skills or to develop these skills among ourselves. Our group, as it shapes up, should include individuals capable of planning and coordinating a sustained program of action, of interpreting the movement to the opponent and to the public through speaking and writing, of carrying out tactical actions of symbolic significance to illustrate our motives and aims, of administering funds, arranging meetings, handling correspondence, etc. A maximum of versatility is to be cultivated within the limits of individual aptitudes and the needs of the program.

We should begin very early to study and discuss the theory and history of nonviolence and to engage in training sessions among ourselves, not only seeking to adapt historical strategies to our own needs but also to acquire a sufficient knowledge of theory to be able to speak fluently about it to others. It is part of the leadership's responsibility both to master nonviolence beyond our immediate needs and to equip ourselves not only to practice it but to teach it to others. This is even more important in our leadership training and subsequent teaching of socio-drama, in which we rehearse not only in words but in actions the various kinds of encounters we expect to have with our opponents. It is here that we test out our theories and beliefs and learn how to maintain nonviolent conduct and discipline under conditions of stress. (See page 165.)

Once our training program is under way, we map out a suitable constructive program and begin to recruit potential cadres, joining with them in the constructive work, which should be intrinsically beneficial and noncontroversial in its content—ideally, some form of service that is of real benefit to a segment of our community and that can elicit approval from our opponent and from neutrals. Some nonviolent campaigns have done without a constructive program or have relied on normal community activities to balance the strain of protest action, but they have usually had to pay an unexpected price later on for this deficiency. A clean-up campaign or a series of week-end work camps to repair dilapidated buildings might be particularly well suited to the purposes of a localized campaign. Proponents of national and international actions have recommended ongoing service work of the kind done by the Peace Corps and by such agencies as Ecumenical Voluntary Service, Eirene and Service Civil Internationale.

In the more typical domestic situation of conflict along racial lines in an American city, let us assume that we are a Negro leadership group. The immediate issue is not building maintenance but access to public facilities that are denied to us, or some such grievance that involves asserting our rights, making a claim, securing concessions from the dominant white community which holds effective political power. Nevertheless, if we mount a constructive effort to repair buildings in the Negro community we thereby demonstrate our solidarity as a community and also tangibly undercut charges that we are only concerned with wresting our rights from the whites, only asking them to do something for us. We also exercise self-respect and heal inner divisions that may exist within our community. This makes possible the interpretation of our protest activity as a basically positive action and identifies the nonviolent cadres as helpful and generous persons. Even more important, this image is not a fake, concocted merely for publicity; it rests on an authentic foundation. This foundation also serves directly to undergird the struggle itself, since we need a healthy cohesion that goes deeper than the immediate issue, while it likewise provides the leaders and cadres with the valuable experience of working together in a common cause under an agreed-upon discipline prior to the onset of direct action.

Through the constructive program, which existing community organizations may be invited to join, an avenue is opened through which such organizations can subsequently link themselves with a campaign of nonviolent action. Meanwhile, their support of the constructive program need not imply anything beyond the immediate work.

Once we have completed our own basic training in theory and practice, we turn to the training of our cadres, with whom we continue working on the constructive program. As their number grows, we select those who are best qualified and assign them to posts of responsibility. The primary organizational unit for both constructive work and protest action is a team ranging in size from eight to sixteen persons, with one team member taking responsibility for the others. Lines of authority should be clarified to avoid confusion and to coordinate the actions of all teams. Ideally, each team of cadres should be a duplicate of the leadership team, capable of interpreting fully the principles of nonviolence and of the campaign, and potentially able to succeed to the leadership if necessary. Definite procedures should be established within each team and within the movement as a whole for making decisions democratically and carrying them out authoritatively.

This means, among other things, that members of the initiating leadership group must eventually be prepared to yield their positions to leaders chosen by the masses. Continuity of symbolic leadership is highly desirable, but there are dangers in its concentration in one person. Flexibility of effective administrative and strategic leadership may be an overriding asset.

The Campaign Begins

We are now ready to initiate the campaign on the level of conventional action and are prepared to follow it up with a nonviolent strategy. Possibly our work in the constructive program has by this time resulted in a change of attitude by the opponent which makes a crisis unlikely. If this is the case, we may find him ready to consider our petition without pressure, and we shall continue to emphasize the constructive work and broaden it. But we shall assume that conditions have shown no sign of improvement.

It is hard to prescribe the next step in general terms. If there has been a series of incidents such as the mistreatment of bus passengers in Montgomery, to which we referred above, the wise course may be simply to wait for the next incident in the series. Or it may be desirable to initiate action through a deliberate act of defiance—not a mass action but an individual or small-group action calculated to precipitate conflict, that is, to bring latent conflict to the surface.

Here we must proceed with caution, selecting as our target a potential issue that can eloquently articulate the mood of the masses and thus bring forth their response—an issue which at the same time can be most readily communicated in simple human terms to the opponent's masses and to neutral or "outside" elements. An example is the sit-in for "a cup of coffee." Another might be defiance of a curfew. The persons chosen to undertake such an action should be well-trained cadres who are able to conduct themselves in an impeccable manner. Particularly in this event, but also at later stages, it is important that the opponent be deprived of the opportunity to muddy the issue by stigmatizing these cadres in any way. A strong factor in the case of Rosa Parks is that she was known to everyone in Montgomery as a highly respectable person. An injustice to a slovenly person is still an injustice, but the psychological impact is keener when the victim is well-dressed, clean-shaven, clean-cut and well-behaved.

If these cadres are arrested or mistreated, we check the response of the community to which we are offering our leadership. If it is weak, we have miscalculated the situation and had better try another approach. But if it is strong, if people are saying that "something must be done," it is time for us to make our bid for leadership. Depending on the mood of the people and other factors in the situation, we may issue a call for a public rally or mass meeting at which to present our petition to the people, or we may assign our cadres the task of circulating the petition. Or the social structures may be such that we choose to obtain the signatures of key community leaders rather than of the masses. The time element is a factor here, too, and we must choose a course that enables us to move quickly while the issue is hot and before it is taken up by violent elements.

With the petition we are ready to go to the opponent and present our demands. If he refuses to deal with us, we publish our demands and proceed to stage a public demonstration to dramatize the issue, mobilize our masses in support of it and appeal to the opponent's masses to influence their leaders in the desired direction. The appeal to the opponent's masses may take a number of forms such as radio announcements and distribution of leaflets. One of the most difficult but also most promising is door-to-door calling and telephoning by cadres who are prepared to explain our cause and discuss the issues on which the petition is based. A measure of success in direct dialog of this kind can not only open the possibility of early settlement but if we move on to mass protest action it will enhance the likelihood of a sympathetic response.

We are not using the petition as an ultimatum but as a basis for negotiations and as an occasion for man-to-man encounter at the top levels of our respective groups.

Kaspar Mayr has remarked that of the various types of nonviolence

The most effective form has always been civil disobedience against users of violence, against usurpers. [But] the goal remains to convince the opponent in his heart that he is in the wrong and that he is doing wrong.[5]

Much wishful thinking has been devoted to the notion that nonviolence works chiefly through moral persuasion. Mayr's emphasis is correct; it would be a mistake to abandon the goal of converting the opponent just because it is harder and less likely than the method of compulsion and coercion through nonviolent pressure. The fact is that the two methods are complementary, as April Carter has pointed out:

In any nonviolent campaign two broad categories of power are operative: psychological power and the social power which results from an alteration of political, social or economic relationships. . . . A nonviolent campaign involves a blend of psychological power and social power, the relative emphasis on conversion or coercion determining the over-all future of the campaign.[6]

An individual's position in the power structure is likely to decide his responsiveness to a moral appeal if it touches upon a substantive matter—that is, something his job depends on. In the bottom strata there may be an unwillingness to risk the job by responding, but if caught in a conflict of conscience the individual functionary may look for loopholes to accommodate us without jeopardizing his position. If there is latent conflict between him and his superiors, as is often the case, he may even be capable of rebelling against orders to perpetrate injustice, if the moral appeal is overwhelming. A policeman, for example, has a certain amount of discretion in dealing with demonstrators. We may succeed in getting more or less gentle treatment from him, but only in the extreme case can we call upon him to come over and join us, or to take a position of neutrality. As a rule, this is possible only in a revolutionary situation.

The position of the leadership person is different, whether he is an elected official, an appointed executive, a military officer or a management spokesman. Whatever his personal feelings, he holds his position and the power that goes with it as the agent of a constituency, a company, a class or some other entity. Though accustomed to exercising power, his loyalties to the source of that power are usually much firmer than in the case of the functionary. If the group he represents has a vested interest in its side of the issue we are concerned with, it is likely—and he as its agent is likely—to have strong, built-in defenses against a moral appeal. Part of this is the result of compartmentalizing personal and official decisions in the ordinary exercise of his leadership role. Even in the rare case of conversion, such a man is more likely to step out of his leadership role than to take the system with him. Pragmatically, pressure and coercion are more reliable here than persuasion. If he is an elected official, for example, it is more effective to change the mood or composition of the electorate than to try to get him to take a public stand which throws him into opposition with it.

Nevertheless, it is important in the encounter with the opponent to seek to establish personal rapport. There is the outside chance that the issue at stake hinges on the intrusion of his private attitudes into his official actions, on knowledge or ignorance of the situation, etc. There is also the likelier chance that courtesy, courage and honesty on our part may win us his respect and lead him to curb excesses that are not basic to the system it is his duty to uphold. This is to be desired as affording a better climate in which to wage the struggle. It is also morally sound. But the compelling strategic reason for good conduct on our part is to clear the path for our use of pressure.

It is our task in any encounter with the opponent to strip away his fears and apprehensions and to deprive him of any rationalizations he may be using to distort the facts. It is distinctly to our advantage if we can summon sufficient empathy to see matters from his point of view so that we can help him to see the situation as it actually is.

The fact that we have initiated the conflict is upsetting. It poses a threat of unknown proportions which our opponent is anxious to dispose of. If we confront him with too much meekness, he will be glad to pounce on this as a sign of weakness. If we confront him with overbearing boldness, he will exaggerate the threat we pose to the status quo. Our job is not to wheedle or to bluff, but to show him that we are responsible persons seeking a change of conditions to which the opponent's social structure can adjust, and that we have adequate support for a course of action that will deepen and prolong the conflict. As Martin Luther King has stated, the purpose of direct action is "to create a situation so crisis-packed that it will inevitably open the door to negotiation." [7]

We will reassure him as much as we can, without concealing our ultimate aims and, by indicating our willingness to negotiate, offer some latitude for compromise. In every aspect of our appearance, bearing and conduct, we should avoid provoking the opponent in any way. We should speak distinctly and choose our words with care; and we should remain calm and composed in the face of any provocation he may offer. We do not seek to throw him off balance, though we may permit him to throw himself off balance—a feat which is not so advantageous to us as our gracious act of presently setting him on his feet. We show him by our actions that we are in control of the situation no matter what happens, and that we will not misuse our power. By being honest and fair at all times ourselves, we give him no excuse to be dishonest or unfair to us. In explaining to him our choice of nonviolent means, we not only make a gesture of good will but we also convey the impression that we are secure enough in our strength that we can confidently set our own limits upon it. Thus our moral position psychologically enhances our coercive power.

The attempt to begin negotiations should be pursued throughout the campaign until they occur and move to a satisfactory conclusion. They may take the form of direct bargaining or of arbitration by an impartial arbitrator. If the opponent contests our facts, we do not hesitate to propose an independent fact-finding commission.

We must recognize that the opponent may consent to negotiations or to other such measures, not to work toward a solution of the conflict but as a delaying tactic to undermine our movement and terminate the conflict on his own terms. He may stipulate that we cease demonstrations or direct action while negotiations are in progress, or for a stated period of time, counting on the resulting inertia to give him a chance to smash the movement. As a general rule, therefore, we should never consent to suspend our activities for longer than a few days and always have new plans in readiness. Exceptions would have to be justified by tangible evidence of the opponent's good faith.

Throughout the campaign, mass demonstrations can serve as a convincing index of numerical strength. To get a maximum turnout, however, they should be wisely spaced, adequately publicized and imaginatively staged with full use of vivid symbols of the movement's purpose and unity as well as devices to amplify the message and boost morale, and to make unmistakably clear the fact that the leadership group and the cadres have the full support of the masses. A mass demonstration is not a specifically nonviolent action. The larger it is, the more vulnerable it will be to provocation by the opponent. Serious risks are involved in staging such demonstrations during periods of acute conflict. The dangers can be reduced if sufficient numbers of cadres are present in the demonstration to keep it under control and head off rioting if it should occur, but provisions should also be made to disperse quickly and calmly in case of disorders. And there will be times when we shall want to exercise our discretion not to demonstrate en masse but to indicate numerical strength and solidarity in less volatile ways.

In addition to numerical strength, expressed through demonstrations, the readiness of our movement to act can be shown by symbolic acts such as picketing, poster walks and silent vigils carried on by small groups—usually one or more teams of cadres—on a continuous basis: around the clock for several days, once or twice a week for months, etc. In India, fasting was used by cadres, and it has been used by pacifist groups in the West, but in the latter case it has not always communicated. Mass marches and prayer pilgrimages can be very effective symbolic actions if discipline can be maintained. The need for careful planning here is even greater than in stationary mass demonstrations.

All of these actions have value as morale-builders as well as showing the opponent our strength. Other devices should be developed to express our solidarity and purpose. Slogans, emblems, forms of greeting and the like can have strong effect. Winston Churchill's famed World War II "V for Victory" sign, the Communist clenched-fist salute and other such gestures had wide effect and communicated readily. The distinctive white cap of the Indian National Congress, the shout of the word *"mayibuye!"* (freedom) in South Africa and the hymn "We Shall Overcome," adopted by Negro students in the American sit-in movement, are among numerous examples from nonviolent movements. Each is a valuable means of expressing what we stand for in the simplest terms. We shall therefore devise our own and make it a point to display them whenever we can. They should be simple enough for a child to recognize and emulate, clear enough to state the issue at a glance. "Jim Crow Must Go" and "Ban the Bomb" are slogans that meet this specification. They are not only short but have rhythm and ring that make them superior to, let us say, "End Jim Crow" or "Scrap Nuclear Weapons." The same factors should be borne in mind when devising a variety of slogans to be painted on picket signs or banners. The solidarity symbols have their place among the latter, but there should also be signs that have the more prosaic function of explaining the issue or stating the facts in a rudimentary way, like tabloid newspaper headlines. The lettering should be large and bold enough to be read at a distance and also to be photographed. The publication of a news photo showing our poster walk or our march with banners means free publicity among the opponent's masses and among neutrals and sympathizers. Here again, incidentally, the value of presenting a good appearance through neat attire, erect posture, etc., is obvious.

Initiating Direct Action

Sooner or later, if a date is not set for negotiations, or if negotiations have begun and stalled, we shall announce our intention to launch concerted direct action or to expand those actions which we have already initiated. We work out our timetable and instruct all the cadres, who pass the word to the masses. If we have radio facilities, we may alert listeners to the fact that an important announcement is to be made. In most cases it will be wise not to inform the opponent of the full details of the action that is planned until it is certain that he will be unable to forestall it. We may announce the day and even the hour, but not the content; or we may announce the content of the action but not the time. When we make this announcement, we combine it with an ultimatum, stating that we are prepared to suspend the action or call it off if the opponent meets our demands (for negotiation or for settlement) by a specified time.

The first line of direct action may be symbolic rather than coercive: a symbolic on-the-job work stoppage for fifteen minutes at a prearranged time (with exceptions for certain types of work in which this gesture would be damaging or dangerous) or a one-day stay-at-home strike. At the time the action is about to begin, or as much earlier as we safely can, we announce to the opponent and to the general public exactly what we are going to do, specifying time, extent, location—all the external details. We also indicate that we are prepared to take further action if this one does not bring results. By announcing in advance just how long the work stoppage is going to last, and then carrying out our plan exactly as stated, we indicate clearly that we are in control. We leave the opponent no loophole to explain the event away or to divorce it from its leadership.

Mass actions such as this should be used sparingly, so as not to deplete the morale of the masses. We must always bear in mind the distinction between the thoroughly trained and disciplined cadre and the more loosely involved masses. If the masses are asked to do too much, they will become tired and the conflict will disintegrate into chaos or apathy. On the other hand, if they are asked to do too little their enthusiasm will wane and the movement will coast to a halt. A wise leadership must have a good sense of timing. We should be able to assess the mood of the masses well enough to know when to call them into action and for how long—and this also means judging when to call a halt so that an action does not end in straggling.

If the symbolic work stoppage does not bring results, we may turn to a number of tactics that do not demand the full participation of the masses and which focus attention on several different teams of cadres, such as picketing beamed at the opponent's masses alternating with a sit-in at one or more offices or stores involved in the issue. Aspects of the constructive program might be given extra emphasis at this stage, along with small-scale prayer vigils, deputations to influential individuals among the opponent's masses (e.g., clergy, professionals and others outside the administrative apparatus) and rallies, prayer meetings and other morale-building events that involve no strain and no struggle.

The next step, which may supplant but more likely will supplement these diverse tactics, is sustained mass noncooperation or passive resistance, focused on the immediate issue. Before this step is taken, we should consult with our cadres to determine how long this action can be sustained. If it is a selective buying campaign, for example, we may be able to count on the masses to change their shopping habits with relatively minor inconvenience for an unlimited period. But if it is a boycott against a needed commodity we must be prepared to terminate it when the required sacrifice begins to tire the masses, or else take steps to produce substitutes through the constructive program. Gandhi's twin emphases on the boycott of foreign cloth and on hand spinning was a stroke of genius in this respect.

When we begin selective passive resistance of this kind, we should also make plans to expand or intensify it in the event the opponent takes a serious step in reprisal, or as a means of renewing the effort if the initial phase begins to fade. A boycott of certain goods, for example, can be broadened into a complete boycott of the stores which sell those goods. Or it may be extended to another sector—from merchandise to transport and other facilities. In India at one stage, resisters refused to use British law courts to settle civil disputes, but this probably did more to promote the resisters' solidarity than to exert pressure on the British in a direct way.

Although in many situations it may be desirable to hold off from direct action of the assertive type until passive-resistance methods have first been used, there is no intrinsic reason for not using direct action first. Some situations will provide a foothold for the latter and not for the former. Where access to services and facilities is the major issue, there is often little scope for passive tactics except to augment the nonviolent demand for such access through direct action—going and attempting to get service. The two may be phased in sequence or used simultaneously, depending on the situation itself. A key question would be: do we have sufficient purchasing power that its withdrawal could be decisive in altering the policies of a store which bars us from lunch counters, fitting rooms, etc., or must we rely more heavily upon sitting at the lunch counter or entering the fitting room? Suppose we want admittance to theaters, libraries, public parks or other places where passive resistance would be inapplicable? Here the attempt to enter would be the only alternative to picketing and the like—the only possible form of specifically nonviolent protest.

Before engaging in nonviolent direct action, however, we should examine two factors affecting the context of law and order. First, even if we are only transgressing established customs we may encounter forcible resistance from store owners or employees, hecklers, hoodlums and the like. To what extent can we depend on law-enforcement officers to be on hand to maintain order and protect us from bodily harm, and to what extent are we on our own? What will we do in the latter event? First-aid, rescue and escape preparations will have to be made as well as rigorous selection and training of cadres. In many such cases the police will intervene, often belatedly, and arrest us for "disorderly conduct" or some other specious charge, maintaining both order and the status quo. We shall have to plan to replace the arrested cadres in successive waves as they are removed from the scene, repeat the action after an interval of hours or days, or turn to another tactic.

Second, there is the question of the legality of our action as such, apart from what may happen as a result of it. If we are breaking local ordinances that give police the technical right to arrest us, we may want to initiate court action or we may decide on the basis of higher-court rulings that we have some legal justification for going ahead. Here we must consider the question of civil disobedience as discussed in Chapter 4. With or without a secure legal basis, however, we must also weigh carefully the penalties which the authorities can actually inflict, as well as our own resources to absorb and overcome them. Can we muster enough cadres to fill the jails and "clog the machinery" or at least render ineffectual the opponent's efforts to dispose of our protest in this way? Ideally, we should be able to fill the jails and still have enough cadres left to fill the lunch-counter stools or otherwise carry on the action. If we do resort to such a tactic our organizational structure should be carefully reviewed and modified to assure continuous leadership, dividing our forces into several strata so that if our top-level leaders are arrested another group can step in and fill their places. For maximum effectiveness it may also be necessary to recruit large numbers of new cadres from among the masses and to bring in cadres from outside the community. By all means, the constructive work should be kept going and stepped up if possible.

Filling the jails is the virtual end of the line for nonviolent strategy, once the point is reached when either all of our forces are behind bars or the authorities are unable or unwilling to put them there. It is not necessarily the end of the campaign, however. The arrested cadres can appeal to their jailers and government officials, who may be moved by the degree of commitment shown in the cadres' willingness to endure imprisonment for the sake of their objectives. In extreme situations that afford no other alternative, those in jail can use the hunger strike as their last weapon of nonviolent coercion, resolving to fast until released. Short of this, efforts to change social policy through appeals to jailers have not been notably successful. Direct appeals to the policy-making officials themselves have a better chance, and psychologically the moral substance of the appeal from jail may not only add to socio-economic pressure such as that created by the boycott or other actions, but it may also provide the officials with a face-saving rationale for meeting the demands: they are giving in to the moral appeal rather than to pressure.

Perhaps the crucial factor at this point, however, is the effect on public opinion. More people can be swayed by the simple fact of suffering than by a righteous cause that does not vitally affect them. Our going to jail may bring the issue to life for them and cause them to exert pressure on those who make policy. Officials who imagined that they were only maintaining law and order may see themselves cast in the role of oppressors and find the image uncomfortable, leading them to rethink their position. Even among the opponent's masses there may be a change of attitude. Going to jail potentially raises the question whether the offense at issue is so vital to the existence of the opponent's way of life that its whole system of law enforcement must be made to hinge on it.

If this does not bring victory, all is not necessarily lost. Recourse to higher courts, higher governmental intervention and other possibilities may still be open. Or it may be necessary to turn to another strategy for a new campaign.

REFERENCES IN CHAPTER 8

1   Kaspar Mayr: *Der Andere Weg* (Nürnberg, Germany: Glock und Lutz, 1957), p. 260.
2   Lewis Coser: *The Functions of Social Conflict* (Glencoe, Ill.: The Free Press, 1956), p. 95.
3   M. K. Gandhi in *Young India,* September 23, 1926.
4   *Harijan,* February 22, 1942.
5   Mayr, *loc. cit.*
6   April Carter: *Direct Action* (London: Peace News, 1962), p. 30. A pamphlet.
7   Martin Luther King Jr.: *Letter from Birmingham City Jail* (Valley Forge, Pa.: American Baptist Convention, 1963), p. 5.

9

Nonviolent Conduct
and Discipline

Undergirding every tactic of nonviolence is the conduct of the individual cadre. Whether he acts alone or in a team, it is the nonviolence of his individual conduct that gives the tactic its nonviolent character. Although uncoordinated individual acts do not add up to a movement or a strategy, there can be no such thing as a nonviolent movement or a nonviolent strategy without the disciplined nonviolent conduct of its individual cadres. A thorough understanding of this basic fact, leading to study and training to implant it, is a prerequisite for any campaign that chooses nonviolence as its strategy. The ability of each cadre to adhere to a code of strict discipline under stress is a matter that cannot be left to chance, and in some situations where a tinge of violence might spell disaster, the cadre's firmness in nonviolent conduct becomes a strategic imperative.

The essentials of any code of discipline are relatively simple. Its keystone must be: Don't strike the opponent. But this dictum alone will not cover the other contingencies of nonviolent conflict, nor does it explain the why and how of the conduct which discipline is to secure. Let us first outline a basic discipline and then discuss the dynamics of conduct and its effects, together with the basic training that is required. The following is a composite of several codes that have been used:

1. Maintain an attitude of good will at all times.

2. Avoid malicious language, slogans or labels to stigmatize or ridicule the opponent.

3. If force or violence is used against you, your teammates or others, do not retaliate. Never use violence.

4. Do not carry weapons of any kind. Do not carry implements that could be used or interpreted as weapons, such as a pocket knife.

5. Abide by decisions of the group or, when in action, follow orders given by the authorized group leader. Avoid maverick behavior.

6. Without abrogating the above, exercise creative judgment and initiative. Be flexible, willing to experiment.

7. Be ready to assume leadership of the team if required to do so.

8. Submit to arrest promptly and politely unless a policy of noncooperation has been decided upon.

9. Be punctual and precise in carrying out all tasks.

10. Maintain neat appearance and dignified posture at all times, in conformity with the moral image of the cause. This includes speaking simply, clearly and to the point. Avoid tendentiousness and be prepared to give a straightforward reply to relevant questions as well as to ignore with good grace any inflammatory remarks, jeers or other verbal abuse from the opponent.[1]

To these we may add a pertinent point: the team and the movement have a responsibility to give the individual cadre their full support when he acts on their behalf, sharing their available resources to the fullest extent in providing bail if arrested, medical aid if hurt and in general doing whatever is possible and necessary to help him out of any trouble arising from his involvement.[2]

Turning now to the dynamics of nonviolent conduct in face-to-face encounter, let us first examine what Richard B. Gregg, in his book *The Power of Nonviolence,* has called "moral jiu-jitsu":

The nonviolence and good will of the victim act in the same way that the lack of physical opposition by the user of physical jiu-jitsu does, causing the attacker to lose his moral balance.[3]

According to Gregg, the element of surprise is initially the key factor in this process, but it is to be understood in relation to a number of other factors which we may summarize as follows, omitting those portions of Gregg's analysis that are perhaps not central to the process:

1. Lack of physical retaliation disorients the immediate opponent, making him unsure of his ground. The fact that the nonviolent cadre stands his ground without fighting back, manifesting both courage and good will, mobilizes an inner conflict in the opponent between his initial aggressive stance and his latent or habitual tendency to meet good will with good will.

2. At a deeper level, the opponent's "unsureness" is diffuse and undefinable, calling in question a whole configuration of prejudices and value judgments, and making him suggestible. That is, his psychological defense mechanisms are unplugged and he becomes amenable to the well-integrated structure of values which the nonviolent cadre is able to maintain.

3. The juxtaposition of the angry, violent attacker and the calm, unretaliating resister mobilizes spontaneous human sympathy for the latter on the part of any onlookers, and a concomitant censure of the attacker's conduct, which tends to impel him to disengage himself from the immediate conflict.

4. By showing through conduct that he is willing to suffer for his beliefs, the nonviolent cadre wins respect for those beliefs on the part of both opponent and onlooker. This would be the case also if he were to "stand up and fight" with counterviolence, but nonviolent conduct enhances the effect because the cadre thus clearly demonstrates also his respect for the assailant and his steadfast resolve to do him no harm.

5. By controlling the conflict in this way, maintaining his balance while the assailant is thrown off balance by his own unretaliated thrust, the nonviolent cadre is in a position to help the assailant to his feet in a moral sense.

6. Incipiently, at least, by his refusal either to flee or to fight, the nonviolent cadre communicates to the assailant a gesture of

trust which invites reciprocation. This may contribute to conversion, but whether this happens or not it builds an image of the cadre which reflects favorably on his cause and allays the assailant's suspicions.

Gregg acknowledges the difficulties posed by an unusually cruel and insensitive opponent, but counts on "dramatic scenes of prolonged nonviolent resistance" to penetrate eventually. Central to his conception of nonviolence is the belief that the nonviolent individual or group can convert the opponent to an awareness of "essential human unity" in terms of which a common bond is established between the two parties to the conflict.

The French psychoanalyst Maryse Choisy gives a different interpretation of the process:

All the dynamism of nonviolence consists in the fact that it succeeds in totally liquidating the nonviolent person's unconscious guilt feelings, while at the same time in the same degree it activates the opponent's guilt. And it is this bad conscience of the other which renders him more vulnerable. But in the degree that the nonviolent person acts out of love, not only has he brought the other's guilt to consciousness but he has made him *accept* this guilt. It can no longer change into paranoid projection. On the contrary, it inhibits the aggressive *élan*. Because at the instant when it manifests itself, it feels itself already forgiven by the nonviolent one. Thus, in this inner dialog, there is a triple dialectical movement of contradictory relations: the nonviolent one is exalted, the violent one is moved to compassion and the nonviolent one is raised up with him.[4]

Two salient principles are evident in the dynamics of nonviolent conduct: integrity and empathy. Integrity signifies consistency and wholeness, the resolution of contradictory impulses in terms of what is basic to health. Hatred is a disintegrative emotion; it divides and fragments. Evil is the basic principle of disintegration, symbolized in chaos and disorder or equally in an order based on disunity. Gregg's emphasis on "human unity" is one way of stating the essential wholeness and integrity of humanity, but the same principle applies at every level of existence, authenticating the individual self which becomes integrated as it resolves its inner conflicts, authenticating relations between persons as they resolve interpersonal conflicts and establish common grounds, and likewise authenticating intergroup relations in the same way. This is what Choisy is referring to when she speaks of the nonviolent person having liquidated his guilt feelings. This is also the objective of the Gandhian concept of "self-purification" through fasting and other acts of self-denial. It is all a matter of sweeping out of oneself whatever blocks one's resoluteness of purpose.

There are varieties and degrees of integrity within certain closed orbits. A white supremacist may be a man of honesty and honor in his dealings with white persons, and he may try to act with honor and honesty on a different scale in his dealings with Negroes, but the cleavage between the two orbits with their different concepts of integrity constitutes a flaw in his integrity as a total person—and consequently it is a source of guilt.

We must not suppose that it is impossible to be effective in nonviolent conduct unless we are perfect, nor that adherence to a nonviolent discipline results in perfection. To be operative it is sufficient that outward conduct exhibits integrity, even if it is forced, but it must be undergirded by a certain minimum of inner attitude if it is to be sustained. We run a tremendous risk if we attempt to counterfeit these attitudes or to hold them merely as abstract principles, for ultimately the source of nonviolent power is rooted in love and hinges upon our ability to express that love at a crucial moment in the form of empathy.

Empathy is, quite simply, seeing things from the opponent's point of view. It does not mean feeling sorry for him or merely calculating how we would act if we were in his position. It means understanding him as he understands himself, with all his foibles and prejudices, momentarily setting aside our own standards of value. Only through empathy can we search out and discover the inherent integrity of the opponent's personality which it is our task to enlarge. And we cannot do this empathically if we have not already developed a degree of integration within ourselves and among one another within our own group.

Romano Guardini has stated this brilliantly in another context:

Everything, to remain human and be spiritually successful, must first pass through the "personal center," that inmost core of the responsible human heart. The true, the good and the right are realizable only if accepted by living poeple with inner, genuine conviction, and to bring this about requires reverence, encouragement, patience. He who would be truly effective with men must respect *their* freedom, stir *their* initiatives, awaken *their* creative centers.

The greater a man's power, the stronger the temptation to take the shortcut of force.[5]

If we take "power" in our context to mean the sheer technique of "moral jiu-jitsu," it is not difficult to imagine the misuse of the latter in an attempt to embarrass the opponent and throw him off balance. A superficial understanding of nonviolence may result in just such tactics, which antagonize the opponent and destroy rather than establish rapport. There is latent in such a view the strong temptation to inflict psychic injury, to damage the opponent's self-esteem while refraining from overt violence against him—in short to use abstention from physical violence as a means of provoking "unwarranted" attack, thus tricking the opponent into a position of moral disadvantage and making him lose countenance. There may be some immediate satisfaction in making a fool of the opponent in this way, but its net effect is to stiffen his opposition and encourage him to engage in further repressions despite the refusal of the "nonviolent" persons to employ violence.

The pressures used in a nonviolent campaign are social and strategic. The object of nonviolent conduct is not to carry them into the realm of interpersonal encounter, but just the opposite. Nonviolent conduct is predicated on the assumption that hostility and moral disintegrity will be manifested by the opponent as part of his response to social conflict, and that these may take violent forms which we shall then not resist in kind, but on the contrary meet with good will and forgiveness, ready to relieve the opponent of his guilt and establish a new relationship of mutual respect *which we have already unilaterally begun.*

As Maryse Choisy indicates above, nonviolent conduct brings the opponent's guilt to the surface and meets it with forgiveness that inhibits its "aggressive *élan.*" Culbert G. Rutenber gives us a working definition of its implications:

forgiveness must never be interpreted as condoning evil or acting as though its existence really did not make any difference. . . .

Forgiveness, to be morally effective, must satisfy the conscience and moral sense of the one forgiven. . . . [It] must be offered in such a way that the forgiven one is not humiliated and his self-respect is not taken away.[6]

He adds that, to be authentic, forgiveness must be motivated by love, without which it may be nothing more than a gesture of condescension or of contempt which implies that the forgiven one is not worth getting upset about. The occasion for forgiveness should not be glossed over, as if to say "there is nothing to forgive." It should be made clear, verbally or otherwise, that insults and injuries which are forgiven are real insults and real injuries.

The Principle in Action

James Baldwin has written: "I imagine that one of the reasons people cling to their hates so stubbornly is because they sense, once hate is gone, that they will be forced to deal with pain." [7] Hostility is a kind of shield, and in inviting the opponent to dispense with it we are asking him to emulate our vulnerability, which we demonstrate by accepting suffering. In our encounters with individual persons in the opponent's ranks we should consider the extent to which their solidarity is based on conformity to a group standard of hostility. It may be difficult for an individual opponent to respond overtly with good will toward us because of the pressures exerted upon him by his group, and we should respect his reluctance for this reason. A question to be asked in the situation is whether we seek to pry individuals loose from their group or whether we want to have a more diffuse effect on the group as a whole, prying it loose from its hostilities toward us. In some situations, the two possibilities may work together; in others we may have to choose between them.

We must be careful not to corner our opponent. "Confronted with the impossibility of remaining faithful to one's beliefs, and the equal impossibility of becoming free of them," writes Baldwin, "one can be driven to the most inhuman excesses." [8] Firmness should never become dogmatic rigidity. Although nonviolence places a premium upon the capacity of the nonviolent cadre to endure suffering, each team of cadres should have sufficient tactical flexibility to be able to choose whether to extricate the individual members from a catastrophic situation or, if this alternative is foreclosed, to endure martyrdom with a composure that may cause their attackers to repent afterward.

Charles Walker offers some specific suggestions for nonviolent conduct in direct encounter. First, in response to provocations, cadres should be careful to avoid clever remarks, intemperate statements, name-calling or other inflammatory behavior and should not break ranks or otherwise display disunity. In addition, when actually under attack, he suggests the following procedures:

1. Adhere to group discipline and do not intervene except to help an injured person. Each team member should be prepared to endure attack and not expect it to be warded off by his teammates.

2. Pray for the victim and the attacker. Walker does not state whether to pray aloud or silently, but if sincere prayer is voiced aloud it may communicate moral support to the victim and help to inhibit the attacker's aggressive impulses.

3. If the victim is able to do so, he may try to interrupt the attack by calmly saying to the attacker: "Sir, may I ask you a question?" and transferring the conflict to a verbal level.

4. The group leader gives all instructions and supervises removal of injured persons, assigns cadres to administer first aid or provides for medical attention.

5. Team members may express solidarity by spontaneously singing a hymn or reciting a prayer together. They should generally avoid loud talk, outcries, vigorous gestures or sudden movements. Unless agreed upon in tactical decisions made beforehand to meet the needs of the situation, they should not scatter when attacked but remain close together and maintain uniform bearing, e.g., all standing or all kneeling.

6. Do not appeal to police or bystanders for aid, but be prepared to accept any such aid or intervention with poise and equanimity.

7. Note carefully the attitudes of onlookers, with a view to follow-up as well as to the possibility of their immediate effect on the struggle. Depending on the issue that is involved, they may comprise a source of support for either resisters or attackers, and any shift in their attitudes may be crucial.[9]

If arrested, cadres should comply courteously and promptly with the legitimate orders of police and jailers. There is a school of thought which advises personal noncooperation by "going limp" and compelling the arresting officers to carry the resister, but careful thought should be given to this tactic before using it, since it is likely to exacerbate hostility and may provoke brutality by the police and weaken rapport with neutral onlookers.

If a nonviolent strategy terminates with arrest and a new line of strategy of legal action is begun, cadres may be content to accept bail; but if nonviolent strategy is to be carried into this area the most effective course will be for cadres to refuse bail, to insist on individual trials and thus to fill the jails and glut the court calendar. In jail and in the courtroom, of course, cadres should maintain nonviolent conduct at all times. They may keep up their morale and enhance their image in relations with the authorities by developing some kind of constructive program inside the jail, rendering service to other prisoners. Those who remain outside should take responsibility for the families and dependents of the imprisoned cadres, as well as for the welfare of the prisoners, in case the latter are subjected to mistreatment of any kind.

Finally, perhaps the severest test of nonviolent conduct occurs outside the situation of direct encounter in team actions. The worst elements among the opponent's masses may inflict brutal reprisals. Homes, churches and other buildings may be bombed or fired upon by anonymous night-riders. Leaders and cadres may receive written or telephoned threats and their children or relatives and friends may be harassed. Individual leaders or cadres may be ambushed or abducted and beaten, tortured, mutilated or killed. They may be fired from their jobs or refused service by merchants. All of these and other reprisals may be taken to break resistance or to provoke retaliatory violence.

There is no panacea for such reprisals. If the situation or the issue is highly charged, some types of vicious action are to be expected, often as a spontaneous response to the conflict. We must entertain no illusions about the depths of human depravity. But by the same token we must look to the creative resources of nonviolent conduct for solution. If individually attacked we must attempt to remain steadfast in our composure and in our manifestation of courageous good will toward the attackers, even if it seems hopeless that we can thereby avert harm to ourselves. Martyrdom is not to be courted, but it may have an indirectly redemptive effect even when it is not directly effective. Scornful defiance or appeals for mercy are likely to destroy this possibility.

In any event it is seldom possible to work through to a conversion of the immediate assailants without appealing to the more responsible elements in their community to quarantine them. Another alternative is to make use of the moral leverage arising from unretaliated persecution to invoke public censure, pressuring the authorities to act against violence and lawlessness. This of course means mobilizing lawful force against the perpetrators of violence. Any nonviolent movement which on principle rules out this step may find itself confronted at this point with the dilemma of capitulation or extermination.

The Socio-Drama

In order to learn a discipline for nonviolent conduct, it is not enough to memorize a set of rules, even if the theoretical implications of these rules are thoroughly understood. Not only study and discussion but actual training is required. Part of this training will consist of learning teamwork through experience in constructive work and by sharing in spiritual fellowship, meditating together and developing a vocabulary of songs, hymns, slogans and other symbolic devices for building solidarity. But of crucial importance is the socio-drama, in which we actually rehearse nonviolent conduct, putting theory into simulated practice. This is the basic combat training of the nonviolent cadre. It is as vital to him as bayonet drill or target practice is to the recruit in infantry training.

Socio-drama begins with role-playing, in which each cadre becomes a character in an improvised drama without a script. Taking more or less commonplace situations that do not involve conflict, the first sessions aim at articulating empathy by literally trying to understand and act out a given situation from a standpoint not one's own. By doing so in a group setting it is possible afterward to discuss and evaluate one another's performance, not from the standpoint of external details or mannerisms that might be important in the theatrical world, but from the standpoint of inner motivations and impulses. The process may be helpful to many cadres also in understanding themselves, and indeed some of the early role-playing should involve cadres in playing themselves as they would react to given circumstances. It may be as simple as asking a group of cadres to imagine that they have just been caught in the rain while on their way to a meeting, and improvising conversation and gestures appropriate to such a situation. Later the same cadres may be asked to imagine that they are members of a different group—i.e. with different customs and habits—caught in the same downpour.

After a few such sessions, the cadres will move on into situations of verbal disagreement and eventually to those in which insult and abuse and actual violence are involved. Some of the cadres will assume the roles of antagonists and attackers, hurling abuse and grabbing or shoving other cadres, whose task it will be to respond creatively while adhering to nonviolent discipline. Partly, socio-drama is a psychological and spiritual exercise, but it also includes practice in a number of physical details. Cadres must learn the gymnastics of receiving blows—chewing gum in order to relax tensions and so ease the impact when struck, clasping hands behind the neck and shielding the face with one's arms, drawing the knees up to protect the abdomen when lying down and being kicked, learning how to fall down gracefully when it is impossible to remain sitting or standing. These and other techniques must be both memorized and practiced. Judo or karate training may be an asset in learning them, but in nonviolent conduct only self-protection is permissible. When pulled by an assailant, for example, the nonviolent cadre may attempt to slip his grasp but he must learn how *not* to wrestle, how *not* to cause the assailant to lose his balance, how to avoid any action that could be interpreted as retaliatory.

If the group is serious about its training, those cadres who take the role of the opponent will be sharply criticized if they fail to use the typical language of the actual opponent, obscenities and profanity included. It is not their task to create a mild caricature of the opponent, but to represent him as exactly and as authentically as possible. The purpose is twofold: to accustom the cadres to experiencing such situations with calm and without surprise, and to develop the ability to respond calmly when an untrained person might understandably panic. Also, of course, by rotating the responsibility for enacting the role of the opponent, each member of the group has a chance to acquire empathy for the latter, as well as to try a wide range of possible situations.

The value of such training can hardly be overstressed. Mere talk about "what you would do if—" is no substitute for the direct sensory experience of being confronted with someone who is shouting at you, calling you dirty names not with a snicker but with menacing conviction, trying to humiliate you, to provoke you to anger, to push you off balance physically or verbally. With prolonged training through socio-drama, non-violent conduct becomes an easy reflex that can place the cadre in command of a volatile situation. The Congress of Racial Equality has made considerable use of this type of training. Periodically it has held workshops of nonviolence in which, after a series of socio-drama sessions, a seasoned veteran of nonviolent campaigns supervises the trainees in an actual conflict situation of limited scope, in which they can test what they have learned. The presence of an experienced leader is an asset to such training, but his absence does not seriously handicap a group, since imagination and resourcefulness combined with serious study are the chief requirements. There is no elaborate technique to be mastered.

A final consideration in nonviolent conduct is the very ordinary matter of personal appearance and habits. As we have observed elsewhere (see page 146 above), the opponent will seize upon any shortcomings to stigmatize nonviolent cadres as slovenly, undependable, outlandish or crackpot. Cadres must therefore take special care to overcome habits of tardiness, slouching posture and the like, and make it a point to dress neatly, speak clearly, look the opponent directly in the face and in general create an image of self-respect without being overbearing. There is an unfortunate tendency among certain self-styled "radicals" to indulge their personal idiosyncracies under the cover of rationalizations which convince no one but themselves. As Herbert Read has observed:

To wear "rational" clothes, to eat "rational" foods, to establish "rational" schools—these well-meaning exemplary methods too often tend to create a barrier of suspicion and reserve which makes the communication of any truth impossible. There are, of course, degrees of compromise which are also impossible because they demand participation in evil actions. . . . But perfect love demands not only that we should sup with publicans and sinners, but also that we should not offend them on such occasions by our ineffable superiority.[10]

In a word, nonviolent conduct is designed not only to reduce disorder but also to keep the door open to reconciliation even during the conflict, and to keep the issues in focus. We need not force ourselves to conform to the opponent's whims, but if we want to communicate we owe it both to him and to ourselves not to indulge our own whims, which could become a distracting side issue.

There is a point at which all rules and prescriptions fail and success depends on common sense, timing, imagination, inspiration and the providence of a loving God. In addition, there are human and individual limits. Leaders and cadres should try to extend them but plan their tactics and strategy to allow for them, relieving and rotating frontline activists in alternation with the less strain-provoking tasks of the constructive program. Like any method, nonviolence has its characteristic weakness, which Clarence Marsh Case has called "its tendency to fail from apathy on the one hand or to be betrayed into the use of violence on the other." It demands, he adds, "a stronger self-control, a more enduring solidarity of purpose, a greater capacity for passive suffering, a higher ethical development, than most human beings have thus far attained." [11] Consequently, victory must come swiftly unless great stamina can be mustered to face prolonged adversity.

Partly this may require phasing strategy in such a way as to score a series of minor gains or to secure a single major victory in the most accessible sector, rather than trying for a cluster of major objectives at the same time. Partly it may mean augmenting nonviolence with other types of action. But in the realm of conduct itself, it also means a further dimension of training.

Gandhi recommended and rigorously practiced a number of bodily disciplines adapted from Hindu asceticism, among them strict vows of celibacy and restricting the diet to bland foods, counting these as prominent among his "experiments with truth" as an important source of power for social struggle. Others, such as Nehru and Subhas Chandra Bose, who diverged from Gandhi's commitment to *ahimsa* as a religious duty, bound themselves to similar vows in order to facilitate the struggle.

In the West, much less attention has been given to such practices except in monastic orders and among adherents of health cults, moralistic abstainers and the like. If we set aside Gandhi's own example and take that of the more pragmatic Nehru, it is still hard to say how much these practices were a feature of the distinctive Hindu background. The Hungarian passive resistance leader, Ferencz Deák, was an habitual cigar smoker. Meat, alcoholic beverages and sex have not proved to be stumbling blocks for other leaders or cadres of nonviolence.

For the Christian, self-denial has no intrinsic merits. It is not a way of salvation, and when it has historically been claimed as one its devotees have been regarded as heretical. Yet it does have a legitimate place in the Christian life. As Dietrich Bonhoeffer has stated the case:

The spirit assents when Jesus bids us to love our enemies, but flesh and blood are too strong and prevent our carrying it out. Therefore we have to practice strictest daily discipline; only so can the flesh learn the painful lesson that it has no rights of its own. Regular daily prayer is a great help here, and so is daily meditation on the Word of God, and every kind of bodily discipline and asceticism.[12]

Some advocates of holistic nonviolence have gone so far as to argue that cadres must rid their lives of music and art, and sacrifice even personal friendships for the sake of an abstract love of humanity. This chimerical notion has nothing to do with the real issues. Nonviolent conduct does not require the rejection of the normal pleasures of life. But it does mean, as Bonhoeffer suggests, freeing oneself from their domination, ceasing to be possessed by attachments to persons or things, getting rid of unnecessary clutter, disorder and excess.

To achieve this, part of a nonviolent cadre's personal training should involve periods of acute self-deprivation, not to destroy his enjoyments permanently but to purge them of their burdensomeness. A day of solitary contemplation can freshen one's outlook as well as preparing him for the eventuality of solitary confinement in jail. Those who have not tried it will be surprised to find how easily they can endure a three-day fast, and will find the experience of self-control of the will a useful asset in the struggle, in addition to the physiological benefits. To do these things it is not necessary to make vows. Unless a particular habit is decidedly harmful, it is sufficient to interrupt it; it need not be permanently broken. The aim is to develop sufficient inner strength that one can move comfortably from strict solitude to any sort of interpersonal encounter; to be self-contained or self-giving; to eat heartily or go hungry.

Voluntary Suffering

In Chapter 11 we shall return to a fuller discussion of spiritual resources. Now let us consider whether the capacity to withstand suffering has a part to play beyond its function as a necessary ingredient of nonviolent conduct. Does it have any positive tactical significance?

Gandhi set great store by voluntary suffering as a powerful and primary means by which he hoped to touch the hearts of the British rulers in India, and if he did not succeed in influencing their policies thereby he nevertheless demonstrated some such power to sway his own people and to draw sympathy from all parts of the world.

Not all suffering has such an effect. Much of it is in fact useless, though it may produce sympathy. If it is senselessly self-inflicted, it may even provoke scorn and contempt. To have redemptive possibilities, suffering must be meaningful. Where does such meaning come from and how can it have power to work changes either in the sufferer or in the world?

Simone Weil sees the acceptance of evil done to us as a remedy for evil that we have done. The resulting suffering must be unjust, not self-inflicted. The perfect example is the transmutation resulting from the crucifixion of Jesus, the "perfectly pure being," on behalf of a sinful world. "All the criminal violence of the Roman Empire ran up against Christ," she writes, "and in him it became pure suffering." She adds that "redemptive suffering has to have a social origin. It has to be injustice, violence on the part of human beings." [13]

Romano Guardini asserts that "inwardly accepted suffering transforms the sufferer" and "all existential growth depends not on effort alone, but also on freely offered sacrifice." [14] It is not the suffering but the sacrificial act of willing acceptance that makes it spiritually effective, and sacrifice is an act of agapaic love. As Berdyaev has observed, "Psychologically, fear is always the fear of suffering." [15] That is why voluntary suffering is redemptive—because divine love both wills the endurance of suffering and because in this way it casts out fear. As Simone Weil says, "The extreme greatness of Christianity lies in the fact that it does not seek a supernatural remedy for suffering, but a supernatural use for it." [16]

It is no accident that Gandhi considered "fearlessness" indispensable to true *satyagraha* and regarded the capacity to endure suffering as an index of nonviolent power. Commenting on this, however, Régamey reminds us: "The trouble is that the fear of specific danger is frequently contaminated by what Ribot has called 'a primitive, instinctive fear, anterior to all individual experience,' and which is *anxiety*." [17]

Brewster Kneen argues that voluntary suffering has a redemptive effect by terminating a process whereby violence and involuntary suffering have been passed from person to person. The redemptive sufferer thus "removes any threat to others of having the suffering inflicted upon them. The removal of this threat has the effect of increasing social solidarity . . ." [18]

This may well be true in situations that involve misunderstanding, alienation and tension, though even here the presence of diffuse anxieties may prove to be formidable obstacles, but the matter is greatly complicated if the situation is one of overt social conflict, with the would-be redemptive sufferer actively engaged in creating pressures to coerce the very same persons from whom he seeks to remove the threat of suffering.

In such a setting, says Galtung, much depends upon interpretation:

Even if it is intended to symbolize the willingness to suffer unto death rather than submission or [recourse] to violent means, the interpretation may be as a symbol of innate, cowardly masochism or even as lack of will to resist, since the usual symbols—weapons of violence—are absent. [19]

In a similar vein, Leo Kuper has observed that the active courting of suffering by the nonviolent resister is not effective "where the ruler is a collectivity and responds to the subordinate as a collectivity, and where the suffering is a challenge to the ruler's ideology of domination." [20] Thus what may work in simple interpersonal relations does not necessarily work in relations between two large and well-defined groups. At the same time, Kuper acknowledges that the acceptance of suffering has a liberating spiritual effect among the resisters, creating morale and solidarity within their ranks. Galtung describes this as the expressive rather than instrumental value of the act, and notes that

the gratification from an expressive act is immediate and certain, whereas instrumental acts must be brought from the personal system out into the social system, where the causal chains are uncertain and effects may be positive, but only in the long run. When the expressive need is present, therefore, the temptation will be high to resort to expressive acts even at considerable cost along the instrumental dimension.[21]

For suffering to be instrumental and lead to reconciliation, it must operate through a nexus of shared values which provide a basis for empathy. Given the opponent's distaste for avoidable pain, and given also an ideology (such as white supremacy or anti-Semitism) which effectively destroys that nexus, voluntary suffering can only tend to confirm the estrangement and justify the opponent in accommodating the resister's seeming appetite for pain. Hence the initial effect of voluntary suffering in such a context is not to bring reconciliation but to exacerbate conflict.

If sadistic tendencies are already present in the opponent, his confrontation with an apparently masochistic resister will be tantamount to an invitation to inflict pain. The use of redemptive suffering therefore demands a maximum effort to establish rapport and to present the opponent with an image that commands respect and can lay a basis for empathy. Kuper suggests, following Georg Simmel,[22] that the resister may appeal to a third party with whom there is an overlap of his own and the opponent's values, and thus set in motion such forces as moral suasion and secondary boycott. A case in point would be the appeal by black Africans to whites who share with them opposition to white supremacy and share with the white supremacists the fact that they are white.

In addition to its expressive value in building interior solidarity, successfully publicized voluntary suffering may focus public attention on the group and thus on its leadership. Even if the act of suffering and by implication the movement that engages in it appear to be despicable, perverse or incomprehensible, they have attained the status of public facts, and the leadership emerges from anonymity and assumes recognizable (even if distorted) personal identity in relation to the opponent. If repressive measures fail, the opponent now knows whom he must deal with.

Kierkegaard writes of the good to be derived by the incurable sufferer who not only accepts but embraces his suffering and invests it with meaning. There is a similar benefit to be derived by the involuntary sufferer of injustice who volunteers to bear a heavier but more meaningful burden of suffering with dignity and group support, perhaps adding to the burden but enduring it knowingly and purposefully with a moral resistance that was formerly lacking. Only the oppressed can fully appreciate Berdyaev's statement that the acceptance of suffering is "an experience of freedom" that can lead to "spiritual victory." [23] Thus by an act of will the sufferer ceases to be an inert object and becomes a freely acting subject. Instead of cringing under the blows and kowtowing to his persecutor, he now stands erect to take the same blows and exercises his power to forgive offenses that he dares to call offensive. In this lies its expressive value.

In addition to voluntarily accepted suffering, there is self-imposed suffering such as the hunger strike and the fast, which may serve to underline the seriousness of a given protest. Such suffering is often coercive rather than redemptive. The hunger strike or prolonged fast (Gandhi's repeated "fast unto death") is an implicit suicide threat which places responsibility for one's life gratuitously in the opponent's hands. Far from being convinced of Gandhi's good will when he undertook such fasts, the British regarded them as an acute form of blackmail. On more than one occasion they were spurred to action by such fasts, not because they were converted but because they feared the repercussions if they were blamed for Gandhi's death. I. N. Steinberg has called the hunger strike "the sharpest weapon in the arsenal of the disarmed" and tells how on several occasions it was used effectively to secure decent treatment for political prisoners under Bolshevik rule in 1919-1920 in Moscow's Butyrki prison.[24] Much depends, however, upon the character of the participants and their demands. If the former are obscure and the latter excessive, the authorities may feel justified in allowing hunger strikers to perish. It is not a weapon to be used recklessly.

Suffering that is voluntarily accepted rather than self-imposed surely plays an important part in nonviolent conduct, but it is doubtful whether its role is ever more than supportive or that the sufferer himself can derive any earthly benefit from his sacrifice unless it is augmented with tactical and strategic pressures. Although indispensable in maintaining spiritual integrity that has far-reaching implications in the larger context of the struggle, it is no substitute for strategy. Its redemptive value is indirect, through purifying one's own heart in relation to an eternal dimension and liberating oneself from fear and thereby offsetting the demonic element in protest action, but it is the latter that usually must carry the main thrust.

REFERENCES IN CHAPTER 9

1   See Charles C. Walker: *Organizing for Nonviolent Action* (New Delhi: Gandhi Smarak Nidhi, 1962), p. 22. A pamphlet.
2   See *CORE Rules for Action,* a leaflet (New York: Congress of Racial Equality, 1961).
3   Richard B. Gregg: *The Power of Nonviolence* (Nyack, N.Y.: Fellowship Publications, 1959; second revised edition), p. 44.
4   Maryse Choisy: *Yogas et Psychoanalyse* (Geneva: Éditions du Mont Blanc, 1949), p. 240.
5   Romano Guardini: *Power and Responsibility* (Chicago: Henry Regnery Co., 1961), p. 62.
6   Culbert G. Rutenber: *The Reconciling Gospel* (Philadelphia: Judson Press, 1961), p. 51f.
7   James Baldwin: *Notes of a Native Son* (Boston: Beacon Press, Inc., 1955), p. 101.
8   *Ibid.,* p. 171.
9   Compare with Walker, *op. cit.,* p. 31f. The outline given here slightly modifies Walker's presentation, but is the same in its essentials.
10 Herbert Read: *Anarchy and Order* (London: Faber, 1954), p. 31.
11 C. M. Case: *Non-Violent Coercion* (New York: Century Co., 1923), p. 407.
12 Dietrich Bonhoeffer: *The Cost of Discipleship* (New York: The Macmillan Co., 1959), p. 132.
13 Simone Weil: *Gravity and Grace* (New York: G. P. Putnam's Sons, 1952), p. 122.
14 Romano Guardini, *op. cit.,* p. 87f.

15 Nikolai Berdyaev: *The Divine and the Human* (London: Bles, 1949), p. 61.
16 Weil, *op. cit.*, p. 132.
17 Pie Régamey: *Non-Violence et Conscience Chrétienne* (Paris: Cerf, 1958), p. 213.
18 Brewster Kneen: *Voluntary Suffering and Social Change* (New York: Union Theological Seminary, unpublished B.D. thesis, 1961), p. 59.
19 Johan Galtung: "Pacifism from a Sociological Point of View" in *Conflict Resolution*, March 1959, p. 81.
20 Leo Kuper: *Passive Resistance in South Africa* (New Haven: Yale University Press, 1957), p. 91.
21 Galtung, *op. cit.*, p. 70.
22 See Kurt H. Wolff: *The Sociology of Georg Simmel* (Glencoe, Ill.: The Free Press, 1950), pp. 195-197.
23 Nikolai Berdyaev: *Spirit and Reality* (London: Bles, 1939), p. 198.
24 I. N. Steinberg: *In the Workshop of the Revolution* (New York: Rinehart & Co., Inc., 1953), p. 167. See also pages 167-172.

10

Active Love and Reconciliation

Nonviolence, we have said, is not love; nor is it a method for resolving conflict. It is a way of waging social conflict that is compatible with love. It does a minimum of damage and holds the door open to creative, constructive possibilities. But it has no intrinsic power to heal and to build anew. For this we must look beyond nonviolence to active, agapaic love and reconciliation.

This is true in two senses. In the dimension of depth underlying nonviolent conduct it is ultimately love that counts, both as the source of resilient inner strength and as that which authenticates empathy and rapport. Courage based on sheer willpower becomes brittle and will splinter under stress. Likewise, feigned empathy cannot provide true guidance, and ersatz rapport will easily break down. In the dimension of history, of the ongoing interactions of social groups and masses, it is ultimately love that counts in the termination of conflict and the restoration of community between one's own and the opponent's group.

It should not be supposed that nonviolence automatically springs from love or that love automatically follows in the wake of nonviolence. Nor, it is important to note, does the success of a nonviolent campaign necessarily depend upon love. Often in history extraneous events have proved to be decisive. The balance of objective forces such as population and social structures, the presence or absence of the kairotic moment or the charismatic leader—all these and other factors may determine the outcome and compensate for what might otherwise be disastrous defects in conduct, tactics and strategy. There would be no progress if victories in social struggle depended entirely on perfect love. On the other hand, many such victories prove to be hollow, and those purchased cheaply may later reveal a hidden cost.

The kind of love that we are talking about here, obviously, is something more than a natural disposition to treat others fairly or to respond amicably to those we find amiable. It goes beyond the simple moral equation of "live and let live." Nor is it merely an exalted ideal or cosmic absolute. It is not a latent power of human nature, to be activated by discipline and training, nor an overarching principle of human conduct which projects a pattern onto our lives. There is no such thing as love in the abstract—impersonal love, love for humanity. Love is the content of a relationship between persons—between human persons and between the human and the divine. Agapaic love is that kind of love which possesses the power to penetrate barriers. It is love for the stranger, the enemy, the outcast, the ugly, the evildoer. It is love in a different dimension, not only overcoming alienation between oneself and the stranger or enemy, but also deepening and purifying one's natural loves, overcoming residual tensions between friends and resolving inner conflicts within individual persons. It is holy—that is, it contains within itself no mixed motives, no admixture of egotism or pride. Because it is holy, one may agapaically love oneself and one's most dangerous enemy in the same way. But for the same reason, its source and its ultimate focus can only be found in a transcendent God who is a perfect and holy living person.

Romano Guardini has aptly described this love as a "live current" like electricity:

The love Christ means is a live current that comes from God, is transmitted from person to person, and returns to God. It runs a sacred cycle reaching from God to an individual, from the individual to his neighbor, and back through faith to God. He who breaks the circuit at any point breaks the flow of love. He who transmits purely, however small a part of that love, helps establish the circuit for the whole.[1]

Guardini leaves no room for doubt that this applies to the enemy as well. He quotes in full Luke 6:28-36, which begins: "Love your enemies; do good to those who hate you . . ." (New English Bible).

This is no longer mere justice or even goodness. It is no longer the voice of earthly reason that speaks. Something entirely different is demanded—the positive, heroic act of a bounty that can be acquired only from above, a divine generosity that is its own measure.[2]

Referring specifically to the passage which bids us to turn the other cheek, Guardini observes:

This most certainly does not mean that one must behave like a weakling or surrender oneself to force. Rather, that man should extricate himself from the whole earthly business of defense and aggression, of blow and counterblow, of right and usurpation. . . .

Now we begin to see what Jesus is driving at: a bearing in our relationship to others that is no less than divinely free—not what law and order demand, but what true liberty gives. The measure of that liberty is love, the love of God.[3]

The Role of Faith

It is not possible to achieve this liberty by our own will, nor can we simply decide to appropriate it for our use. We know beforehand that we shall fall short, because we are not holy. At our best we are poor transmitters of divine love. Yet the power is given to us to have faith, to stand with openness toward God and toward the enemy, to allow the redemptive current of divine love to flow through us. "It is God who works in you," wrote Paul, "inspiring both the will and the deed, for his own chosen purpose" (Philippians 2:13, New English Bible). This is the work of no mere principle, but of the living God.

Régamey recognizes this fact as he attempts to come to terms with Gandhi's conception of nonviolence as "truth force" (*satyagraha*). The Sanskrit word *sat,* which here stands for "truth," also means "reality" and connotes "righteousness," all of which are attributes of God as revealed in the Bible. But the biblical understanding of God includes also the facts of "work" and "purpose" which are revealed in God's action in history, definitively and consummatorily in the incarnation of holy love in the man Jesus. The actual existence of Jesus as a man among men provides a humanly authentic anchorage for the revelation of God's love, and points tellingly to the real personhood of holy God in a way that would not be possible if Jesus had been a mythical being or a demigod. To be sure, God is truth, and Jesus incarnated truth in human form: he was "the Word made flesh." But it is the dynamic of action which manifests truth as love. The power of truth is no power at all unless it is manifested as active love. As Régamey says,

. . . this power is nothing but a dream, a wish, finally a trap, if Truth is not all-powerful active Love, bestower of grace and strength. Of course certain unbelievers may have enough confidence in the fundamental goodness of men to hope that it can overcome by itself egotistical interests, wickedness, hatred, violence. And so certain "unbelievers" of good will who believe in man can enlist in the ways of nonviolence themselves. But without being aware of it, their optimism implies a belief in God which alone can justify it, since God is the only one to give it its value and to permit its eventual success.[4]

His latter point is consistent with Paul's statement above, for God is no respecter of ecclesiastical credentials, and the forms of faith are not what makes agapaic love accessible to us. The value of Christianity is not that it provides a direct liturgical pipeline to God, but simply that it offers a correct and articulate understanding of the way God works. It would be naïve to suppose that God does not know those who do not know him. To be truly God his reality must be universally true, whether universally acknowledged or not. God's love is not only for

Christians but for all men who open themselves to receive and transmit it. Indeed, the merely nominal Christian who has no real faith is worse off than the non-Christian whose faith is real but inarticulate.

There is a sense in which love is a natural law. Reinhold Niebuhr explains it in terms that are close to our theme:

Man knows, both by experience and by the demand for coherence in his rational nature, that life ought not to be lived at cross purposes, that conflict within the self, and between the self and others, is an evil. In that sense love is the law of life according to the insights of natural religion and morality.[5]

What biblical revelation does is to show us the source of this love which governs life, and to call us to participate in the relationship which it sets in motion. Niebuhr goes on to affirm that there is no limit to the possibility of agapaic love as an admixture in historical processes. "Even the purest form of *agapē,* the love of the enemy and forgiveness toward the evildoer, do not stand in contradiction to historical possibilities." [6] He goes on, however, to qualify this statement by pointing out (as we have already observed) that it is impossible in social action for this holy love to be completely unadulterated. Agapaic love is not irrelevant but its relevance is conditioned by the sinful and demonic elements that are present in history. Though bidden by divine invitation to open ourselves to the live current of holy love, which is the only kind of love that transcends all contradictions, we must also and beforehand establish the very norms of mutuality and civil order that are thereby transcended. Niebuhr's point, which has often been misinterpreted, is simply that the "leap of faith" implied in our opening ourselves to agapaic possibilities must be predicated on a firm footing of established, operative values which may not be recklessly sacrificed in the act of going beyond them. Each of us as an individual or as members of a community who have expressly agreed on such a course of action may indeed throw caution to the winds and abandon all the safeguards of normative justice, knowing what it is that we are risking, but we may not legitimately involve others in our risk. That is, we do not have the right to go beyond self-sacrifice; we do not have the right to require that those with whom we ally ourselves in social conflict should engage in self-sacrifice against their will. For this reason we need always to maintain institutional structures that are not dependent for their success upon a higher level of conduct than may safely be foreseen, yet which do not force that level down but are adaptable upward toward the light of the higher level. With reference to criminal law, for example, there is vast opportunity for enlarging the rehabilitative and reducing the punitive elements of this type of justice, and this cannot be done without recourse to holy love; but the prior consideration is the protection of society. We cannot responsibly let every criminal loose unless every member of society voluntarily assents to take the consequences.

In short, and with specific reference to nonviolence in social conflict, we are not entitled wantonly to abandon existing social conventions or laws simply because we think we are prepared to act in accordance with a higher law of love. The approach of Jesus is instructive here, in his statement: "Do you suppose that I have come to abolish the Law and the prophets; I did not come to abolish, but to complete." (Matt. 5:17, New English Bible.) The gospel penetrates to the very heart of the Mosaic Law and renders its meticulous observance unnecessary by going beyond it and doing more than the Law requires. We need not reiterate our earlier discussion of the basis on which we may defy unjust laws. The point is that in social conflict we have no responsible recourse against justice in the name of love. Our concern must be to establish normative, operable justice rooted in actuality and relevant to historical conditions. It cannot be based on purely hypothetical possibilities or absolute demands.

Nonviolence does not require perfect holy love for its success. For nonviolent conduct a strong admixture of it is ultimately needed as a source of enduring strength, but the fact should not be overlooked that considerations of prudence, of reciprocation and of normative justice are also part of the picture. In all but the rare case of holistic nonviolence, the nonviolent cadre hopes by his exposure to self-sacrifice to gain a realizable historical objective from which he may benefit individually and from which at all events the group he represents will benefit collectively. His prudence consists in a willingness to forego the immediate gratification of violent revenge against injustice for the sake of the higher satisfaction of later enjoying a situation in which injustice has been removed. Further, it is his aim to elicit a reciprocal response from the opponent, leading finally to the establishment of new or altered conventions and laws that are mutually acceptable to both the opponent and himself, terminating the condition of crisis and conflict and allowing him to relax. Indeed, these considerations exert a strong temptation merely to "use" agapaic love as a means to selfish ends.

This, by definition, is impossible. A humanly sinful counterfeit of agapaic love may serve selfish ends, but only authentic love of divine origin can serve God's purposes. Are the aims of our particular social conflict identical with the latter?

Surely it would erroneous to suppose that the alternatives are so starkly opposed—our sinful selfishness versus a perfectionistic conception of discipleship. What introduces relativity and latitude into the picture is the very ambiguity of love. To be sure, we can readily define distinct categories of holy and profane love, and it is true that these operate at different levels of reality. Sometimes, perhaps, they may collide and force us to choose. But they also blend and interact. The mutual love that binds together a man and a woman may be very superficial, undermined by deeper currents of egotism, or it may be undergirded by agapaic depths in which the separate egos are all but lost. In either case, each person at the surface level of mutuality exerts a reciprocal claim against the other. The difference is that in a crisis the latter couple will not be driven apart if the reciprocal relationship is somehow upset or damaged. A marriage may be based solely upon mutual sexual attraction, mutual vocational interests or other forms of reciprocal compatibility, but it will be very precarious unless the couple somehow learn to value one another at a deeper, finally agapaic level.

The function of love in social relationships is naturally more complex and diffuse, and not everything that is said about love between two persons can be true between two groups of many persons on each side. As Howard Thurman has said, "to love means to have an intrinsic interest in another person." [7] When directly confronting an individual opponent, the nonviolent cadre's first task is, through nonviolent conduct, to leave this possibility open by showing a certain minimum of friendliness in response to hostility. This means, in addition to the "moral image" we have mentioned elsewhere, presenting to the opponent what Kenneth Boulding calls a "value image" that is large enough to be accessible to both partisans in a conflict. Martin Luther King has done this by repeatedly stressing the objective of inclusive justice rather than a one-sided aim of securing civil rights for Negroes.

The nonviolent cadre's second task is to communicate the live current of agapaic love, to show authentic concern for the hostile person. This is hard to do, and without faith it is impossible. This is the "leap of faith" in interpersonal encounter. Let us suppose that after several such encounters the opponent's hostility gives way to a friendly response. It is true that this was made possible by *agapē,* but the new relationship now established may well be fairly tenuous. Unless the response is exceptionally strong it is likely to be on a much more mundane, sub-agapaic level on which the opponent is not ready to engage in self-sacrifice for the sake of the nonviolent cadre but is simply willing to refrain from violence and otherwise to accord the cadre elementary respect.

Bridging the Chasm of Estrangement

In the context of the conflict, *agapē* has thus served its purpose and is no longer required in that relationship, which can now stand on its own equilibrium of give-and-take. At this point perhaps we can afford the oversimplification of saying that this process is just a matter of adding up all the encounters between nonviolent cadres and opponents until a certain minimum of community is established between them as sets of persons. But we shall have to bear in mind always the complexities of social structure and the fact that the opponent's leadership group may succeed for a long time in insulating itself against interpersonal contact of this kind. Also the leadership group may exert pressure to induce or force those of its followers who are in interpersonal encounter with the nonviolent cadres to do violence to them against their will. This may severely tax the capacity of the cadres to remain open to *agapē*. Hence the need for a strategy to exert social pressure beyond the possibilities of love.

"The opposite of love is not hate," writes the psychologist Rollo May, "but indifference." [8] Although in many cases overt conflict may bring with it manifestations of hatred, and the precipitating issue may have arisen out of a hostile act, the underlying cause is invariably estrangement between the conflicting groups. The dominant group, often reciprocated negatively by the aggrieved group, has turned its back on the personhood of the latter, imposing restrictions without the latter's consent. It may or may not be doing so with conscious hostility or desire to harm, but what is basic is the withdrawal of human concern, the exclusion of the other, the denial of his real existence as a person—in short, not caring instead of caring. In essence, this is the same as sin, for sin is estrangement from God. The latter may take the form of active rebellion or waywardness, but in any event it implies the statement: "You are unimportant" or "You don't exist." Inasmuch as love of God and of neighbor and enemy are inextricably interrelated, the indifference that causes conflict is a form of sin, for it implies the same type of statement.

Sin has its consequences, and one of them is that indifference and estrangement provide fertile soil for irrational hostility. Unrepented sin breeds guilt, which in turn creates fear. The next step after denying that God exists is to accuse him of being evil, and the next step after turning one's back on one's neighbor is to fear that the latter will plant a knife in it. In the absence of love the other becomes a blank screen onto which we project our anxieties: the stranger is always potentially a scapegoat for our own unconfessed sins. C. G. Jung confirms this fact:

Anything which disappears from your psychological inventory is apt to turn up in the disguise of a hostile neighbor, where it will inevitably arouse your anger and make you aggressive. It is certainly better to know that your worst adversary is right in your own heart.[9]

The natural human response to indifference is counter-indifference, and to projected hostility, hostility. Man's natural egotism, which is at the root of sin and is, as we have already seen, the antipode of agapaic love, makes him susceptible of rationalizations which place the burden of blame outside himself, whether on a scapegoat or on circumstances or elsewhere. We tend to reason directly from unevaluated experience to what we construe as objective fact: "It is true because I saw it." We do not make allowance for the subjective factor in experience, or if we do we evaluate it invidiously, assigning temperate and benign motives to ourselves and rash, malicious motives to those from whom we are estranged. In the end, a situation develops in which we and our opponent face each other not as we are but as ugly stereotypes which, ironically, tend to confirm each other in fact as well as in fantasy.

Bruno Bettelheim, in his highly perceptive study of the alienated relations between Nazi concentration camp guards and their Jewish prisoners, says that members of both groups "behaved as if psychological mechanisms comparable to paranoid delusions were at work in them." [10] Each thought of the other as representatives of a type rather than as individual personalities, and this had the effect of creating in each group an illusion of desperately needed emotional security based on uniform conduct in relation to a uniform, hence predictable, image of the other. By investing the SS guards with uniformly bestial, inhuman traits which were often enough actually present, the prisoners were able to retain some measure of self-respect in submitting to the guards' degrading commands.

In order to understand SS behavior the prisoners had to fall back on their own experiences. The only way they could explain and understand the actions of the SS was by imputing to them motives they were familiar with. Thus they projected into the stereotype of *the* SS most, if not all, of those undesirable motives and characteristics they knew best, namely, their own.[11]

The real problem, it is easy to see, is not hatred as such but depersonalization. So long as each party to the conflict stands behind the defensive armor of stereotype there is an unbridgable chasm between them. Somehow the nonviolent cadre must dispense with this type of armor, bridge the gap and penetrate the opponent's armor. Only agapaic love can do this, and here it will be wise to remember that we are speaking of relation, not emotions. Here, particularly, this calls for more insight than feeling. Partly this means restructuring one's understanding of the situation and of the opponent, but this involves more than an exercise of rational intelligence. It involves an act of faith. Often, by the time conflict has been precipitated, estrangement has reached such a point that the only convincing clues to the opponent's motives would readily persuade us that the stereotype is very nearly true. Our task, then, is to take upon ourselves the risk of attributing to him a basic, underlying good will for which we cannot expect at first to find much evidence.

In order to do this, we have to set aside our own defensive

stereotyped behavior, trusting primarily in God's grace and also provisionally in the putative good will of the opponent until the agapaic love that we are thus enabled to transmit establishes elementary respect. The specific nature of a given conflict will of course dictate much of what is required, but the central focus, initially, should be on the common humanity of oneself and the opponent—that is, those features of personality and experience which do not presuppose specific knowledge of the individuals or their groups.

Any exhibition of defiant bravado or undue deference may be misunderstood as a threat or a weakness. We must begin with the fact that, rightly or not, our opponent is suspicious of our motives. The only way we can make clear both our good will and the issue of conflict is by simplicity which avoids extraneous matters—and by God-given courage and love.

The Place of Reconciliation

The whole process of overcoming estrangement is reconciliation, which is the biblical term that stands for the circuit of love as a live current to which Guardini refers. Reconciliation signifies not the bringing together of entities that are intrinsically estranged but the healing of broken communion between persons. It is based on the primal created unity of mankind, which has been disrupted, fractured by sin. Reconciliation is the paramount expression of love as the "law of life" which proclaims that the only ultimate justification of conflict is the achievement of a higher integration of harmony. Reconciliation between God and man occurs when man turns from sin and, with repentant faith, opens himself to receive God's holy and redeeming love. Reconciliation between man and man is part of the same process, in which man turns to his fellow man with trusting openness to transmit this same love and thereby to complete the circuit. The actual process is not instantaneous like plugging in a lamp. It takes time to be consummated, and to the extent that our human wiring is defective it is never perfectly consummated in history.

Within the relativities of history, however, we may still speak meaningfully of reconciliation as we speak of agapaic love, in admixture with stable norms of mutuality. Just as we may overlook the manifold fissures within each of two communities that are sundered from each other by a deep cleft of estrangement, so we may consider reconciliation as practically complete when conflict between those communities has ended on a basis of operative harmony. Ultimately the process is endless within historical time: there is always residual estrangement, and when healing has taken place between ourselves and our opponent we may find ourselves allies in facing some new conflict with a third party; or our own internal dissensions, held together by the unity demanded for the conflict that is now resolved, may surprise us from within. In this sense, conflict is never-ending and the need for reconciliation is ever-present.

But within these relativities, each discernible conflict ends sooner or later, whether by reconciliation or in some other way. It may be strategically concluded by conquest or disengagement without being resolved. It may be resolved by compromise, through the adjusting of claims and counter-claims, without reaching any deeper accord, or through arbitration in which a neutral party makes the decision. Only in reconciliation, however, is there a settlement which results in what Kenneth Boulding calls "convergent modifications of the images of the two parties." [12] It is a rapprochement in depth, based not only on a formal adjustment but also affecting attitude and outlook. Boulding sees this as the result of "conversation, argument, discussion or debate," but he makes it clear that something more than talk is involved—something akin to Martin Buber's concept of "meeting" or "dialog." He introduces the useful idea of the "value image" consisting of a vital, irreducible core and a variable outer shell. Representing the constellation of values which a given group lives by, the value image bears a resemblance to the moral image of the person. Boulding continues:

The success of the reconcilation process, then, clearly depends on how far the value structures of the parties in the field of conflict occupy the core or the shell of the value image. . . . The problem is complicated by the fact that the boundary between the core and the shell is not fixed but is itself a result of the general value system and of the process of communication and argument to which the party has been subject in the past. Unskilled argumentation that seems to threaten the person of the other party may only serve to harden and widen his core of values and so make agreement all the more difficult. On the other hand, a dramatic act of renunciation symbolizing concern for the person of the rival may produce a drastic reorganization of his value structure with a shrinkage of the inflexible core and an extension of the malleable shell.[13]

In our present context we may well question the value of a dramatic act of renunciation as such, since the whole tenor of a nonviolent campaign would presumably serve the same purpose even more convincingly. Otherwise, what Boulding is saying accords perfectly with the theological conception of reconciliation if we take the core of the value image to mean that which corresponds to the inner integrity of the person and of a community of persons. In these terms, then, reconciliation is consummated when we and our opponent establish a common shell within which the two separate cores can exist side by side. In a formal sense this would mean, for example, agreeing to share equitably in a public facility that our opponent has denied us the use of. With the support of a certain minimum of mutual respect established in the course of the campaign by the initiative of active, agapaic love, this formal agreement would eventually blend into the larger picture of habit and convention in which we and our opponents virtually obliterate the memory of the situation that created the conflict.

The process can be exemplified from the experiences of Irish immigrants and their descendants: 1) mutual hostility and distrust between Irishmen and non-Irishmen; 2) action to achieve justice; 3) termination of conflict; 4) crumbling of barriers accompanied by discovery of common bonds; 5) celebration of distinctive Irish traits by the non-Irish; 6) lessening of distinctiveness in the awareness of both parties; 7) actual lessening of distinctiveness. In the earlier stages, whether positively or negatively, there is something "special" about being Irish; when Americanization is completed, Irishness is simply part of one's ancestry. Allowing for the factor of color, a somewhat similar pattern may be seen in the history of the Negro, including the occasional exaggerated celebration of acceptance that springs from the effort to assuage guilt.

What we are left with finally is not a stabilization of agapaic love nor even an appreciably heightened articulation of mutual concern, but simply a normalization of relationships with the lines of group conflict removed. Again, this is a temporal process and it may pass through a period of heightened concern, but the end result is nothing more than mutual acceptance, leaving scope for new invitations to transmit God's holy love in completely different patterns of conflict.

There is, to be sure, a certain exuberant type of perfectionist who envisions the coming of the kingdom of God as the result of the infusion of *agapē* and reconciliation into situations of social conflict. Perhaps indeed, amid advances and reverses, this is how the kingdom will eventually bring history to its consummation and conclusion at the end of time, but in the interim we should not scant the very appreciable immediate fact that when reconciliation has run its course at the end of conflict, both we and our opponent unite in a common victory of mutual integrity. Could we ask for any better culmination after that than to return the glory of it to God and go our way together as ordinary men?

REFERENCES IN CHAPTER 10

1 Romano Guardini: *The Lord* (Chicago: Henry Regnery Co., 1954), p. 70.
2 *Ibid.*, p. 74.
3 *Ibid.*
4 Pie Régamey: *Non-Violence et Conscience Chrétienne* (Paris: Cerf, 1958), p. 256.
5 Reinhold Niebuhr: *The Nature and Destiny of Man* (New York: Charles Scribner's Sons, 1953), Vol. 2, p. 82.
6 *Ibid.*, p. 85.
7 Howard Thurman: *Mysticism and the Experience of Love* (Wallingford, Pa.: Pendle Hill Pamphlets, 1961), p. 13.
8 Rollo May: "The Art of True Love" in *United Church Herald* (New York), October 6, 1960, p. 4.
9 C. G. Jung, quoted by Rajendra Prasad in his introduction to Pyarelal: *Mahatma Gandhi: The Last Phase* (Ahmedabad: Navajivan, 1956), Vol. 1, p. ix.
10 Bruno Bettelheim: *The Informed Heart* (Glencoe, Ill.: The Free Press, 1960), p. 221.
11 *Ibid.*, p. 223f. Careful study of pages 218-231 can provide a firm foundation for interpreting many situations involving estranged groups.
12 Kenneth E. Boulding: *Conflict and Defense* (New York: Harper & Brothers, 1962), p. 310.
13 *Ibid.*, p. 312.

11

Sources of Strength

"All nonviolent action that is to any degree broad, vigorous and sustained," writes Régamey, "presupposes the attainment of a fairly high spiritual level." [1] Beyond such techniques and methods as socio-drama, how do we develop the capacity both to withstand violence without retaliating and to maintain openness and rapport to communicate active love under conditions of prolonged or acute stress? Training in technique is invaluable for eliminating the anxiety of uncertainty and surprise, but it cannot produce courage. Likewise, rational understanding of both the situation and the opponent is vital to the initiative of love, but if love itself is lacking in us, if we do not feel the live current passing through us, what are we to do?

In many cases, strategic advantages can go far to make up for serious shortcomings in both personal conduct and teamwork, and of course no level of a nonviolent campaign should be neglected or left to chance. But often the pivotal factor may be precisely the will to sustain nonviolent conduct or to show concern for the immediate opponent as a person, and an otherwise well-prepared campaign may founder on just this point where personal courage and love are demanded. It is at such a moment that we appreciate the truth of Gandhi's statement: "A nonviolent man can do nothing save by the power and grace of God." [2]

Gandhi recognized the importance of prayer as a means of receiving this power: "Prayer is not an old woman's idle amusement. Properly understood and applied, it is the most potent instrument of action." [3] We are referring here, of course, not merely to the recitation of some fixed form of words in a casual or perfunctory manner. This vitiates the very meaning of prayer, which is ultimately a dialog between man and God or, in Martin Buber's phrase, "the speech of God to man." That is to say, in its depth and fullness, prayer is not only man's quest for God but it is also and paramountly God's response. The highest form of spiritual prayer is a form of acute listening and receptiveness to the Divine Presence. But preceding this stage are a number of preparatory steps.[4]

Prayer is first of all a discipline of mental hygiene, of freeing one's consciousness from distractions and readying one's whole being to respond with "unreserved spontaneity" to this Presence. Jung, in his "Answer to Job," testifies that prayer "reinforces the potential of the unconscious."[5] However stated, the effects are real. Paul E. Johnson refers to the achievement of an awareness of needs and realities, a sharpened perspective, renewal of emotional energy and integration of personality as being among ten discernible psychological effects of prayer,[6] and Walter G. Muelder attributes these benefits to a well-developed life of prayer:

There is a growth in faith and the capacity for faith . . . there is a release of new energies, a purgation of incentives, an overcoming of guilt feelings, and a release of compassion.[7]

Empirically, the externals of a prayer discipline may be nothing more than psychological conditioning, the ordering of consciousness by acts of the will. We begin by making ourselves relax and proceed to focus our thoughts.

Some devout persons find the presence of a cross or crucifix or ikon extremely helpful in focusing their thoughts, while others regard any such object as a distraction. Psychologically, the decisive question must always be which usage is most effective for the individual who is trying to pray. Different temperaments may lean toward different conditions.

Given these conditions to produce a relaxed state of mind, the next step is to concentrate our thoughts. Repetition of a simple formal prayer such as the Lord's Prayer, the Jesus Prayer or some such form of words can be very helpful in doing this, provided the words are not merely mouthed but are dwelt upon by the mind so that the meaning they embody sinks in.

The essence of this stage of prayer is to organize our thoughts around God—as Nels Ferré says, to recall "who God is. God is sovereign love. He is both ultimate reality and our most intimate friend." [8] Second to this, we should recall that "God loves everyone completely." [9] In prayer we do not simply note these facts and set them aside, nor do we reason about them, but we hold them exclusively in our consciousness and allow them to suffuse our whole being. This is a habit that has particular value in the immediate context of the conflict situation. The further stages of prayer, which Ferré designates as adoration, gratitude and thanksgiving, and finally intercession, should flow easily from this state of recollectedness. Adoration is not a matter of debasing oneself, of bowing and scraping, but of awe, reverence and wonder—not of "praising" God in the human sense of bolstering his ego, but of sensing how one's own inadequacies and weaknesses are overcome by the fullness and grandeur of God's love. Gratitude and thanksgiving might well be called rejoicing in this love, knowing and feeling that it is for us, that every moment of true joy and hope springs from it. Intercession, finally, is our asking God that his love be given, his will be done for persons we think of—for our friends and comrades, for our enemies. In conclusion, we plead for strength and courage, for power and love and faith that we may do God's will ourselves.

Resources for the Mind and Spirit

The whole process can be understood and justified as a form of psychotherapy to purge the mind of rancor and confusion, to restore balance and perspective, and to instill wholesome thoughts and motivations—and indeed that is what it is. The capacity for nonviolent action has been explained by the French Catholic writer, Hervé Chaigne, as

primarily the result of a whole cluster of psychological and moral forces, the highest state of equilibrium attained by the man who is master of himself and humble before the truth that surpasses him . . .[10]

Many people may be capable of experiencing the therapeutic effects of prayer without conscious reference to God and, indeed, without calling it prayer at all. This may itself be an indication of humility and of candor if they are unable to name the power and presence of divine love as God, if their faith is real but unformed. But for many the absence of an articulated religious sense is a serious handicap. We can better understand the full implications of prayer if we recognize God's part in it.

Nels Ferré takes us a long way toward this kind of understanding in this theological explanation:

Prayer is living with God through the universal love of Christ and in the Spirit. Prayer is talking with God as our Father. Prayer is identifying our lives with the will of God, first for himself and then for all people. Prayer is finding the strength to overcome self, to transcend the battle of the ego and to loose the tensions which hinder seeing, by the power of the Spirit within the reality of our new creaturehood in Christ.

Thus the Holy Spirit, through prayer, gives us the fruit of the Spirit. The world is looking for genuine love and true community. Only as we *are* the truth more than merely speaking it can God utter his truth effectively to us and through us.[11]

Faith, it has been said, can move mountains. The New Testament records an episode in which the disciples of Jesus tried unsuccessfully to cure an epileptic boy (Matthew 17:14-20). Romano Guardini observes: "They had tried to effect a cure by an effort of the will, possibly bordering on magic. He teaches them that the healing of God's disciples is healing in confidence of mission and in faith—pure faith utterly submissive to the will of God." [12] The disciples had good intentions.

Moreover, they had been instructed in right conduct. What they lacked was adequate power, which could come only through trusting God. It was only with the coming of the Holy Spirit at Pentecost that they were imbued with a living faith. Of this event, Guardini says:

It is as if everything Jesus had said and done . . . has sunk into their consciousness only as seed sinks into dumb and passive earth . . . Until now they have been untouched by act and word. But when the Spirit descends, the dormant seed suddenly swells and unfolds, and at last the men who were to be his faithful witnesses spring up, who in turn spread the seed of the Master's sacred word abroad.[13]

The whole process of prayer, then, is first a matter of plowing our consciousness and implanting in it the seed of faith. The harvest is up to God, in his loving response through the Holy Spirit. In this sense, as Ferré says, "prayer is communion." It is consciously entering into relation with God and seeking to elicit his response.

Time should be set aside for regular prayer as a discipline, but we can also learn to pray more and more in every situation in which we find ourselves—to praise God for every joy at the moment we experience it, to ask for guidance and strength at every moment of challenge and, in short, always to keep God close to the edge of consciousness—to be in constant communion, to "pray unceasingly." In periods of crisis and stress especially the nonviolent cadre can find sustenance in this ingrained habit of prayer. Gandhi found it in the ceaseless mental repetition of "Rama," the Hindu name of God. Others have found it in the Lord's Prayer and in other formulas such as the Twenty-third Psalm, portions of the "peace prayer" of Francesco d'Assisi or sentences of their own devising. In each case, the purely psychological effect is to stabilize one's thoughts by providing them with an unshakable center, with the deeper religious effect also of holding open the channel through which agapaic love can flow, overcoming fear and strengthening faith for the immediate task.

In addition to daily devotions it is wise to cultivate the habit of retreat. Gandhi made it a practice to observe strict silence one day a week, but many persons find it adequate to retire into solitude once a month for a few hours or a day, spending this time in silent meditation, perhaps focused on a devotional text, on the love of God or on no specific theme, as a kind of broadened, free-form extended prayer.

During the course of a campaign of nonviolent action, cadres should meet frequently for group meditation. Richard Gregg suggests that they sit together in silence for fifteen to thirty minutes or longer, either simply ridding their minds of all conscious thought and all awareness of sensory perceptions, or focusing their thoughts on an agreed-upon theme such as "an incident in the life of some great exemplar of nonviolence." [14] Gregg asserts that this practice is essential for building a firm sense of unity among members of a team of cadres. The aim is not merely formal unity but a deep sense of shared commitment to the cause, to one another and to God. The dimension of common worship in *koinonia* is perhaps as vital as personal prayer itself and is in fact a communal expression of the same thing.

Annually or more often in a protracted campaign, nonviolent cadres may benefit from a group retreat for a week end, going away to some secluded place and submitting themselves to a regimen of alternating corporate and solitary devotions, manual work, worship and fasting.[15] If jail looms as an imminent possibility, the time in enforced inactivity which this involves may be adapted to serve the purpose of retreat. Certainly jail need not be an occasion for stagnation but can be an opportunity for renewal and spiritual revitalization.

From Praying to Working

Work in the constructive program can also serve as an important source of strength. The tasks which it imposes may be gratifying in the results they produce and enable the constructive workers to experience a sense of satisfaction that binds the group together. Even if results are thwarted or destroyed by the opponent, however, the experience of shared effort and struggle can contribute a bond of unity among the cadres. Not only teamwork but many kinds of team activities can also do this—the use of common symbols and slogans, group singing of songs and hymns, the sharing of inspiring stories of saints and heroes in the nonviolent tradition. These practices build morale or "team spirit." There is always the risk of promoting an exclusive in-group attitude, however, which may be sufficient for endurance but tends to narrow and finally to close off the possibility of rapport and reconciliation with the opponent. For this reason we must take care to introduce into our group meditations and other morale-building activities themes that encompass the opponent as well as our own group.

Even though we may begin with a degree of group solidarity and wish only to heighten it in a nonviolent context, we shall find ourselves enmeshed in a contradiction if we try to go very far in combining nonviolent conduct with an attitude of irreconcilability. Hatred, we must admit, can be a strong motivation to action that involves risks and mobilizes courage. But it is too volatile as an emotion to be successfully repressed for very long. When the lid flies off, there is literally hell to pay. That is one reason why we need prayer that includes as part of its content the affirmation that God's love is for our enemies as well as for ourselves and our friends. That is why, too, in prayer we need to habituate ourselves to deferring our selfish wishes to the wiser will of God.

Prayer might well be preceded by reading 1 Corinthians 13 or 1 John 4, both of which are testimonies to the power of divine love. If we set out to pray with openness toward this power, however little we at first believe in its reality, and with willingness to take the leap of faith that is required, we can become instruments of redemption even as we engage in unremitting conflict. "Not only can we bring about a whole new world through prayer," says Nels Ferré, "but one's own life can by its means become astonishingly new." [16] The power does not reside in the act of prayer, but in God's love itself which prayer helps to mediate to us. God's love is always there for us. Prayer is the key with which we unlock our ego and open ourselves to receive it.

Public prayer meetings, marches and vigils partake of this same reality if their content and motivation are truly humble and loving. They are a means of communicating with the opponent on a spiritual level. But their authenticity presupposes a high spiritual level in our own lives, without which the public manifestation is likely to smack of hypocrisy and to offend the opponent and observers as an exhibition of spiritual pride. For this reason, too, it is extremely poor strategy to combine such events directly with acts of protest or of pressure. Prayer is not a weapon but a resource. It must be used with fidelity to its intrinsic purpose if it is to yield strength.

REFERENCES IN CHAPTER 11

1   Pie Régamey: *Non-Violence et Conscience Chrétienne* (Paris: Cerf, 1958), p. 294.
2   *Harijan,* June 18, 1938.
3   *Harijan,* June 4, 1946.
4   See Martin Buber: *Eclipse of God* (New York: Harper & Brothers, 1957), p. 126.
5   C. G. Jung: *Collected Works* (New York: Pantheon Books, 1958), Vol. 11, p. 456n.
6   See Paul E. Johnson: *Psychology of Religion* (Nashville: Abingdon, 1945).
7   Walter G. Muelder: "The Efficacy of Prayer" in Simon Doniger, ed.: *Psychological Aspects of Prayer* (Great Neck, N.Y.: Pastoral Psychology Press, 1954), p. 10f.
8   Nels F. S. Ferré: *Strengthening the Spiritual Life* (New York: Harper & Brothers, 1951), p. 29.
9   *Ibid.,* p. 30.
10 Hervé Chaigne: "The Spirit and Techniques of Gandhian Nonviolence" in *Cross Currents,* Spring 1961, p. 125.
11 Nels F. S. Ferré: "Theology and the Devotional Life" in *Theology Today,* April, 1955, p. 9. Used by permission.
12 Romano Guardini: *The Lord* (Chicago: Henry Regnery Co., 1954), p. 63.
13 *Ibid.,* p. 67.

14 Richard B. Gregg: *The Power of Nonviolence* (Nyack, N.Y.: Fellowship Publications, 1959), p. 162.

15 See the following pamphlets: Constance Garrett: *Renewal Through Retreat* (Bernardsville, N.J.: St. Martin's House); Gilbert Kilpack: *The Idea of Retreat* (Wallingford, Pa.: Pendle Hill Pamphlets); John Oliver Nelson: *Retreats for Protestants* (Bangor, Pa.: Kirkridge).

16 Ferré: *Strengthening the Spiritual Life*, p. 26.

12

Christian Nonviolence and the Church

Nonviolence has deep historical roots in the Christian faith and in the church of Jesus Christ, exemplified in its Lord, whom Gandhi once called "the prince of *satyagrahis*." The record of the early church is, among other things, that of a fellowship of nonresistant martyrs. Even after the decline of its original perfectionism in the era of Constantine, currents within the church preserved this witness through monastic orders and such lay movements as the Devotio Moderna, as well as among the early followers of Wycliffe, Waldo, Hus and Wesley. Even Calvin was subjected to its influence in an early version of his *Institutes,* and a vital influence in John Wesley's experience of conversion was the nonresistant Zinzendorf, one of several figures on the radical fringe of Protestantism who have carried this historic witness. Such dissenting Russian sects as the Dukhobors and Bezmolitovtsy have had much in common with the Shakers, Quakers and Inspirationists of the West. Sometimes determinedly biblical, as with the Mennonites, or with admixtures of spiritualism verging on heresy, these many groups have not let the world forget that nonresistance is a Christian teaching.

The main line of church history after Constantine took a different course. Few Christians today can thinkingly rejoice in the savage excesses of violence done in the name of Christ between Catharists and Catholics, Catholics and Protestants, Anabaptists and Lutherans, Christians and Turks or Saracens, to mention only some. Yet even within the main-line churches, whether Catholic, Orthodox or Protestant, nonresistance has never been wholly repudiated, and hardly a movement for reform or renewal has been able to ignore its claims. Even when ruled out of the sphere of social action, it has been recognized as holding a place in the way of life of the devout, at least in personal affairs.

Nonresistance is a difficult doctrine, and it is not surprising that even the radical sects which officially honor it either dwindle in numbers and disappear or become lax in its observance from generation to generation. For them and for the individual perfectionist within the larger churches, a special problem exists. We are not indifferent to it, but more urgent problems must claim our attention.

Their full dimensions greatly exceed the scope of this book. We can only note some of the elements—the fact that so many Christians today lack vitality of faith; that so many churches have wandered off into pious irrelevance; that we are besieged with the problems of a technological and ideological revolution and divided in our understanding of it. It does not deny the eternal truth of our faith to admit that the era in which we live increasingly predicates its values and standards on new gods of reason or science which are decidedly "post-Christian." Even if a return to the pure nonresistance of the early church should prove to be part of the answer to these problems, it is not an immediate option for the millions of half-believers within the church as it exists, nor can it be offered as such by those committed Christians who have taken it as their task to find answers to the immediate problems.

Thus we find that, of the three kinds of Christians—perfectionist, nominal and realist—it is the third we must be chiefly concerned with. The nominal Christian is content with religion as a commodity; the perfectionist may be content with a verbal semblance of nonresistance, or he may be anxious to make it relevant to the world. The realist has no alternative but to demand relevance.

Christian realism emphasizes responsibility both for the

church, with all its nominal Christians, and for the world which the church is committed to redeem. The realist does not categorically repudiate the nonresistance taught in the Sermon on the Mount, but he is more concerned with acting effectively and is disinclined to increase the risk of failure, which is great enough, by insisting on means which exceed the capacities of those who are called upon to use them. He cannot embrace merely suppositious programs. Experience has taught him to be skeptical about the possibilities of human nature and candid about the obstacles to be confronted by any form of social action.

This does not mean that the realist is unmindful of moral distinctions or the high demands of the gospel, which are most readily conceded in the direct encounter of the individual, but in confronting problems that involve social responsibility he cannot insist on applying them in an absolute way. Even here these distinctions and demands are not discarded, however. But instead of being applied directly to problems they are used as absolute standards against which to assess whatever means are at hand. This involves a high degree of pragmatism, but it is never an unbridled pragmatism. A truly Christian realism never ceases to seek out the most moral of the workable alternatives that present themselves, and to devise and introduce new alternatives that are relevant. It would be a serious mistake to identify this approach with a timid acceptance of the status quo. Realism necessarily involves risk-taking and even sacrifice, but always in a context of responsibility.

Beginning with a commitment to relevance and responsibility, the realist is free to choose from a wide variety of means, including nonviolence. The perfectionist, beginning with a commitment to nonviolent conduct at all times and in all situations, is not free to choose other means, but he is free to enter situations in which nonviolence may be relevant and to work to adapt it effectively. From a realistic viewpoint, this may seem to be sheer realism. For some perfectionists it may in fact be a coincidence, while for others it is a compromise which means moving out from the pure witness of strict non-resistance to the less clear types of nonviolence that involve pressure and coercion bordering on force.

Restricted to it as he is in principle, the perfectionist has traditionally been eager to imbue nonviolence with his whole outlook. And of course to him the relationship is obvious: nonviolence goes hand in hand with conscientious objection to military service, and it is closely related to other articles of his faith, whatever they may be. If he is a vegetarian, for example, it is for the same underlying reasons that lead him to embrace nonviolence. Within the churches, this circumstance has tended to polarize opinion on the question of nonviolence. It is surely understandable if many realists, habituated to the pragmatic use of force and accustomed to hearing about nonviolence as an adjunct of pacifism, have tended to ignore nonviolence. Having settled the pacifist question, they have unwittingly thrown out the separate question of nonviolence. It has generally required a new and urgent context to force a confrontation with this question, and even in the setting of the nonviolent demonstrations that swept the United States in the 1960s, the burden of old arguments exerted considerable inertia. Virtually all of the pioneering work in developing nonviolent methods of struggle was done by pacifists. Gradually, outstanding Negro leaders took it up and some of them also became pacifists. Only then did nonviolence begin to gain currency among realists in the larger community: only after it had proved itself. And even then the movement from grudging to positive support indicated a continuing lag.

Not all realists lagged. A quarter of a century before the Montgomery bus boycott, Reinhold Niebuhr wrote: "There is no problem of political life to which religious imagination can make a larger contribution than this problem of developing nonviolent resistance." [1] For Niebuhr the criterion was that the racial situation is of such a kind that it offers a good chance of success. Events proved his thesis correct. This assessment did not, however, hinder Niebuhr's choice of other means when considering the aggressions of Hitler and Mussolini. Both nonviolence and military resistance were within the scope of his realism. But, caught up in the debate over pacifism, the majority of Christians who flocked to the banner of Niebuhrian realism in the 1930s and 1940s lost sight of these distinctions.

What once seemed obvious was later to become absurd— the assertion, endorsed by perfectionists and realists alike, that it is impossible to achieve results through nonviolence in one situation unless those who use it are committed to use it in all situations. It has long been a neglected fact of history that most of the major campaigns in which nonviolence has been used effectively have neither required nor resulted in such a sweeping commitment. "The advantages of nonviolent methods are very great," wrote Niebuhr, "but they must be pragmatically considered in the light of circumstances." [2] Those who found themselves in such circumstances were seldom pacifists, and proved their realism by having the imagination to exploit these advantages while, ironically, many who called themselves Niebuhrians were at a loss to do more than issue resolutions.

Sources of Revitalization

How far and how fast the church can move toward regaining the initiative in the understanding and use of nonviolence is a question that is bound up with the larger problem of renewal. The three types of Christians to which we have referred are not, in actual fact, so easily compartmented. Much that passes for perfectionism is nothing but a pious pretense, and much so-called realism is sheer bravado. Granted that there are outstanding individuals, even authentic saints, in both categories, the two groups blend into a total picture that is blurred. This is true even of the background of nominal believers and those estranged from the church. There is flux and movement; there are degrees of commitment even among the largely uncommitted. The church of Jesus Christ, even at its moments of lowest ebb, possesses through the Holy Spirit that works within it and authenticates it, a resilience and capacity for change exhibited by few if any other institutions. The Reformation came not from external incursions but from monks, priests and theologians nurtured within the Catholic faith, and the great reforms inaugurated by Pope John XXIII were made possible by the selfsame cardinals who had been chosen by predecessors who were unready for these steps—or, more accurately, by the Holy Spirit at work among them.

This is not the place to attempt a survey of the widespread currents of reform and renewal, nor is it relevant here to assess their success or their pace. It would be easy to exaggerate how much is actually happening, and disastrous to minimize the need for vastly increased efforts on all fronts. In every era there have been those to whom the Bible is an honored but purely ornamental object, and those actively engaged in relating its truth to the world. The fact we wish to single out and stress is that nonviolence as a form of Christian action does not go against the grain but points in the same direction as other currents of renewal. It can contribute to the process of transforming the church from what Edwin T. Dahlberg once called "a 'reservation' for people with 'religious' needs" into an authentic community of faith.

One distinguished theologian, Culbert G. Rutenber, has spoken for many proponents of renewal:

The fact of the matter is that much—perhaps most—of what goes on in the local church should be scuttled. Every organization should be forced to justify its existence in the light of the church's mandate from its Lord.

Most of all, the preacher-centered church should be transformed. The church must see itself as primarily a ministering community, not a talked-at congregation. . . . The work and witness of the believing church is inevitably the work and witness of the membership. This is the meaning of the doctrine of the priesthood of all believers.[3]

In contrast with an earlier generation which tended to fragment itself into denominational resolutions, unofficial reform agencies and congregational complacency, Rutenber's views and others like them are backed by efforts within the churches themselves which seek tangible ways of affecting life at the parish level. Though many of these efforts are faltering and inconclusive, they are being made. One of the forms they take is the establishment of small face-to-face groups to develop new leadership and lay participation, overcoming the audience structure of the congregation. Surely this is one essential step, but when such groups fail it is often for lack of definite tasks to be carried out which can involve their members in both mission and fellowship. They thrive on a well-balanced program of worship, study, discussion and action projects, with the last of these often proving to be the most crucial.

Where Churches Choose Action

While not every house-church group may have occasion to use nonviolence in its community, it is worth noting that nonviolent demonstrations require action by groups of approximately the same size. Christian students who became involved as cadres in the Nashville sit-in movement in 1960 said that their experience of committed fellowship gave them new insight into what the church could be like. The same response was found in the Norwegian church under the Nazi occupation. These were largely nominal, churchgoing Christians, but it is also a fact that more than a few individuals who had turned their backs on the church found their faith rekindled and returned to the fold. In many places where cadres of the Southern Christian Leadership Conference sought to establish a base in the local church, they at first encountered the most apathy in the minister, fearful of jeopardizing his stable position in the community or losing accustomed comforts. Just as often, however, such men became caught up in the atmosphere of commitment and carried forward to leadership in fulfillment of their vocation, surely a testimony to the power of the Holy Spirit.

Even though belated, the response of major denominations to the nonviolent movement for civil rights exhibited a similar spiritual contagion. Many of the official resolutions seem remarkably diffident. The American Baptist Convention, meeting in Detroit on May 17, 1963, stated: "While we regret the need for . . . nonviolent demonstrations, we deplore even more the injustices which provoke and make them necessary." This tepid language, however, was accompanied by the formation of Baptist Action for Racial Brotherhood to spark among local churches "participation in nonviolent demonstrations for civil rights," further specified to include "demonstrations, parades and rallies" and "nonviolent demonstrations of protest" in addition to conventional types of social action. Among the BARB committee's members was Harold E. Stassen, former Governor of Minnesota, who led a Baptist contingent in the massive March on Washington, August 28, 1963.

The United Church of Christ said virtually nothing about nonviolence as such at its Fourth General Synod, but established a Fellowship of the Committed which included these words in its membership pledge: "I commit myself as a Christian to engage now in responsible nonviolent demonstrations when such actions are necessary for racial justice." This body had scarcely been formed before a number of ministers, including some in denominational staff positions, were arrested for carrying out this pledge.

In 1961 the North American Area Council of the World Alliance of Reformed and Presbyterian Churches resolved that "when a law prevails that keeps people from securing justice . . . a Christian, after serious and careful consideration and after sharing his concern with other members of the household of faith, may engage alone or with others in an act of civil disobedience." Two years later Eugene Carson Blake, chief executive officer of the United Presbyterian Church in the USA, was arrested and jailed in a nonviolent demonstration in Baltimore. With him were Msgr. Austin J. Healy, representing the Roman Catholic Archdiocese of Baltimore; the Rt. Rev.

Daniel Corrigan, director of the Home Department of the National Council of the Protestant Episcopal Church; Rabbi Morris Lieberman of the Baltimore Hebrew Congregation; and nearly three hundred others, including numerous Protestant ministers. Undertaken a few weeks before the great March on Washington—itself a tribute to nonviolence, in which more than 200,000 demonstrators maintained model discipline—the Baltimore action was only one of many to come, and not the most challenging.

Other major Protestant bodies, such as the Disciples of Christ, whose United Christian Missionary Society formally approved "direct action," took similar steps to join actively in the broad nonviolent movement for civil rights. Consistently the emphasis was placed on involvement and commitment rather than, as formerly, on paper pronouncements. The United Church's pledge referred not merely to good will but to a "risk-taking witness." A statement of the National Council of Churches not only authorized "the encouragement of nego-tiations, demonstrations and direct action." It also stated as among "the first actions of a continuing strategy of corporate witness . . . to commit ourselves, as members of the General Board, to engage personally in negotiations, demonstrations and other direct action in particular situations of racial ten-sion." It was in his capacity as a member of the NCC Board that Dr. Blake was jailed, as were others who were to follow.

The Roman Catholic Church, with its distinctive traditions and institutional structure, was slower to articulate a definite program. Nevertheless, individuals from laymen and priests to members of the hierarchy stood shoulder to shoulder with Prot-estants and Jews. A number of parish priests in the Deep South withstood physical assault in a lonely nonviolent witness to papal and archdiocesan utterances affirming racial equality. One such statement was embodied in these words of Patrick O'Boyle, Archbishop of Washington, as he led the freedom marchers in prayer at the Lincoln Memorial: "May we shun violence, knowing that the meek shall inherit the earth. But may this meekness of manner be joined with courage and strength." Various Catholic writers such as Mathew Ahmann, William J. Kenealy, S.J., and Thomas Merton adumbrated this sentiment in relation to the growing nonviolent movement. Few, however, within the Protestant or Catholic churches, had begun to develop a theoretical understanding of nonviolence even in pragmatic terms as they awakened to its relevance. Like most Christian social action, nonviolence tended to be viewed either as a direct expression of Christian love or as a lubricant to secular processes of justice, and little attention was given to its theological or ecclesiological dimensions. The following words from a pastoral letter of the Roman Catholic Archdiocese of New York is not unrepresentative:

Demonstrations and other activities of these [civil rights] organizations, in which the good that is reasonably expected through these demonstrations outweighs the accidental unfortunate effects, when they are carried out in a responsible and peaceful manner within the bounds of Christian charity and justice and finally when they are undertaken as a last resort in the struggle to overcome the second-class citizenship of American Negroes, are deserving of the support and participation of Catholic American citizens.

Other statements have emphasized Christian motivations more explicitly, but virtually without exception both Protestant and Catholic statements have made it clear that nonviolence is seen as external to the church as such, an incidental, even regrettable feature of events in the world which, with proper stipulations, oblige Christians to take part in them. The note of prudence is legitimate, but while it varies in emphasis it has tended to be predominant. The situation is urgent; we must act in it. It is in fact so urgent that we must even go so far as to take part in, or initiate, public demonstrations. But they should be peaceful. That is the role of nonviolence.

There is nothing precisely erroneous in this perspective, and we have already noted some of the vigorous and committed actions that have stemmed from it. What has been generally lacking, however, is any conception of nonviolence as a generic type of social action having special relevance for the church. The conception has been almost uniformly adjectival rather than substantive, a brake rather than an engine.

Yet viewed substantively as a method and a dynamic of action capable of being harnessed to social objectives, nonviolence has a demonstrable contribution to make in the church's encounter with the world. Although many types of community organization—schools, labor unions—can provide a basis and an organizational structure for nonviolent-action teams in the event of a national emergency, nonviolence has a special task to perform in the context of the church. In its fulness, a nonviolent campaign offers a challenge to many aspects of ongoing or sought-for renewal, energizing conventional social-action programs, giving urgency and focus to prayer cells and knitting together the loose strands of church membership into a living fellowship. Even formal worship may gain new vigor.

John Oliver Nelson, who has had long experience both in Protestant retreats and in field work with ministerial students, has indicated how a serious venture into Christian nonviolence might begin in a local church:

It requires patient, prayerful exploration of the meaning of the New Testament, examination of the actions of inspired social leaders in all the years, and lessons in teamwork among a committed group. A minister can raise up within his congregation such a trained nucleus, or any dedicated Christian can draw together a circle of men and women and young people with this aim—if there is directness of purpose and the insight that here is the key answer for our generation amid world tensions.[4]

This is a modest enough beginning. Further steps have been outlined in an earlier chapter (see pp. 131–154). Whether nonviolence is in fact the "key answer," it is certainly a possibility that should be explored. Even if Christians choose realism rather than perfectionism, they should not deny themselves access to Christian nonviolence. Even if they may decide in a given situation that nonviolence is inapplicable, they should be able to do so on the merits of the case and not because they

are unprepared. Being prepared, they will be enabled sometimes to reduce the prevalence of less moral conduct, including
the immorality of inaction. Of all people, Christians should
not allow themselves to be in a position where legal remedies,
conventional social action, brute force and acquiescence are
the only alternatives they know how to handle.

To look honestly and without illusion at the church as it is
today is a sure cure for the temptation to think of nonviolence
as a panacea. We are already getting by with too much easy
verbiage unsupported by risk-taking action. The task is a formidable one, and it would be wild optimism to think that a
sudden transformation, however urgently needed, is anywhere
in sight. The challenge is all the more staggering when we
turn from the encouraging upsurge in the area of civil rights
to consider the twin forces of hedonistic materialism, bour-
geois and Communist, that are ranged against us. The only
choice we have, however, is between capitulation and resistance—to let religion become increasingly the irrelevant and
obsolescent commodity of happy robots or Orwellian proles,
or to assert what little understanding and faith we still possess
and pray for more. In a world of increasing depersonalization,
nonviolence has much to recommend it as a safeguard against
too much remote control in the social order and as an aid in
enriching the resources of the human person, not merely to
stand alone in a mass or against it, but to work toward its
transformation and redemption.

If we approach this task with Christian realism, drawing
upon the lessons of the past, we may be enabled to avoid some
of the mistakes of the future. But history is not a blank sheet
on which we are at liberty to write our own destiny, guided
unerringly by experience and theoretical principles, even with
the most effective use of the best means. The God who is love is
also the Lord of history, a living God whose actions condition
all of our historical possibilities. Under his hand seemingly
disconnected events fortuitously combine to produce surprising consequences for good or ill that can be evaluated only

in retrospect. Christian nonviolence is ultimately Christian not simply because it is used by Christians, nor even because its ethic seeks to make Christian love relevant to social conflict, but also theologically in recognizing that its power is not absolute but derivative. Nonviolence shares with all forms of human actions the fact that it can never exhaust the fulfillment of God's will. In his own unfathomable wisdom he may reprieve us from the consequences of our folly or chastise our self-righteous pride. Our actions, our skill in strategy, our steadfastness in conduct are all important, but they are not the whole story. In the end it is faith, hope and love—all in relation to God—that are decisive. Whether we win or lose in history hinges on God's grace and God's judgment. It is always God who has the last word.

REFERENCES IN CHAPTER 12

1   Reinhold Niebuhr: *Moral Man and Immoral Society* (New York: Charles Scribner's Sons, 1932), p. 254.
2   *Ibid.*, p. 252.
3   Culbert G. Rutenber: *The Reconciling Gospel* (Philadelphia: The Judson Press, 1961), p. 127.
4   John Oliver Nelson: "New Testament Power for Social Change" in *The Journal of Religious Thought,* Autumn-Winter 1957-1958, p. 12.

A Casebook of
Nonviolence

13

Purported and Authentic Nonviolence

Since the publication of Adin Ballou's *Christian Non-Resistance* in 1846 there have appeared occasional compilations of brief accounts purporting to show the power of love, kindness, empathy, honest dealing or other virtues to overcome evil. Most often these accounts are very sketchy, carelessly documented (frequently from second-hand sources) and bathed in syrupy sentiment. Some of them are remarkable testimonies to the working of the spirit of Christ in men. But many are plainly trumped up, based on questionable information, faulty reasoning, a misunderstanding of the real situation or a biased and gratuitous interpretation. Such anecdotes may edify the naïve but to a critical mind they can only cast doubt on the whole idea of nonviolence.

The purpose of this chapter is twofold: to puncture these half-true fantasies and to present a picture of actual instances of historical nonviolence, indicating both its strengths and its limitations in practice. Only by such critical study can we equip ourselves to interpret new occurrences of nonviolence or to anticipate problems that theory alone cannot adequately envision.

A large share of these edifying tales are clearly irrelevant to the subject of nonviolence. Although they may be worth telling for other reasons, stories of international mediation, the peaceful settlement of border disputes and the like are in this category, as are tales of the "pacific monarch"—Asoka, Pericles, Queen Jadwiga, "the lost Tsar," etc.—which merely show that some nations and heads of state are wise enough or prudent enough not to stir up trouble. More characteristic of the genre, however, are stories of individual encounters that hinge upon a battle of wits or a benign misunderstanding by the participants, which are then embroidered in such a way as to inject them with a factor of moral uplift or spiritual power that is quite specious.

One such story is based on the fact that in October 1942 near Stalingrad a wounded German corporal was bandaged by a Soviet medic and then permitted to return to the German lines. This is the factual core of the story. Somewhere between the original report and the second or third retelling, the following embellishments have been added. First, the narrator expresses incredulous amazement that the Russian did not wantonly kill the wounded German. If, as is probable, it was the German soldier who first told the story, it may well be that he *was* amazed because Nazi propaganda had led him to expect nothing but barbarous ruthlessness. The real meaning of the fact might be simply that, in this instance at least, the Nazi stereotype of the Soviet soldier had no basis in fact. The narrator, however, makes no effort to evaluate this amazement or the fear with which it is bound up. It does not serve his edifying purpose to do so.

Second, the author makes the assumption that the Russian was "obeying the moral law" and that he was motivated by simple compassion. This may be so, but it is pure conjecture masquerading as self-evident fact, and it ignores possible alternative explanations. Maybe the Russian was just tired of taking prisoners. Maybe he liked the German's looks and would have shot him if he hadn't. Maybe he reasoned that it would be more patriotic to let the German government hospitalize the man. We have no way of knowing what his motive actually was. The facts are so meager that the field of speculation is wide open. For all its good intentions, such a story shows, among other things, how ambivalent is its author's view of human nature, since in the process of showing that a highly exceptional Russian soldier could obey the moral law he implies that the average Russian soldier conforms to the Nazi stereotype of Slavic bestiality.

Another example of what often passes for a testimonial to nonviolence is the following episode from *Victories Without Violence* by the English Quaker Anna Ruth Fry. The book repeats almost word for word many of the quaint anecdotes in Ballou's century-old book. This is a more recent one.

In a suburb of Berlin toward the end of World War II there lived a "Mrs. H.," Miss Fry tells us, who "did all she could to help poor Jews when persecuted, hiding them as best she could." One day at the town hall members of the Gestapo warned her and others "not to say a word against the regime."

The impetuous Mrs. H. "lost her temper. 'And I will talk!' she yelled. 'It is a shame what is being done. I don't hate the Jews, no, I don't. And I don't love your Hitler, who is responsible for all this misery.' "

These were bold, heroic words. Having said them, Mrs. H. left the room. The police soon brought her back, "wanting to carry her away." But they let her go. Why? Because they respected her courage or because her compassion for the Jews touched their hearts? Not at all. Some of Mrs. H.'s neighbors interceded for her, explaining that she "hardly knows what she says when she loses her temper." So what we are supposed to believe is a moral issue turns out to be a case of nerves. Apparently Mrs. H. was happy that it worked out that way, since she let it go at that.

We next find the irrepressible Mrs. H. in trouble with the Soviet occupation a few months later. She has been complaining that Russian soldiers are stealing watches. The Soviet commandant calls her in and interrogates her. "Did you protest in the same vigorous way when the Nazis ill-treated the Jews?"

"Certainly I did," she says, and "someone" corroborates her testimony.

The Soviet officer responds warmly to this. He does not say anything about rectifying the injustice that Mrs. H. had been complaining about, but Anna Ruth Fry and her Mrs. H. are glad to forget about that. "You go home now," says the Russian, "and nothing will happen to you. And try to forget the wrongs you have suffered." Forget about the stolen watches, too!

Perhaps it is belaboring the obvious to say that it is hard to see any "victory" in either of these episodes, which together occupy a little less than one full page in Miss Fry's slender, often-reprinted booklet. The most that can be said is that Mrs. H. made two unheeded protests and got off unharmed. A critical reader is tempted to think that in both cases the authorities wrote her off as a harmless screwball. Yet in the book's introduction Miss Fry claims to give illustrations of a mysterious spiritual power which she identifies as "nonviolent resistance," a "pacifist technique" that can serve as "a possible alternative to the futile crime of war." Mysterious it is indeed; if such an alternative is embedded in the story of Mrs. H., it is hard to fathom.

Most of Mrs. Fry's stories tell of unarmed religious people (usually Quakers) minding their own business when a conflict of some kind arises in which they do not take part, and the outcome of which they do not in any way influence. The "victory" invariably is nothing more than the fact that they manage to scrape through unmolested, or are even taken under the protection of one of the warring groups, as in the case of the Shakers who had Morgan's Raiders as their uninvited protectors during the Civil War. Stories about night-riding bandits and Chinese river pirates always cast the villains as ruthless cutthroats who are touched by the uprightness and Christian courage of their intended victims, as if transformed. But may it not be that their range of responses is wider than Miss Fry gives them credit for? One suspects too that many encounters might be reported in which the good Quakers or missionaries did not live to report victory.

In his book *Shall Our Children Live or Die?* Victor Gollancz tells of a Jewish rabbi tormented by Nazi SS men. On Yom

Kippur, the Day of Atonement, they whipped him, forced him to stand knee-deep in a pile of human excrement and then ordered him to preach. "My friends," the rabbi said to the SS men, "the fundamental principle of the Jewish religion, as of all the other great religions of the world, is: Love thy neighbor as thyself." A cynic might suggest that this was a shrewd way of asking for mercy, but a more generous interpretation—the one intended, which I am inclined to share—sees here evidence of dignity that cannot be defiled, moral nobility and unconquerable good will. The anecdote thus says much about the rabbi. What is missing is the SS men's response to it. Having made his point about the rabbi, Gollancz leaves the story suspended in mid-air. Were the SS men moved to shame, or did they perhaps guffaw and walk away? The story makes no claim to illustrate "nonviolent resistance," but it is one of many that are pacifist favorites and as such often lumped together with accounts that do make such a claim. A book titled *Above All Nations* gives many examples of "enemies" saving the lives of children or other civilians or refusing to shoot wounded soldiers. Such stories remind us that humane responses are possible even in many situations where they are unlikely. They may serve the cause of nonviolence by supplying a source of morale, but their relevance is marginal.

John Lewis, in his provocative book *The Case Against Pacifism*, disposes of many incidents claimed by pacifists as illustrations of nonviolence. In particular he singles out William Penn's honest dealing with the Indians, which understandably won the latter's respect for the Quaker settlers and relieved them of any occasion to choose between armed force and nonviolent resistance since the Indians did not attack them. He also points out that the courageous abstention from violence by Edward Richards and Theodore Pennell in Afghanistan when accosted by "fierce tribesmen" constitutes isolated individual exceptions that have no social validity. Much the same could be said of missionaries and doctors spared by marauders elsewhere. They are exempted because they pose no

threat and perhaps are even respected for their good works—
and above all because they are, in effect, considered either
friends or neutrals. To be sure, there is an element of danger
and risk, but it hinges on the possibility of misunderstanding
rather than conflict. To refrain from the use of arms in such a
situation is, as Lewis points out, only good sense. If it happens
to conincide with a temperamental aversion to violence or a
principled adherance to nonviolence, as in the case of Richards,
that only provides an additional bulwark to enable one to do
the sensible thing. But basically it is not nonviolence as such
and it is a mistake to extrapolate from such experiences the
possibility of engaging in unarmed conflict with those who in
fact are simply respecting the neutrality of such individuals.
Had Richards, for example, been the leader of a nonviolent
compaign to obtain certain concessions from the Kurds, they
might well have butchered him on the spot. This is Lewis' con-
tention, and whether he is right or not in his estimate of these
specific situations it is clear that there is no warrant but a
partisan and propagandistic one for mixing the category of
individual witness indiscriminately with that of social action.

Once we have set aside the spurious and the marginal, what
are we left with? Historical crises resolved solely by "pure
nonviolence" are virtually nonexistent. Yet there have been
episodes in which a strategy of nonviolence has been the decisive vehicle in waging and winning a campaign. There have
been other episodes in which nonviolence functioned as a
catalyst, precipitating a victory through legal or political channels. There have been episodes of nonviolence within a context
of largely violent struggle, and there have been situations in
which an incipiently nonviolent type of moral appeal has
yielded to armed struggle without any consistent attempt to
test the further possibilities of a systematically nonviolent
struggle. An important borderline area includes the tactics of
strike and boycott in labor struggles and similar kinds of civil
resistance—seldom clearly nonviolent, yet often approximating
nonviolence in a refusal to be provoked to counterviolence

when attacked. Given the actual record of civil resistance, punctuated as it is by departures from its own standards, this is a difficult and problematical category. Barthelemy de Ligt in *The Conquest of Violence* goes so far afield as to call "nonviolent" the action of the German Social Democrats under Bismarck in going underground and deciding against sabotage as a weapon of struggle.

If we set aside Ligt's loose usage of the term and allow for the "impurities" suggested above, the one distinct hallmark of nonviolence in all its authentic varieties is the meeting of actual or threatened violence unarmed and purposely, whether pragmatically or by conviction, making a stand without resorting to physical force against the enemy.

We have had to be selective in choosing the examples that comprise this casebook. Those given range from one case of Christian nonresistance to the incidental, spontaneous nonviolent episodes of the East German and Hungarian revolts of the 1950s. In between are significant cases of major passive resistance and direct-action campaigns. Rather than cram this section with many brief snippets to prove only that nonviolence occurred, we have preferred to devote the available space to a more comprehensive account of fewer cases, giving in each as much detail and historical context as is known and necessary for an adequate appraisal. To do this, we have had to forego the inclusion of Gandhi's campaigns, which in fact pose special problems and deserve detailed study. Perhaps the best source currently available for these is Joan V. Bondurant's *Conquest of Violence* (Princeton 1958). Additional cases from other countries can be found in Mulford Q. Sibley's *The Quiet Battle* (Doubleday Anchor 1963). Both books contain helpful bibliographies.[1]

REFERENCE IN CHAPTER 13

1 See also the extensive bibliography in the book edited by Peter Mayer: *The Nonviolent Tradition* (New York: Orion Press, Inc., 1964).

14

Nonresistance: The Moravian Indians, 1782

Although Christian nonresistance may sometimes achieve a socio-political objective, its intrinsic purpose is not this but a way of faithful obedience. As subsequent chapters will make clear, nonresistant martyrdom is by no means the only way Christians have used nonviolence, but it is a way that is close to the literal teaching of the gospel. Related to the case that follows is a long history that ranges from the crucifixion of Jesus to the massacre of Christian Kikuyu tribesmen in Kenya in the 1950s at the hands of the Mau Mau. Its legacy may be described as "how to die like a Christian." Our purpose in including this example is not to recommend it but to provide a clear illustration of the difference between nonresistance and strategic nonviolence.

In the mid-eighteenth century Count Nikolaus von Zinzendorf, bishop of the Moravian Church and heir to the nonresistant wing of the Hussite Reformation, founded an Indian mission at Shekomeko, New York. Within a few decades the work and witness of his followers had led to the conversion of considerable numbers of Delaware Indians in Pennsylvania, of whom Theodore Roosevelt was to write:

The zeal and success of the missionaries were attested by the marvelous change they had wrought in these converts; for they had transformed them in one generation from a restless, idle, bloodthirsty people of hunters and fishers, into an orderly, thrifty, industrious folk, believing with all their hearts in the Christian religion in the form in which their teachers both preached and practiced it.[1]

Chief among the Moravian missionaries was David Zeisberger. Born in Moravia in 1721, he emigrated to Georgia at the age of sixteen and, after a few years there, went north and almost returned to Europe with Zinzendorf. He was already aboard ship when he was moved to jump ashore and join the Shekomeko Mission. By the time he was ordained to the ministry in 1749, he was fluent in the Mohawk and Delaware languages. After a year-long visit to Herrnhut, Zinzendorf's model community in Germany, Zeisberger embarked on an impressive career of evangelism among the Iroquois of New York and Pennsylvania.

In March 1771 Zeisberger went out to the capital of the Delaware Nation in Ohio at the invitation of its grand council. The following year, as a result of his talks with the Delaware chieftains, he returned with an aide, the Rev. John Heckewelder, to found Schoenbrunn, the first of several settlements which he populated with Indian converts to Christianity. The settlements flourished until a few years after the outbreak of the Revolutionary War. Located midway between the American outpost at Fort Pitt and the British at Fort Detroit, the nonresistant Moravians were in fact neutral, but this did not keep them from being an object of suspicion. They earned the hostility of non-Christian Indians, too, by their frequent appeals to them to turn back from the warpath.

In 1781 the warrior Indians, at the instigation of the British, made several raids on the Moravian settlements but failed to deter Zeisberger or his followers. Finally in September, Zeisberger and other missionaries were seized and taken to the Delaware camp, where they found a British captain in charge. Their mission house was sacked, many of the Christian Indians were dispersed and the missionaries were taken to Detroit. For a time, however, they and a large number of the converts were held in a "captives' village" not far from the colonies. The winter was a hard one, and some 150 of the Christian Indians were granted permission to return to the settlements to get food which had been stored there.

One of the settlements was Gnadenhütten, in the Tuscara-was Valley. When they arrived, together with John Martin and five other mission assistants, they learned that only a short time earlier a war party of Sandusky Indians had attacked a farm, butchering a woman and her five children. It was widely rumored that the Christian Indians had committed the crime or had given shelter to the criminals. A man who had been taken captive by the Sanduskys warned them that a party of two hundred frontiersmen was on its way to destroy the settlements.

The Moravians counseled with one another and decided to leave by March 7, counting on their innocence to protect them in the event the frontiersmen arrived earlier. On the morning of March 6 they were busily sacking corn when the latter appeared, headed by Colonel David Williamson. Williamson was very friendly, offering to place the Moravian Indians under his protection, and he set his men to helping them recover goods which they had hidden in the forest when the mission had earlier been sacked. He persuaded the brethren at Salem to set fire to that place, saying that he would soon build them another.

There is some conflict in the precise details of what followed. Probably the best account is that of Bishop Schweinitz:

The white men seemed deeply interested in religion, asked many questions with regard to it, and listened to what they told them of their personal experiences with the profoundest attention. . . . "Truly, you are good Christians!" exclaimed the militia. Meanwhile the Indian boys sported with some half-grown lads of the command, taught them to make bows and arrows, and frolicked gleefully through the forests.

On the bank opposite Gnadenhütten the eyes of the deluded converts were suddenly opened. Coming upon a pool of fresh blood and a bloody canoe, they stopped in mute surprise; but in that moment the militia seized them, bound their hands behind their backs, and hurried them across the river, where they found the rest of the Indians also prisoners, confined in two houses, and closely guarded.[2]

They were vilified and accused of many crimes in addition to the recent one. The frontiersmen were in a lynching mood. Williamson assembled them in a single row and asked: "Shall the Moravian Indians be taken prisoners to Pittsburgh, or put to death? All those in favor of sparing their lives, advance one step!" Only eighteen stepped forward. Then the frontiersmen debated whether to burn the Indians alive in their houses or to tomahawk and scalp them, finally deciding on the latter.

Although startled to learn of their fate and continuing to protest their innocence, the Indians begged only time to prepare for their death. They were given until the next morning. Through the night, says Schweinitz, "shut up in their two prisons, the converts began to sing and pray, to exhort and comfort one another, to mutually unburden their consciences and acknowledge their sins. . . . As the hours wore away, and the night deepened, and the end drew near, triumphant anticipations of heaven mingled with their hymns and prayers."[3]

The next morning the converts were taken in pairs, men to one "slaughterhouse," women and children to the other. One of the women, Christiana, had once lived in Bethlehem, Pennsylvania, in her youth and spoke fluent German and English. She begged Colonel Williamson to spare her life. "I cannot help you," he said coldly. John Martin's two sons escaped the day before the massacre and were shot down by sentinels. Otherwise all were scalped after being felled by tomahawk, spear or warclub. And all died except two boys who, only stunned, played dead and slipped away. The death toll included twenty-nine men, twenty-seven women and thirty-four children. All but twelve babies and five adults were baptized Christians.

After the massacre, the frontiersmen spent a day securing their plunder before setting fire to Gnadenhütten and moving on to Schoenbrunn to repeat their barbarous act. But messengers from that place had gone to Gnadenhütten on an errand, returned and gave the alarm.

Zeisberger was deeply saddened by the news when the two boys reached him on March 23. For the rest of his life he continued to shepherd what remained of his Indian flock, leading them from one place to another along Lake Erie and finally settling them at Goshen in the Tuscarawas Valley, where he died in 1808.

The effect of the Gnadenhütten massacre recoiled upon its perpetrators. Theodore Roosevelt tells what happened to a body of 480 Pennsylvania and Virginia militiamen that included "most of those who had taken part in the murderous expedition." In a skirmish with Shawnees and Delawares, seventy of them died of wounds, were killed outright or were captured. The head of the expedition was burned alive. Says Roosevelt:

The Indians were fearfully exasperated by the Moravian massacre; and some of the former Moravians, who had joined their wild tribesmen, told the prisoners that from that time on not a single captive would escape torture.[4]

One man who was condemned but managed to escape saw a number of his comrades tomahawked or tortured to death. And, concludes Roosevelt, "until the close of the year 1782 the settlements along the upper Ohio suffered heavily, a deserved retribution for failing to punish the dastardly deed of Williamson and his associates."[5]

The piety of these "holy innocents" did not save them from death as they had hoped, but it did provoke a terrible and costly vengeance upon their slayers which the Moravians could neither have foreseen nor asked.

REFERENCES IN CHAPTER 14

1 Theodore Roosevelt: *The Winning of the West* (New York: G. P. Putnam's Sons, 1920), p. 6.
2 Edmund de Schweinitz: *The Life and Times of David Zeisberger* (Philadelphia: J. B. Lippincott Co., 1870), p. 545. See also Eugene F. Bliss, editor: *Diary of David Zeisberger* (Cincinnati: Clarke, 1885), Vol. 1, pp. 78-82. Also Georg Heinrich Loskiel: *History of the Mission of the United Brethren Among the Indians in North America* (London, 1794).
3 Schweinitz, *op. cit.*, p. 548.
4 Roosevelt, *op. cit.*, p. 103.
5 *Ibid.*

15

Passive Resistance in Hungary, 1859-1867

From January to June 1904 the weekly Dublin newspaper *The United Irishman* published a serial by Arthur Griffith titled *The Resurrection of Hungary: A Parallel for Ireland.*[1] Reprinted in booklet form and widely distributed for more than a decade, it has been described as "a milestone on the road to Easter Rising,"[2] the armed rebellion of 1916 which led through protracted guerrilla warfare in 1918-1921 to the founding of the Irish Free State. Its thirty-two-year-old author was the principal organizer of the Sinn Fein movement that began in 1907.

Many things have been forgotten since then—for instance, the fact that Sinn Fein, later known for its terrorism, originated as a movement of passive resistance with hunger strikers as its early heroes. Griffith's record of an earlier Hungarian movement has often been retold in pacifist circles, handed down from one author to the next and becoming ever more abbreviated and cryptic while the sole source, Griffith's booklet, became a rarity. Although most of Griffith's text has recently been reprinted, there are important aspects which it does not cover and which are only now made public beyond the specialized range of the sources. Most striking of these is the crucial role of the Protestant churches. In addition to my own research, I have relied to an incalculable extent on the assistance of Elemer Bako, Hungarian Research Librarian of the Library of Congress, who provided bibliographical data and translated

Magyar sources on the church struggle that forms part of the following account.

The Mounting Storm

Hungary, once an independent kingdom, had been under Austrian rule for more than a century when, in 1828, its people refused to recognize the right of the Habsburg emperor to order a levy of troops. Only a Hungarian Diet, they insisted, had the power to do this. Thus began five years of agitation climaxed by an imperial decree ordering elections to be held which gave Hungary limited autonomy in the conduct of its internal affairs. This concession did not placate the Magyars, however. After 1833 they clamored for more—first for such limited goals as a national education program and later for restoration of Hungary's independence.

In 1847, under the leadership of Lajos Kossuth, the Magyars succeeded in wringing a constitution from the Habsburgs, but the following year was a hectic one. Wallachian, Serbian and Croatian troops attacked the forces of Kossuth but were repulsed. The Austrian viceroy arrived in Budapest to revoke the constitution and was assassinated. A democratic revolution broke out in Vienna and Kossuth sent Hungarian troops to its aid. An Austrian counterinvasion was thrown back by the Hungarians. In April 1849 Kossuth proclaimed Hungary a republic but fled into exile when forces of the Russian Tsar moved in and returned control to the Habsburgs. The Diet was suppressed, the constitution abrogated; even county councils were banned and the nation was carved up into military districts administered by Austrian officers.

Lutheran and Reformed churches bore a heavy brunt for their support of the short-lived Kossuth regime. Following its defeat many pastors and several bishops were imprisoned. Protestants were forbidden the title of bishop and autonomous church organizations were dissolved. Imperial administrators adjusted church districts to correspond to military zones and

sent Austrian officers to watch over church meetings. A decade
passed before Hungarian churchmen were able to make any
concerted effort to overcome these disabilities, which in any
case were for the most part lifted in a year to be reimposed
later.

On the political scene, meanwhile, who was to fill the position of leadership vacated by the exiled Kossuth?

One of the men who had been elected to the Diet of 1833
was a twenty-nine-year-old lawyer named Ferencz Deák, a
member of the Roman Catholic landed gentry and a descendant
of Verboczy, the author of Hungary's ancient Corpus Juris. Not
only an able jurist, Deák possessed wide knowledge of the
judicial systems of other countries. A monarchist and tradition-
alist who was once likened to Edmund Burke, he was of such
moral caliber that he refused to accept re-election to the Diet
in 1843 because of unscrupulous conduct ending in bloodshed
by members of both parties. He explained to a friend that he
would "always see bloodstains upon the mandate." Nevertheless, it was Deák who drafted the Liberal Program of 1847,
and in the following year he accepted the post of minister of
justice in Kossuth's government, parting with the latter when
the republic was declared.

After the debacle of 1849 the nation looked to Deák for
leadership, regardless of class or party, and it was to him that
the Austrian minister of justice turned in 1850 to confer on
Hungarian affairs. Deák, however, declined, stating that such
a conference could have no legal basis unless the constitution
was restored. He cautioned his countrymen to be patient and
neither concede the right of the Austrians to rule nor seek to
repel them by force. "The publication of his letter of refusal,"
wrote one historian, "made the nation understand that hence-
forth the watchword of all patriots must be 'passive resistance.' " [3]

At first this was largely a waiting game. When the Austrians
in 1850 began to replace the military districts with civil administration, many Magyars grudgingly accepted minor offices, but

most of the educated held aloof from taking posts of responsibility. Except for the abortive Makk conspiracy of 1852, said one of Deák's biographers, the people "refrained with striking unanimity . . . from isolated acts of violence." [4]

The 1850s were a hard period for Hungarian Protestants especially. In 1855 the Habsburgs signed a concordat with the Vatican, giving Catholic bishops authority over the state educational system and attempting to integrate the institutions of Hungarian Catholicism within the structure of the Catholic Church of Austria, a move that provoked opposition from Hungarian Catholic clergy. A similar attempt was made to bring the Hungarian Protestant churches into a unified empire-wide arrangement in which they would forfeit their autonomy.

The Protestants resisted stubbornly. In 1857 a deputation of Hungarian Calvinists went to Vienna to explain their position to the Kaiser and received a polite but deaf hearing. A few months later, at the August session of the Trans-Tisza Church District in Debrecen, Hungary's "Calvinist Rome," it was decided to regard the government order as a mere "proposal," and a plan of educational administration was submitted as an alternative to the official Austrian one. In retaliation, Vienna revoked the right of the University of Debrecen to award diplomas, and added other penalties.

Both sides moved slowly until September 1859, when Vienna began concerted efforts to impose its will in a vigorous eight-month campaign, beginning with the issuance of an Imperial Patent which forbade church autonomy, together with an implementing decree detailing the steps to be taken by the churches.

On October 8, under these laws, Austria prohibited the holding of church district courts and authorized its military forces to disband them if they were held, unless they were reorganized according to the new plan.

At the October session in Debrecen, the Reformed Church's leaders gave their answer. Kálmán Tisza, who was later to become Hungary's first Protestant prime minister, declared the

Austrian move "a grave act, the intentions of which cannot be accepted or promoted without the coercion of our conscience and without contradicting our vows of office and making us renegades to our religious principles." [5] District Superintendent Emeric Révész drew up two detailed memoranda stating the church's case and not only presented them to the government but published them abroad, where their appearance in the *Edinburgh Review,* for example, garnered strong support in Scotland. He also made contact with British, Prussian and Dutch diplomats in Vienna and impressed them with the Hungarian Protestants' plight.

The Austrians countered with raids on the homes of bishops and moderators, many of whom were arrested and brought before magistrates. When these leaders were removed from their positions, the churches refused to fill the vacancies. The situation among the Lutherans was complicated by the fact that many of their congregations were not Magyar. The church historian, Mihály Bucsay, shows the extent of the resistance:

Among the Reformed there were only 25 congregations, i.e. about 1%, ready to let themselves be organized according to the Patent. Of the Lutherans, there were about 226 communities that went along, mostly German and Slovakian, with 333 resisting in spite of promises and threats. [6]

When the Trans-Tisza council, spearheading the struggle, met in Debrecen as scheduled on January 11, 1860, in defiance of the government order, the Kaiser's representative was at a loss to prevent it. Churchmen turned out in full force—500 church officials alone from the nearby parishes, in addition to thousands of laymen. Another church historian tells of the encounter:

Immediately after the opening prayer, the Austrian Imperial Government representative . . . stood up and called upon the meeting to disperse. The chairman [Deputy Bishop Peter Balogh] then asked those present whether they wished to disperse or not, whereupon the huge crowd roared in reply: "We shall hold the meeting;

we will not disperse." Then as the meeting proceeded, fear began to show on the face of the Imperial representative, as he saw thousands of angry eyes turned in scorn upon him. Finally, he could bear the situation no longer, and got up and left; and no one did him harm.[7]

Although he had troops stationed outside, he was evidently reluctant to use them in the face of such determined and unanimous opposition. Attempts were made to persuade a Debrecen delegation to yield to promises of monetary aid for parish administration and teaching personnel, but to no avail.

Turning to another tactic, the government bypassed church officials and ordered pastors directly to accept a slightly modified decree, which they were instructed to read from the pulpit on two successive Sundays. Emeric Révész immediately sent out a message to all churches reiterating the council's position and indicating that the amended decree was to be resisted as firmly as the original one. With the exception of one area which did not receive the message, every minister in Hungary, some 1,500 in all, refused to read the Patent from his pulpit. Many of them were arrested as a result.

Vienna pressed its offensive. During February and March the arrests continued. Not only pastors but bishops were taken to jail. Police broke up church meetings again and again, though sometimes the churchmen succeeded in keeping their meetings going in defiance of the authorities even when government officials were present. "Wherever it was learned that a church leader was to be speaking in defiance of the law," writes Imre Révész, "huge crowds would gather to hear him; the church resistance was thus turning into a national resistance."[8]

Students expressed their solidarity with arrested church leaders by going to the towns where their trials were held and conducting silent demonstrations, dressed in black. In the courtrooms the prisoners rejected any form of legal defense, contending simply that they had acted in accordance with their constitutional rights and liberties. Those who were not arrested proceeded to conduct church affairs as if the hated decree were nonexistent, and formed committees for the defense of church autonomy. When the Trans-Tisza District held its session on April 20 as scheduled, more than 5,000 laymen were present as a gesture of support.

Meanwhile, support from abroad was beginning to be felt. In January there was a mass meeting in Glasgow, and the British Government queried Vienna about the situation. In February the British prime minister spoke of it in Parliament. Leading newspapers in England, France and Prussia took up the cause of the Hungarian Protestants, and it was rumored that the Roman Catholic Primate of Hungary was preparing to lead a delegation of Hungarian Catholics to consult with the Kaiser and seek a solution. Throughout the struggle, in fact, the beleaguered Protestants received moral support from their Catholic countrymen.

Confronted with its inability to break the resistance of the churches by armed force without running the grave risk of precipitating a new national rebellion and piqued by its faltering prestige abroad, the Austrian Government looked for a way to extricate itself gracefully from the impasse. The Kaiser appointed a new Imperial Governor, the Hungarian Protestant, Field Marshal Lajos Benedek, and on May 15 revoked the decree and substituted a mild alternative which exempted all congregations that did not accept it. The Patent remained formally in effect, but its application to the Protestant churches was nullified and all the arrested ministers were freed.

Compromise, Habsburg Style

This setback for the Habsburg monarchy turned the tide not only for the Protestant churches but for the nation as a whole. The example of resistance was to prove valuable in the near future.

At first it seemed possible that a conciliatory course might yield political concessions in the new atmosphere that seemed to be arising. A few months after its revocation of the church decree, Vienna instituted a limited form of self-government in Hungary and asked Ferencz Deák to serve in it as Judex Curiae. Deák declined, but he was elected to the Pest County Assembly the following year and persuaded it to enact laws necessary for recruiting soldiers and levying taxes, even though he still considered these measures a concession to an unconstitutional regime. Again he continued to warn his countrymen of the folly of seeking to win their objectives by violence: "You may blow up whole fortresses with gunpowder, but you cannot build the smallest hut with it." [9]

Deák's cautious optimism was betrayed by a new turn of events with the promulgation of a royal rescript creating an Imperial Parliament without Hungary's consent. It now became clear that the crown's intention was to lead the Hungarians toward amalgamation rather than toward autonomy. Deák gave Hungary's reply in an address to the Diet, which approved it unanimously and dispatched it to Vienna:

If it be necessary to suffer, the nation will submit to suffering, in order to preserve and hand down to future generations that constitutional liberty it has inherited from its forebears. It will suffer without losing courage, as its ancestors have endured and suffered, to be able to defend the rights of the country; for what might and power take away, time and favorable circumstances may restore; but the recovery of what a nation renounces of its own accord from fear of suffering is a matter of difficulty and uncertainty. The nation will suffer, hoping for a better future and trusting to the justice of its cause.[10]

Deák made clear the principle that was at stake: "It is sought to transfer to a foreign assembly sitting in the capital of a foreign country the right to make laws for ourselves and our children. Who will acquiesce? No one!" [11] The only legal solution, Deák maintained, was for the Habsburg Kaiser, Franz Josef, to accept the Hungarian Constitution promulgated in 1847 and come to Buda to be crowned Hungary's legitimate sovereign. Unless these conditions were met, the Kaiser was in effect a usurper to the legally vacant Hungarian throne.

Franz Josef's answer came on August 21, 1861. On that day he dissolved the Hungarian Diet. When the Pest County Council protested, it too was ordered dissolved. Defying the Kaiser's authority to do this, the councilmen refused to leave the council chamber until Austrian troops entered and forced them out. Other county councils throughout the nation followed suit, refusing to transfer their services to the Austrians. The constitution, already abrogated, was formally suspended by a royal rescript in November, and the country was placed once again under Austrian military rule.

In calling once more for passive resistance, Deák said: "Let us make ourselves as disagreeable to them [the Austrians] as we can." Clearly he did not conceive of this strategy as a manifestation of Christian love. But he firmly admonished his people to avoid resorting to acts of violence and to adhere to justice and law—Hungarian justice and Hungarian law. For the struggle as he saw it was precisely against Austrian injustice and illegality. "This is the safe ground," he said, "on which, unarmed ourselves, we can hold our own against armed force. If suffering be necessary, suffer with dignity."

The order was obeyed. Griffith tells us how:

When the Austrian tax-collector came to gather the taxes the people did not beat him or hoot him—they declined to pay him, assuring him he was a wholly illegal person. The tax-collector thereupon called in the police, and the police seized the man's goods. Then the Hungarian auctioneer declined to auction them, and an Austrian of his profession had to be brought down. When he arrived he discovered he would have to bring bidders from Austria too. The Austrian Government found in time that it was costing them more to fail to collect the taxes than the taxes if they were collected would realize. In the hope of breaking the spirit of the Hungarians, the Austrians decreed that soldiers should be billeted upon them. The Hungarians did not resist the decree—but the Austrian soldier after a little experience of the misery of living in the house of a man who despises you, very strongly resisted it. And the Hungarians asserted that from their enforced close acquaintance with the Austrian army they found it to be an institution they could not permit their sons, for their souls' sake, to enter, wherefore they proposed that enlistment in the Austrian army was treason to Hungary, and it was carried unanimously.[12]

When the Imperial Parliament met in Vienna it was boycotted by the Hungarian representatives. Within nine months of the Kaiser's high-handed dissolution of the Hungarian Diet, Austria had become a laughingstock throughout Europe. "Passive resistance," the London *Times* editorialized, "can be so organized as to become more troublesome than armed rebellion." [13]

Although the Diet remained dissolved, its members continued to meet informally under other auspices, not quite "underground"—in agricultural, trade and literary circles: a device practiced by Basque republicans under Franco through soccer teams, and by a later generation of Hungarians in the Petöfi Circle of the 1950s. Hungarian businessmen resolved in their trade meetings of the 1860s, for example, that it was sound economics for Hungarian buyers to choose Hungarian goods rather than Austrian goods. "The results of these discussions," Griffith observed, "had a force as binding as law upon the people." [14]

For a brief period, Austria tried to cope with the Hungarians' economic warfare by issuing an ordinance that declared "exclusive trading" illegal. The Magyars flouted this law with such solidarity that it became unenforceable. "A few months of the jail-filling process," wrote Griffith, "and Austria found herself in another *cul-de-sac*." [15] Nationalism flourished in the Magyar press and "the Hungarian historical novel became a feature of the time." When a minor famine struck the land in 1863 the people's united morale enabled them to endure it.

It was shortly after this, in 1864, that Austria joined with Prussia in a war against Denmark over the question of Schleswig-Holstein. There was talk among some Hungarians of seizing this occasion for an insurrection, but wiser counsels prevailed, recognizing that to be successful Hungary would need the support of larger powers. To revolt at this time would invite collision with the whole North German Confederation. Deák continued to play his waiting game. Meanwhile Bohemia, after participating in the Imperial Parliament at Vienna for two years, had recalled its deputies in derision, thus further weakening Austria's position.

Franz Josef now took tentative steps to mollify the Hungarians. On December 14 he appeared in Pest in person to reopen the Hungarian Diet, in which Deák was the key figure as "minister, jurist, diplomatist and party leader." [16] The Kaiser's motives were not impeccable. Bismarck, the Prussian chancellor, was maneuvering him toward a showdown that was to come in the *Brüderkrieg* of 1866, a seven-week war that consolidated Prussia's hegemony among the numerous German states and laid the basis for the powerful German Empire that was soon to be established. The decisive battle of the war was lost by Austria at Königgrätz on July 3. Before the outbreak of war the Kaiser had been anxious to placate the Magyars to the extent that they would not resort to insurrection. Not only did he have Deák to contend with, but Bismarck had authorized the exiled Hungarian leader, György Klapka, to form a Hungarian legion equipped with Prussian arms. Now the Kaiser was in desperate straits. A few days after the Königgrätz disaster he summoned Deák to Vienna.

Deák arrived at the imperial palace at midnight. The Kaiser said to him abruptly: "Well, Deák, what shall I do now?"

The Hungarian leader's reply was direct: "Your Majesty must first make peace and then give Hungary her rights."

"Will the Hungarian Diet give me men to carry on the war if I grant it the Constitution at once?" the Kaiser asked.

Deák's answer was "No. I will not make the restoration of my country's freedom a matter of barter." [17]

Deák's waiting game was nearing its end. His refusal to accede to Franz Josef's request sealed Austria's defeat in the war.

In the months ahead, the Kaiser made a number of ostensibly conciliatory overtures, hoping to settle the Hungarian question without meeting Deák's demands. On December 15, a communication from the Hungarian Diet, drafted by Deák, was sent to Franz Josef, making it clear that none of the latter's proposals would even be considered until Deák's demands were conceded.

The Kaiser's ill-considered reply was a decree of compulsory military service which, but for Deák's cool restraint, could have plunged Hungary into a desperate insurrection. Deák persuaded the Diet to send a deputation to Vienna to resolve the crisis as a last-ditch effort before yielding to the clamor for revolt. Both for Hungary and for Austria the situation had become most precarious, and an insurrection might have proved costly to both in the face of Prussia's ambitions.

The Kaiser saw the handwriting on the wall and to Deák's surprise rescinded the odious army law. In another two months events moved rapidly to a climax. Franz Josef reshuffled his cabinet, assigning the post of prime minister to Count Beust, a statesman with whom Deák had already reached an unwritten understanding a few months earlier. Julius Andrassy, a Magyar nobleman who had once had a price on his head for his part in the 1848 revolution, was invited to form a national cabinet for Hungary.

On February 18, 1867, the Kaiser restored the Hungarian Constitution. Deák and Beust signed a compact establishing a dual monarchy and Franz Josef was crowned King of Hungary. Deák's work was done. He had accomplished it by a combination of able statesmanship, patience and passive resistance.

The outcome was not greeted with universal rejoicing in the empire. "The dualist system," as Oszkar Jaszi has pointed out, "maintained the pyramid further on its head with the small correction that they heightened the base from six to twelve million by the addition of five million Magyars and a million Magyar-Germans. This new basis was manifestly unstable against the will of eighteen million people." [18]

In forty years the synthesis came apart at the seams and the empire collapsed. Austria became a small republic and Hungary a small, kingless monarchy. Probably for this reason the name of Ferencz Deák, which shone so brightly for a time, has become obscured.

For our present purposes, however, we are not concerned with debating the stature of Deák or to argue for his perspicacity as a statesman. His importance consists in the fact that he used passive resistance successfully as an integral part of a sustained campaign to achieve an historic goal. As the foregoing account shows, passive resistance alone did not bring the desired result, but it formed a crucial element among other factors, and was the only one over which the Hungarians had complete control. Had they not persevered in this strategy over a period of two decades it is highly likely that they would have failed to make use of the gratuitous leverages (such as those arising from Austria's position vis-a-vis Prussia) that developed during that period.

Unlike the Moravian nonresistants, Deák and his followers were in no sense committed to nonviolence as an article of faith. Their choice of passive resistance was made on wholly pragmatic grounds on a realistic assessment of their situation, although it undoubtedly owed something to Christian motives in the church campaign. Insurrection had been tried once with disastrous results. Although it was kept periodically under review, prudence dictated an alternative course of action which in the end validated itself by its results.

REFERENCES IN CHAPTER 15

1 Arthur Griffith: *The Resurrection of Hungary* (Dublin: James Duffy and Co., 1904). Extracts are reprinted in a book edited by Mulford Q. Sibley: *The Quiet Battle* (Garden City, N.Y.: Doubleday & Co., Anchor Books, 1963), pp. 137-155.
2 Edgar Holt: *Protest in Arms* (New York: Coward-McCann, Inc., 1961), p. 24.

3   C. M. Knatchbull-Hugessen: *The Political Evolution of the Hungarian Nation* (London: National Review Office, 1908), p. 147f.
4   F. M. Arnold-Forster: *Francis Deák* (London: The Macmillan Co., 1880), p. 119.
5   Quoted in Mihály Zsilinszky, ed.: *A Magyarhoni Protestáns Egyhas Története* (Budapest: Athenaeum, 1907), Vol. 4.
6   Mihály Bucsay: *Geschichte des Protestantismus in Ungarn* (Stuttgart: Evangelisches Verlagswerk, 1959), p. 175.
7   Imre Révész: *History of the Hungarian Reformed Church* (Washington: Hungarian Reformed Federation of America, 1956), p. 128.
8   *Ibid.*, p. 132.
9   Quoted in Arnold-Forster, *op. cit.*
10 Quoted in *ibid.*, p. 195.
11 Quoted in A. Fenner Brockway: *Non-Cooperation in Other Lands* (Madras: Tagore and Co., 1921), p. 13.
12 Arthur Griffith, *op. cit.*, p. 57.
13 *Times* (London), August 24, 1861. Quoted in *ibid.*
14 Griffith, *op. cit.*, p. 58.
15 *Ibid.*
16 Arnold-Forster, *op. cit.*, p. 224.
17 Quoted in *ibid.*, p. 237. Compare with Brockway, *op. cit.*, p. 20.
18 Oszkar Jaszi: *The Dissolution of the Habsburg Monarchy* (Chicago: University of Chicago Press, 1929), p. 105.

16

Civil Resistance in Finland, 1898-1905

The situation of Finland under Romanov rule in the Nineteenth Century bears some resemblances to that of Hungary under the Habsburgs, aside from the incidental fact of their common ethnic heritage. Conquered by Sweden in the Twelfth Century, the grand duchy of Finland was ceded to the Russian Empire in 1809. Under Russian rule, Finland was autonomous in its conduct of domestic policy, enacting its own laws through its own parliament, but foreign affairs were conducted on its behalf by the Russian Imperial Court at St. Petersburg, and Russian tsars were monarchs of Finland as well.

For nearly a century this arrangement was largely satisfactory to the population of Finland, and the country prospered culturally and economically, without Russian interference in its internal affairs. But the rise of Pan-Slavism in Russian ruling circles led, in the latter decades of the century, to a series of Russification measures. In 1889 Tsar Aleksandr III annulled certain reforms of the criminal law that had been voted by the Finnish Diet; in 1890 the postal service was brought under Russian control; in 1891 certain officials were required to know the Russian language.

Soon after the coronation of Nikolai II more strenuous moves toward Russification were made, largely at the instigation of Konstantin Pobedonostsev, procurator of the Holy Synod of the Russian Orthodox Church, a man identified both with efforts to raise the spiritual level of the Russian clergy and with draconic persecution of dissenting sects and the Russification of minorities throughout the empire. To execute the policy of the new tsar and of Pobedonostsev, General Nikolai I. Bobrikov, who had earned a reputation as a tough Russianizer in the Baltic provinces, was appointed Governor-General of Finland in 1898.

One of Bobrikov's first acts was to call a special session of the Finnish Diet to enact a new army bill. Under an act of 1878 the peacetime strength of the Finnish Army had been set at 5600, with a reserve of 20,000, for the sole purpose of defending Finnish territory. Every adult male was liable to ninety days of compulsory military service, spread over a period of three years. Bobrikov's bill, however, not only raised the term of service to five years but decreed that Finns be conscripted into Russian units, placed Russian officers in command of Finnish regiments, and made the latter an integral part of the Russian armed forces, liable to service anywhere in the empire.

The Diet unanimously rejected the new army bill, whereupon Bobrikov, on February 15, 1899, published an imperial manifesto in which the Tsar arrogated to himself the right to decide what affairs were to be discussed by the Diet and in effect reduced the Diet to a consultative rather than a legislative body.

The Tsar Demurs

Both the Senate and the Diet sent delegations to the Tsar, but neither was received. A constitutional bloc was then formed as a national front representing various political and social groupings. Despite censorship of the press and of the mails, a petition was circulated throughout the nation and 522,931 signatures were secured within two weeks. (The total population of Finland at the time, including children, was about 2,700,000.) Five hundred men from every district of the country made their way to St. Petersburg undetected by Bobrikov's agents, to present the petition to the Tsar. An international deputation bearing a similar petition was also organized. Among its thousand signatories were Herbert Spencer, Florence Nightingale, Emile Zola, Anatole France, Theodor Mommsen and Henrik Ibsen. The Tsar refused to receive either of these deputations. The army bill was implemented by imperial decree. J. Hampden Jackson gives a concise account of the next steps:

There followed a regime of calculated oppression in Finland. Bobrikov abolished all rights of freedom of speech and assembly. He attempted to enforce the Army Bill by calling up a batch of 25,000 conscripts. Of these 15,000 refused to serve. He could not imprison 15,000 men but he could and did banish seventeen publicists who defended them and dismiss fifteen judges who upheld their case. He replaced the Finnish police, provincial governors and mayors by Russians. He dismissed three hundred civil servants from their posts. He disbanded the Finnish Army and filled the barracks in Helsinki and other towns with Russians. And he made the teaching of Russian compulsory as the principal foreign language in schools.[1]

In response to these measures the Finns resorted to passive resistance. Anatole G. Mazour gives an excellent summary of the form it took during its first phase:

High Finnish authorities refused to attach their signatures to official papers as was required by law; judges paid little attention to recently promulgated legislation or executive orders. . . . Parents were advised to overlook orders requiring their children to be taught Russian. A secret patriotic society was organized for the purpose of drafting petitions and drawing up protests, organizing public demonstrations, rendering legal aid and assisting Finnish emigration or disrupting the enforcement of conscription. All this was carried on while Finnish authorities did little to interfere. Teachers openly advocated passive resistance among their pupils. The Lutheran clergy defiantly preached from the pulpits and appealed for aid for the national cause.[2]

To circumvent press censorship the constitutional bloc launched a publication, *Fria Ord* (Free Words), in Stockholm, which was circulated clandestinely among the Finnish populace. These and other activities from underground and from exile kept up the morale of the people and provided links of communication among them in the face of ubiquitous Russian power.

For more than five years the struggle continued. The Finns held fast to civil resistance despite increasing repressions by their Russian overlords. Under pressure from one of Bobrikov's most odious tactics, however, a rift was precipitated in the otherwise steadfastly nonviolent resistance. This tactic was the use of agents provocateurs, men hired by the Okhrana, the tsarist secret police, to commit acts of violence against the Russian authorities in order to provide tangible excuses for repressions against the Finns or to provoke the Finns themselves to adopt violent methods. Thus began a round of violent incidents secretly engineered by the Russians against themselves, then savagely revenged upon the Finns by the Tsar's Cossack regiments. These repressions were authorized by a 1903 regulation giving Bobrikov dictatorial powers "for the maintenance of state order and public peace in Finland." At the same time, additional Russification measures were adopted.

Instead of shattering Finnish resistance, Bobrikov's new actions recoiled upon him. He was assassinated on June 16, 1904, by a young Finnish patriot, Eugen Schauman, the son of a former senator, who then committed suicide. Soon afterward a Russian army officer, Lieutenant-Colonel Kramarenko, was assassinated, and an attempt was made on the life of the Russian governor of Viipuri, M. A. Myasoyedov. These and other such violent acts were committed out of desperation by Finns who were in contact with the Russian Social Revolutionary Party. They also collected arms for a possible insurrection.

An Alliance Takes Shape

But passive resistance was not yet over. Its second phase was to come from a new quarter, the fast-growing labor movement. The first Finnish trade union had been founded in 1883, holding its first political congress a decade later. In 1895 the socialist newspaper *Työmies* (The Worker) was founded, advocating replacement of the old Diet of four estates with a unicameral legislature based on universal and equal suffrage, in addition to free public schools, an eight-hour work day and other reforms. Much of the support of the Finnish Social Democratic Party which had evolved by 1903 came from agricultural laborers as well as urban workers. Though numerically small (13,500 in 1903), it was well organized. When Russia was defeated in its war against Japan in 1905 the Finnish Social Democrats knew exactly what to do. They called a general strike. Jackson provides the details:

Trains stopped, telegraphs went dead, factories stood empty. This lead was followed spontaneously by the whole nation: shops, offices, schools, restaurants, were shut. The police went on strike and . . . university students formed a corps to maintain order. . . . There was no bloodshed; it was merely passive resistance with a whole nation behind it.[3]

On the sixth day the Tsar's government, which was beleaguered by insurrection in St. Petersburg, came to terms with the Finns, rescinding Bobrikov's innovations and re-establishing constitutional government with a new Diet elected by the votes of every citizen twenty-four years old or more, with no property qualifications or privileges, male and female alike. In the first elections under the new system, held in 1907, the Social Democrats won eighty out of the 200 seats.

If the situation had stabilized at this point we could record a magnificent triumph for nonviolence. But within two years, having consolidated its power after the 1905 upheavals, the tsarist government turned once more to efforts at Russification, this time by clever manipulations of law rather than by the outright illegality of Bobrikov. During this period there was sporadic passive resistance, such as the refusal of twenty-three members of the Viipuri Court to give a dictated judgment on a test case. For this they were tried by a Russian tribunal and imprisoned in a Russian jail. Also, two-thirds of the Finnish pilot service resigned in protest against control by Russian maritime officials.

Finland retained some of the gains won through passive resistance. Even through World War I, the Finns were exempt from Russian military service. But at the same time, the Russians with impunity doubled the sum which Finland was required to pay in lieu of supplying soldiers, and the Russian War Office built fortifications and moved its troops freely on Finnish soil. Leaders who dared to speak out against Russification, such as the Speaker of the Diet, Per Svinhufvud, were exiled to Siberia.

During the same decade, Finland—or at least Finnish capitalists—enjoyed unprecedented economic prosperity. Fortunes were to be made supplying the inexhaustible Russian war machine. This fact explains much of the inability of the nation to unite as it had done in 1905. In the end, class divisions were to result in civil war at the hour of independence. Twenty-four thousand Finnish lives were lost in 1918 before a republic was established. Social Democratic leaders were imprisoned or exiled by the nationalist forces of Field Marshal Mannerheim.

As in the case of Hungary, we see once again in Finland the great possibilities inherent in a united nonviolent resistance, but also the extent to which these possibilities hinge upon external factors over which the resisters have no control. The dominant role assumed by the general strike of 1905 depended chiefly upon Russia's defeat in the Russo-Japanese War and upon the subsequent crisis of the tsarist regime in the widespread revolts of that year. Granted these facts, however, the Finnish general strike was a decisive event. It did not usher in the millennium. Many of the gains it achieved were lost in a few years, though others endured through independence and after. And in the end the same people who had managed to hold out against the Russians largely without bloodshed were to slay one another with savage ferocity. There is a profound historical irony here and its salient lesson is that the successful use of passive resistance at one moment in history is a means proportionate to the ends it achieves and not a blank check on future developments.

REFERENCES IN CHAPTER 16

1 J. Hampden Jackson: *Finland* (New York: The Macmillan Co., 1940), p. 68. For further documentation see Mazour, cited below, and the following: Magnus Gottfried Schyberson: *Politische Geschichte Finnlands, 1809-1919* (Stuttgart: Perthes Verlag, 1925); John Henry Wuorinen: *Nationalism in Modern Finland* (New York: Columbia University Press, 1931); and H. Seton-Watson: *The Decline of Imperial Russia, 1855-1914* (New York: Frederick A. Praeger, Inc., 1952).
2 Anatole G. Mazour: *Finland Between East and West* (Princeton, N.J.: D. Van Nostrand Company, Inc., copyright 1956), p. 22.
3 Jackson, *op. cit.,* p. 74.

17

Denmark and Norway, 1940-1943

Nonviolent resistance to the Nazi army of occupation in Denmark and Norway during World War II strongly resembles, in certain respects, the Finnish civil resistance of 1898-1905. The countries invaded were relatively small and ethnically homogeneous, and it was the policy of the German invader not, as in Eastern Europe, to destroy existing political institutions and enslave the population, but to subordinate and manipulate them for the invader's purposes. Although in many ways the Third Reich was more totalitarian than the Romanov Empire, it differed in one point favorable to the Danes and Norwegians. For the Finns were outsiders to the ethnic ideology of Pan-Slavism that figured in tsarist Russia's encroachments, while the Danes and Norwegians, perhaps even purer Nordics than the Germans themselves, were claimed by the Nazis as kinsmen, fellow members of the "master race." Hence, unlike any of the other countries invaded by Nazi Germany, these two nations were given preferential treatment. It is instructive to note, by contrast, that when Germany attacked the USSR many Russians welcomed them as liberators, only to become disillusioned and embittered as a result of the ruthless treatment they received as *Untermenschen* in the Nazi ideology. So rigid were the Nazi racial attitudes that they virtually blotted out any chance of a moral appeal by anyone categorized as racially inferior, such as Jews or Slavs. And by the same token the Danes and Norwegians (and to some extent the Dutch) were punished in a much milder way when they resisted, and not at all when they did not. Hence it is not possible to generalize from the experience of these countries without also altering the basic given fact of the Nazi race theory and its implications. If this is done, however, there are undoubtedly lessons to be drawn from this segment of history which would apply to situations involving a nonracist type of totalitarianism.

Denmark Under the Nazis

Both Denmark and Norway were invaded in 1940. Of the two, the latter is of greater interest from the standpoint of nonviolence, but the story of Denmark must first be told briefly.[1] This country capitulated without armed resistance, submitting to a one-hour ultimatum to admit German troops. In return, it was assured that Germany would not interfere with constitutional liberties. There was a general coldness toward the invaders, but no serious attempt to make their stay untenable. When the Nazis violated the occupation treaty by hoisting a German flag from a Danish public building, King Christian announced that he would personally remove it if the Nazis did not. They did. Again, the Danish Government repudiated the Anti-Comintern Pact after the Germans had persuaded the Danish prime minister to sign it. In 1942, when the Nazis decreed that Denmark's 8,000 Jews must wear the yellow Star of David, the King made it a point to attend a celebration in a Copenhagen synagogue. His stand was affirmed in protests by the Bishop of Sjaelland and other Lutheran clergy.

Not until August 1943, however, did the Danes resort to determined resistance. Demonstrations flared into a general strike in the major cities. These were quickly crushed by German troops. A military state of emergency was declared on August 28 and reinforcements were sent in. The King was placed under house arrest, the cabinet resigned and the Danish Parliament, which had continued to exist as a democratically elected body, dissolved itself. Thousands of Danes were killed in reprisal for their defiance. A rash plan to destroy Copenhagen by artillery fire was thwarted only by the cleverness of an anti-Nazi German shipping expert attached to the German legation, Georg Ferdinand Duckwitz. For the rest of the war the Danish underground fought the Germans with sabotage and guerrilla attacks.

One more episode must be reported. In September, Duckwitz told Danish political leaders of a Nazi plan to round up all the Jews on the night of October 1. With lightning speed the Danes spread the report by word of mouth. On September 30 in the Copenhagen synagogue the news was received. When the raid came, only 472 Jews were caught. All the others had gone into hiding—in Protestant churches, in Catholic cloisters, in the homes of friends and strangers, in hotels and on farms. Subsequently, in a remarkably well-organized fashion the Jews were taken by taxi or other means to the seacoast and from there smuggled across the narrow straits of Öre Sound by fishing boat, rowboat and canoe to neutral Sweden, embarking at night to evade German sea patrols. Some 7,500 Jews were thus taken to safety under the noses of the ruthless enemy.[2]

The Norwegian Resistance

The Norwegians responded more vigorously to the invasion, meeting the Germans with armed resistance which lasted for two months. The King and parliamentary leaders escaped to England and formed a government-in-exile. Once the brief but vigorous armed defense ended, the Norwegians quickly adjusted to the mild terms of the occupation forced upon them by the invaders. Attracted by high profits, Norwegian businessmen accepted contracts to furnish the Nazis with military goods. Trade unions were assigned Nazi puppet officials and although resistance quickly developed, the lure of high wages at first had a delaying effect. These were the first steps in a series of moves by which the German occupation authorities sought to transform the nation's democratic institutions into either German agencies or the tools of an indigenous Nazi-type political organization, the Nasjonal Samling. At the top level, this process was consummated in September 1940 with a series of decrees which abolished all political parties except the Nasjonal Samling.

This puppet government, headed by Vidkun Quisling but under the virtual control of German Reichskommissar Terboven, created a Norwegian equivalent of the Nazi S.A. known as the Hird, which frequently joined with both German and Norwegian political police in combating resistance.

The first real gesture of resistance came when the Norwegian Supreme Court resigned in December in protest against Nazi decrees which violated Norway's democratic laws. During the same period the Nazis dissolved the country's numerous sports clubs and replaced them with new ones, which were so completely boycotted by Norwegian sportsmen that no public games were played throughout the occupation. At the University of Oslo, the student union was abolished, but its Nazi successor was boycotted out of existence, and lecturers appointed to teach Nazi ideology ceased to teach when no one attended their classes.

Regulations were issued which abolished the executive functions of local councilors and appointed new mayors wherever possible, with dictatorial powers. In the dwindling number of communities in which the old mayors remained, they ignored these regulations and continued to consult with their councils in accordance with prewar democratic procedures.

The two most notable sectors of resistance were the churches and the schools. Although teachers bore a harder brunt during this period, it was a time of testing for the church. Bishop Eivind Berggrav wrote in a message to the Swedish Church Assembly in May 1941: "God has led the Norwegian Christians into the great melting pot where everything belonging to us has become small and God has become great." [3] In the midst of hardship there was a great resurgence of faith, symbolized by the return to the church of the noted liberal humanist, Dr. Kristian Schelderup, who was among outspoken and active Christians arrested in 1942. Although the struggle focused on the established Lutheran state church, other denominations rallied to its cause.

The first encroachment on the church was a decree expunging parliament and the King from the official church prayers. Pastors met this decree by saying this portion of the prayers in silence. A more serious clash occurred when Quisling's ministry of church affairs decreed that pastors must divulge to police on request any information given to them by parishioners in the privacy of the confessional, on penalty of imprisonment. This led first to a protest signed by all seven of the church's bishops and then, in defiance of the state authorities, to a pastoral letter that was read from every Lutheran pulpit in Norway and distributed in printed form. In addition to the interference in church affairs, the church protested the illegalities which had led the Supreme Court to resign, and the terrorist actions of the Hird. No concerted action was taken against the churches at this time, though an abortive attempt was made to recruit pastors into a Nazi-style "Christian Unity Movement." Only twenty pastors in the whole country joined, and they were boycotted by their congregations except for a handful of Quislingites.

Simultaneous with the attack on the church, a series of decrees required Quisling's portrait to be hung in school classrooms, made the teaching of Nazi doctrine compulsory, revised the history curriculum along Nazi lines, and substituted German for English as the second language. Backed up by parents and by the church, both teachers and students showed stiff opposition, in the face of which the authorities withdrew the decrees.

The Nazis renewed their attack on church and school a year later. In the meantime they were slowly consolidating their power, which provoked the trade unions to strike on September 8, 1941. With this as a pretext, a state of emergency was declared and terror reigned for a week under Gestapo auspices. Two strike leaders were shot and journalists and professional men were imprisoned along with hundreds of strikers. A thoroughgoing shakeup of the trade unions followed, extinguishing all vestiges of democracy and placing Quisling followers in firm control. Despite this apparent victory, however, throughout the war the industrial workers persistently engaged in slowdowns and in sabotaging machines to hamper war production, under the guidance of underground leaders.

In February 1942 the Quisling government began a new drive to erect a fascist "corporative state," with the Laerersamband, a compulsory teachers' association, and the Ungdomsfylking, a compulsory youth movement, as part of its structure. At the same time that these were set up, the lapsed decrees of 1941 were reinstated and an attack was launched against the church, beginning on February 1 when the dean of Nidaros Cathedral in Trondheim, Arne Fjellbu, was ordered to yield his pulpit to a Nazi pastor. When he defied the order, he was arrested and, after a preliminary hearing, deprived of his office. While this was happening, Quisling promulgated the law requiring children from ten to eighteen years old to join the Ungdomsfylking. On February 14 Norway's seven bishops lodged a protest against this law as abrogating the right of parents to decide about their children's education, and as inculcating the children with ideas that did not have parental approval. This protest was reiterated from the pulpit throughout the nation on February 22 and was followed by an avalanche of letters written by parents to government officials. On February 24 the bishops resigned their administrative posts in the state church, while asserting their spiritual leadership of the church's congregations—in other words, repudiating the authority of an unjust state and disestablishing the church.

The state responded by dismissing the bishops and prohibiting them from exercising any ecclesiastical functions. They arrested Eivind Berggrav, Bishop of Oslo and the titular head of the church, and Bishop Hille of Hamar. For most of the war's duration, Berggrav was kept under guard in his summer house.

The teachers meanwhile were given until March 15 to comply with the order to join the Laerersamband, and in the interval the schools were closed. The deadline passed and the teachers did not give in. On March 20, arrests began and totaled 1,300 by the end of the month. Some were held as long as eight months. In his definitive pamphlet, *Tyranny Could Not Quell Them* (London: Peace News, n.d.), Gene Sharp has told in detail how approximately half of the total number of arrested teachers were turned over to the Gestapo at the Jorstadmoen concentration camp and subjected to "torture gymnastics" and other harsh treatment for a week in an effort to force them to capitulate. Only thirty-two out of 687 gave in. The rest were subsequently sent to Kirkenes, a village in the far north, above the Arctic Circle, and set at hard labor under frugal conditions of clothing and shelter, guarded by Wehrmacht troops. During their imprisonment the underground resistance movement, aided by the government-in-exile in London, sent to the family of each prisoner an allotment equal to the salary he would have been paid as a teacher.

When the schools reopened on April 8, a small number of teachers stayed out, making arrangements to teach privately. The majority returned to their classrooms but remained adamant in their refusal to join the Laerersamband.

Even before this, on Palm Sunday, March 29, a confession of faith titled "The Church's Foundation," drafted by Bishop Berggrav, was surreptitiously distributed throughout the nation and on Easter was read from the pulpit.[4] Congregations were asked to rise as a sign of assent, and only a handful of Nazi sympathizers remained seated. Some ninety-three per cent of all Norway's Lutheran pastors then announced their resignation from the administration of the state church, as the bishops had done earlier. Clergy and church officials were subjected to harassment, placed under house arrest or banished from their homes, and in some cases prosecuted for trumped-up offenses.

Quisling arrogated to himself the position of head of the state church and appointed unqualified laymen and theological students from among his followers to replace the resigned pastors and bishops. The church set up a provisional council to carry on the work of the deposed bishops. Quisling branded it illegal, but parishioners boycotted his pastoral appointees and by the end of the year he was forced to recognize the provisional council and abandon his efforts to control the church.

Likewise, faced with such determined resistance by teachers, students and parents, Quisling abandoned his scheme of nazifying youth and the schools. After a faltering and ludicrous attempt to nazify the trade union movement in similar fashion, Quisling was ordered by Hitler to abandon his attempt to set up a corporative state.

The balance sheet at the close of 1942 showed impressive results for nonviolence, but nothing that could be called victory. The nonviolent movement succeeded in preserving the integrity of the church and of stalemating the corporative state. During the same period, however, a hundred Norwegians were executed, 7,000 were imprisoned in concentration camps and 1,000 were deported to Germany and to Nazi-occupied countries such as Poland. Although as in Denmark the Norwegians made it clear to the German troops that they were unwelcome, no serious attempt was made to persuade them to desert, nor was any effort made to disrupt the economy or the political order so as to make it impossible for the occupation to continue.

In effect, the Norwegian nonviolent resistance was a defensive operation—at best, a holding action which gave way in 1943-1944 to a program of sabotage led by trained guerrillas parachuted from British aircraft, augmented by open clashes between workers and Hird troops and the assassination of SS and Gestapo men.

REFERENCES IN CHAPTER 17

1   For a full account, see David Lampe: *The Danish Resistance* (New York: Ballantine Books, Inc., 1960). Also John Danstrup: *A History of Denmark* (Copenhagen: Wivel, 1948), pp. 173-195.

2 See Harold Flender: *Rescue in Denmark* (New York: Simon and Schuster, Inc., 1963).
3 Quoted in Bjarne Höye's and Trygve M. Ager's *The Fight of the Norwegian Church Against Nazism* (New York: The Macmillan Co., 1943), p. 123. See also a work translated by Laura Wyss: *Norwegische Kirchendokumente aus den Jahren des Kampfes Zwischen Kirche und Weltlicher Macht,* 1941-1943 (Zürich: Evangelischer Verlag, 1943).
4 Full text appears in the appendix to the Höye and Ager work.

18

The South African Struggle of the 1950s

The basic facts of South Africa are a white population of 3,000,000 divided into two cultural groups, the English-speaking and the Afrikaans-speaking, represented respectively by the United Party and the Nationalist Party in Parliament; and a black population more than three times as large which has no representatives in Parliament and is sharply circumscribed by government policies expressing moderate or virulent forms of white supremacy with concomitant oppression of the blacks. In addition there are some 1,360,000 Coloreds of intermediate status and about half a million Indians.

The beginning of organized resistance by black Africans dates from 1912 with the founding of the African National Congress by a young Oxford-educated African, Dr. P. I. Seme, along conventional lines similar to those of the Indian National Congress before Gandhi. Originating as a result of the virtual exclusion of black Africans from the legislatures of the four South African states and from the parliament of the Union of South Africa which they comprised after 1910, the Congress was set up as a consultative body to present the views of the blacks to the country's white rulers. As a later Congress leader, Albert Luthuli, wryly put it, "to begin with, only the ear was appealed to, until we discovered that it was deaf." [1]

Methods other than appeal to the ear were soon adopted, not always by the Congress, and on a haphazard, uncoordinated basis. A prime object of the protests was the pass system, under which all black men had to carry a police pass at all times and be prepared to display it on request. Its revocation could mean loss of employment.

There were widespread demonstrations against the newly instituted pass system in 1913 in the Orange Free State, an Afrikaner stronghold, which resulted in numerous arrests. Again in 1919 an anti-pass campaign sponsored by the African National Congress resulted in some seven hundred arrests in the city of Johannesburg alone. Luthuli reports:

In Capetown 400 dockers staged a strike. In 1920, 40,000 African miners came out on strike on the Reef, and in Port Elizabeth twenty-one people were killed by the police. In the following year 163 people were wantonly massacred by the police at Bulhoek, and in 1924 a hundred Hottentots were butchered for refusing to pay an incomprehensible tax on dogs.[2]

In 1928-29 Natal burst into fits of unrest and violence . . . and there was trouble in Durban over taxation. In 1930 there was an outburst in Worcester, and an anti-pass demonstration in Durban. The cost of white supremacy—paid almost entirely in black corpses —rose steadily.[3]

Such was the situation for nearly forty years under the avowedly white-supremacist government of Jan Christiaan Smuts and his associates of the United Party. With the election of a Nationalist government in 1948, bent on an aggressive program of *apartheid* (segregation) even more draconic than that of the Smuts era—which, as the above citations show, was "liberal" only in a narrowly comparative sense—the desultory resistance embodied by the moderate Congress was galvanized into a widely coordinated, massive campaign of nonviolent resistance.

Under the leadership of Dr. James Moroka, its newly elected president-general, the Congress met in 1949 and hammered out a program of action which represented a sharp break with the conservative past.

Representations were done with. Demonstrations on a country-wide scale, strike action and civil disobedience were to replace words. Influenced by the combined action of the Indian community after the passing of the Ghetto Act [i.e., the Group Areas Act], we agreed to concentrate mainly on nonviolent disobedience.[4]

There are many complexities and details that we have glossed over, and most of these will have to remain obscure for the sake of brevity, but a few must be briefly sketched in at this point. Out of the separate developments of the different states that form the present Republic of South Africa—Natal and Cape Colony, under British rule since 1843 and 1806 respectively, the former having a large population of Indian immigrants and the latter a sizable population of so-called "Cape Coloreds" descended from a mixed parentage of black and English settlers; Transvaal and Orange Free State, strongly Boer or Afrikaner: descendants of the early Dutch settlers— came several of the complexities referred to. In addition to the cleavage in the white-supremacist ranks between the English and the Afrikaner, there is a certain cleavage among the non-whites, who at various times and in different ways have been subjected to victimization by the whites. As Leo Kuper points out, for example, Indians were little affected by the pass laws and Africans little affected by the Group Areas Act, while the Coloreds suffered from neither and possessed certain marginal privileges to boot. However, members of all three groups suffered "more or less equally under discrimination in public services and amenities."[5]

It remains to be added that although the African National Congress was not designed to exclude nonblacks, it was in fact even more a black organization than the Indian National Congress was a Hindu organization. Alongside it were the South African Indian Congress (with which was affiliated the Natal Indian Congress founded by Gandhi, historically the parent of the larger body), the Franchise Action Council and other Colored organizations. Finally, in addition to these, small numbers of whites in the Liberal Party, the Communist Party and the higher circles of the English-speaking Christian churches, as well as in the universities, comprised a tiny and ineffectual bulwark against *apartheid* in various degrees and with various motives that cannot be explored here.

A Joining of Forces

This digression helps to set the stage for the events of the 1950s. The "combined action of the Indian community," to which Luthuli refers above, was a passive resistance campaign waged by the Indians in 1946 on an issue that affected their community but not other nonwhites. This was the first use of *satyagraha* since Gandhi's departure from Africa three decades earlier. In this campaign some 2,000 Indians were imprisoned. No doubt its impact was felt among the younger generation of ANC leaders. Certainly it is reflected in the Program of Action adopted in 1949. The program soon bore fruit. Early in 1950 Moroka called a Freedom of Speech Convention in Johannesburg, followed by a May Day demonstration against *apartheid* sponsored by the Communist Party and other groups allied with it, in which blacks, Indians and Coloreds took part. Many children stayed home from school as part of the protest. Demonstrators were attacked and suffered heavy casualties.

A third demonstration occurred on June 26, called by Moroka, as a day of mourning for Africans who had lost their lives in the struggle for freedom, and as a day of protest against the Group Areas Act and the so-called Suppression of Communism Act, of which we shall hear more later. Again there was interracial cooperation among the nonwhites and between them and the white anti-*apartheid* minority, and again school children took an active part.

On May 7, 1951, Coloreds in Port Elizabeth and the Cape Peninsula staged an effective strike against *apartheid* legislation aimed at them, receiving some support from Indians and blacks. Finally in July a conference was held between national executives of the ANC and the SAIC, with representatives of the newly formed Franchise Action Council, and a Joint Planning Council was set up to coordinate the efforts of these three organizations in a proposed nonviolent "defiance campaign" against the disabilities imposed on each of the groups they represented. According to the Report of the Joint Planning Council, "Defiance of unjust laws should take the form of committing breaches of certain selected laws and regulations which are undemocratic, unjust, racially disciminatory and repugnant to the natural rights of man." [6] A three-stage plan of action was drawn up, the timing of which "would to a large extent depend on the progress, development and outcome of the previous stage." Its three stages were: 1) acts of civil disobedience by "selected and trained persons" in major cities; 2) increase in the number of such volunteers and in the number of cities in which to conduct these acts of defiance; and 3) mass action "on a country-wide scale" embracing people in both urban and rural areas.

The report also includes provisions for the necessary organizational structure. Each of the national organizations was to have its own Volunteer Corps units. Mixed units were to be formed only to defy laws that affected all nonwhites equally. Specific instructions such as the following formed part of the document:

Method of Struggle on the Pass Law. (*a*) A Unit of Volunteer Corps should be called upon to defy a certain aspect of the pass law, e.g. enter a Location without a permit. The Unit chosen goes into action on the appointed day, enters the location and holds a meeting. If confronted by the authorities, the leader and all the members of the Unit court arrest and bear the penalty of imprisonment; (*b*) Selected leaders to declare that they will not carry any form of passes . . . and thus be prepared to bear the penalty of the law; (*c*) Other forms of struggle on the pass laws can also be undertaken depending on the conditions in the different areas throughout the country.[7]

Elsewhere in the report, provision is made for rural action, industrial strike action (to be reserved for the third stage in the plan of action) and a "one-million shillings" fund drive.

Kuper notes, in evaluating the program of action:

The choice of passive resistance as a form of struggle appears to have been governed by considerations of expediency rather than by the ethic of Satyagraha. The planning of the campaign in three stages, culminating in mass action, indicates that we are dealing with a tactical use of passive resistance. A mass movement is clearly aimed at the embarrassment of the rulers, and not their conversion by a change of heart. Moreover, the given historical conditions weighed heavily with the Joint Planning Council, and not the assumed universal efficacy of voluntary suffering.[8]

Accordingly, no provision was made for fasting or other such acts of self-purification or penance which Gandhi, as a Hindu, deemed essential, for the quite simple reason that such practices had no place in the South African context.

To the extent that the South African campaign was governed by religious motives they were chiefly Christian, providing the courage to withstand retaliation but in no sense provoking any more suffering than the situation demanded. Among the principal leaders may be cited such Protestants as Albert Luthuli, who testifies eloquently concerning the relevance of his Congregational faith to his career in the freedom movement, Z. K. Matthews and others. The head of the ANC's Youth League during this period is described by Luthuli as "a forceful and gifted Roman Catholic, Anton Lembede," and undoubtedly there were other Catholics in the movement. By all indications, none of them were influenced by Hindu or other types of mysticism enjoining self-immolation.

The defiance campaign was preceded by a series of mass rallies in Capetown, Port Elizabeth, East London, Pretoria, Durban and elsewhere, involving crowds of as many as 10,000. Letters were sent to the authorities, announcing plans for the defiance campaign. The government's replies were characteristically unconciliatory, threatening "full use of the machinery at its disposal to quell any disturbances, and thereafter deal adequately with those responsible for initiating subversive activities of any nature whatsoever." [9] Also characteristically, the reply quoted was signed not by the prime minister but by his private secretary.

The African movement, like its counterpart in India, made it scrupulously clear that it was not its aim to "turn the tables" on its oppressors:

The struggle which the national organizations of the non-European people are conducting is not directed against any race or national group, but against unjust laws which keep in perpetual subjection and misery vast sections of the population.[10]

On June 26 the defiance campaign was launched on a nationwide scale, except for Capetown and Natal, which required additional time for preparation. The chief brunt of the campaign was the ubiquitous motto "Europeans Only." Luthuli tells what was planned:

Railway stations, waiting rooms, post offices, public seats, train accommodations, all bear this legend. The volunteers were to abandon the "separate but unequal" facilities set aside for us, and to make challenging use of the alternative white facilities. In addition to this, the flouting of curfew and pass regulations was determined upon. . . . Whenever possible, the authorities were forewarned of the detailed intentions of each batch of volunteers—in some cases full lists of the names of the volunteers were politely handed in.[11]

Although the number of volunteers did not come up to the expectations raised by the size and fervor of the mass meetings, the campaign gathered momentum. The African and Indian congresses of Natal joined the struggle in July and by October, 2,354 resisters were in action. Their discipline, according to Luthuli, was excellent; so much so that the nonviolent volunteers on some occasions took charge of traffic control when the authorities were unable to maintain order. A continuing problem was the prevention of disorderly mob action by African bystanders who were not under the volunteers' discipline. Luthuli tells how he, as head of the Natal branch of the ANC, and Dr. G. M. Naicker, president of the Natal Indian Congress, dispersed a large, truculent crowd of sympathizers after he and

Dr. Naicker had been placed under arrest. The police were unable to do this themselves.

Many of the demonstrations out of which the volunteers came took the form of Christian prayer meetings, and at political gatherings, according to Kuper, "speakers stressed the affinity between nonviolent resistance and the ethic of Christianity" [12] while excoriating the white man's perversion of Christianity as an ideology to sanctify the oppression of the nonwhites. In some instances this went so far as an apparent rejection of Christianity. An African speaker, Moses Kotane, is quoted as saying: "These people are Christians but they eat people. . . . If they represent God then they represent a false God. And if God is like that, then God is no good for Africa." [13] Yet the same speaker used a biblical text as the setting for this remark. The gist of many such statements like this would seem to be simply: "Don't let the white man use Christianity to bamboozle you." No doubt some Africans rejected all outward forms of Christian faith, while clinging to an anonymous ethic derived from it; but many others held fast to a clearly articulated and professed Christian faith in terms of which they, like Kotane, judged the white man's piety as hypocrisy.

The Christian spirit was exemplified in the testimony of volunteers when arraigned in court for the breaking of *apartheid* laws. Following are excerpts from a written statement read to a magistrate in Bloemfontein by S. Mokoena, head of the Volunteer Corps in that city:

It is interesting to speculate, Your Worship, what the reaction of the European would be, were he . . . to discover himself an African just overnight and thus be subjected to the thousand and one irksome discriminatory laws that our people have borne for centuries with Christian-like fortitude. . . .

We do not quarrel with Your Worship when you say you have no alternative but to punish us for deliberately breaking the unjust laws; that is the unenviable duty you are bound to carry out. But, with due respect to Your Worship, we wish to state that punishment, no matter how severe, can be no deterrent to us. We have undertaken this campaign fully expecting such punishment.[14]

Such statements as this were unheard by the white public, for the white newspapers published only terse, impersonal reports of the trials. Indeed, the communication of news through non-white channels was also so poor that it had to be supplemented with mimeographed news sheets and with public demonstrations outside the courts, which were then reported in the press. According to Kuper, for example, prayer demonstrations outside magistrates' courts in Uitenhage and East London were reported in *The Star* on July 23, and in August *Press Digest* reported a gathering of 5,000 praying Africans in Port Elizabeth, welcoming 250 volunteers on their release from prison there. When Dr. Moroka and other leaders went on trial in Johannesburg, *Press Digest* reported that there were white university students among the thousands of non-whites who sang defiance songs and demonstrated all day long at a nearby public square.

At the height of the defiance campaign, on October 18, a series of riots broke out in Port Elizabeth, Kimberley and East London, in which there were bloody clashes between African crowds and the police. The latter did not hesitate to fire into the crowds. A number of Africans and a few whites were killed and others injured. A motion-picture theater was set on fire; a Roman Catholic mission and an Anglican church, among other buildings, were destroyed; a white missionary nun was murdered and her body defiled. In all the disturbances no policemen were killed and few were injured. Both the ANC and the SAIC demanded an impartial commission of inquiry, but the government refused even to conduct routine public investigations. There was reason to believe that the riots were the work of agents provocateurs; the director of the South African Institute of Race Relations was told by Europeans in both Port Elizabeth and Kimberley that "strangers had come into the neighborhood previously to the riots." [15] In East London more than half of the Africans arrested were juveniles: anti-social *tsotsis* not unlike the teen-age gang boys of American and European cities. By all accounts it is clear that the riots were unrelated to the defiance campaign and very likely were instigated by the government.

The Apartheid Strategy

Whether the government instigated these events or not, it quickly utilized them as a pretext to smear and to smash the defiance campaign. Luthuli sums up the implicit reasoning behind the government's move:

The Defiance Campaign was far too orderly and successful for the Government's liking, and it was growing. The prospect before the white supremacists, if they were going to react to our challenge in a civilized way, was that arrests would continue indefinitely. Behind the thousands already arrested there were more, many more. The challenge of nonviolence was more than they could meet. It robbed them of the initiative. On the other hand, violence by Africans would restore this initiative to them—they would then be able to bring out the guns and the other techniques of intimidation and present themselves as restorers of order.[16]

In a leaflet distributed early in November by the National Action Committee of the ANC and SAIC, the shootings were described as a deliberate attempt to weaken the defiance campaign, and nonwhites were warned not to listen to talk that would divide blacks, Coloreds and Indians among one another. And scarcely three weeks after the first riots, the ANC made so bold as to hold a one-day work stoppage in Port Elizabeth to protest the imposition of a curfew. The strike was estimated to have involved ninety-six per cent of the Africans in the town. Also at this point there was an increase of activity by white sympathizers of the defiance campaign. On December 8 a mixed group of thirty-eight men and women, white, black and Indian, were arrested in the Witwatersrand for entering a "native" location without permits. (The Indian group included

M.K. Gandhi's son Manilal, editor of *Indian Opinion*.) On the following day four white volunteers were arrested for occupying non-European booths at the General Post Office in Capetown, and a week later a white trade-union organizer was charged with the same offense in Johannesburg.

Despite these new steps, however, the campaign was in evident decline, slumping from its October peak of 2,354 volunteers in action to only 280 in November and December. Among the factors accounting for the decline were the jailing of the top leaders and a split in their ranks which occurred when Dr. Moroka broke discipline by choosing to be defended by his own lawyer (instead of jointly with the other nineteen codefendants in his case), and pleading mitigating circumstances instead of being prepared to accept the full penalty of the law. If the president-general of the African National Congress could stoop to currying favor with the whites in this fashion at such a moment, what was the rank-and-file volunteer to think? At the same time, the government issued a proclamation, soon bolstered by legislation in Parliament, which gave it far-reaching powers to suppress and punish any defiance. Under this combination of factors the campaign collapsed.

In December at the national conference of the ANC, Albert Luthuli was elected president-general. So far had the campaign ebbed by now that at a meeting near Johannesburg shortly afterward, when volunteers were called for, only one man responded, "and he was tipsy." The campaign was officially brought to an end on June 26, 1953, the anniversary of its launching, with a message in which Luthuli bade Africans and their allies to light bonfires or lanterns outside their homes "as a symbol of the spark of freedom which we are determined to keep alive in our hearts, and as a sign to freedom-lovers that we are keeping the vigil on that night." [17]

The conclusion of the defiance campaign did not mean merely a return to the status quo ante; it meant a new period of reaction and repression. Although sentences decreed by magistrates in court were seldom severe, prison guards went out of their way to make life hard for convicted resisters, beating or humiliating them and depriving them of food on the slightest provocation. Clergymen were denied certain privileges, subsidies were withdrawn from schools employing teachers who aligned themselves with the freedom movement, students were refused readmission to school, workers were fired from their jobs, municipal officials canceled the right of black resisters to remain in their location. These and similar tactics were used, or threatened, by the whites.

Under the Riotous Assemblies Act, magistrates were authorized to prohibit specific public meetings in their district and the minister of justice was empowered to bar all public meetings within a specified area for a stated period of time and to prohibit specified individuals from attending public meetings of any kind when the latter were permitted. Additional powers were granted by the Suppression of Communism Act, which made it possible to proscribe organizations and to declare even private gatherings illegal.

Instead of using these powers to the full, however, the government chose to exercise comparative restraint to achieve the same ends, holding the more extreme provisions in reserve. In July 1952 ANC and SAIC and nonwhite trade-union offices were raided, as were the homes of officials of these organizations, and their records were seized—a disruptive tactic that was to be used again after the campaign ended. The planting of police spies in Congress ranks sowed suspicion and distrust. And resistance leaders were often given suspended sentences on condition that they did not commit another offense under the proscriptive acts.

Under the Criminal Law Amendment Act the government authorized flogging for political crimes and provided for confiscation and sale of a resister's property to pay fines levied by the courts. If a banned leader's speech was played on a recording, not only the listeners but the leader was liable to a penalty. Letters could be intercepted and inspected by the government on suspicion of illegality, thus eliminating the privacy of the mails. Various laws contained overlapping provisions for prosecuting "incitement to civil disobedience."

Luthuli had hardly assumed office when he was banned from entering any of the large population centers of South Africa and forbidden to attend public meetings. Subsequently he was subjected to virtual house arrest, precluding travel outside his home district without express permission for a period of years.

Despite these intimidations and restrictions, however, there were local economic boycotts on a minor scale, as well as other sporadic acts of resistance, and plans were laid for a broad-based Congress of the People, embracing the ANC, the SAIC, the South African Congress of Trade Unions, the South African Colored People's Organization and the Congress of Democrats. The last of these was composed chiefly of whites with a belief in racial equality. The Congress of the People, comprising delegates from every South African ethnic group and from every quarter of the country, met for two days, June 25-26, 1955, at Kliptown, near Johannesburg. This meeting adopted a Freedom Charter which declared that "South Africa belongs to all who live in it, black and white" and that "our people have been robbed of their birthright to land, liberty and peace by a form of government founded on injustice and inequality." The charter set as its goal the establishment of "a democratic state, based on the will of all the people" to "secure to all their birthright without distinction of color, race, sex or belief." [18]

In his book *Inside Africa,* published in 1955, John Gunther concluded his chapter on South Africa with these words: "Is South Africa fascist? Not quite. Not yet." Without venturing a more decisive answer, we may observe that worse was to come. On December 5, 1956, not long after the expiration of his two-year ban, Albert Luthuli was arrested on a charge of high treason, along with 155 other leaders of the freedom movement. Many of them were noted African Christians such as Z. K. Matthews, who lectured at Union Theological Seminary in New York as Visiting Professor of World Christianity

in 1952-1953, as well as a number of Anglican priests and ministers and laymen of the Congregational, Methodist and other churches. Also imprisoned were Dr. G. M. Naicker, president of the Natal Indian Congress, and many other Hindus, Muslims and, of course, persons of no religious affiliation, including Communists.

This is not the place for a detailed account of the celebrated treason trials. After being held in prison for a brief period, Luthuli, Matthews, Naicker and the others were released on bail while the tedious processes of the trials went on, consuming time, money and organizational activity for five years. Much of the money needed to meet the expenses of the trials was raised by the Defense and Aid Fund of Christian Action in London and by the Africa Defense and Aid Fund of the American Committee on Africa in New York, which also placed many distinguished Britons and Americans on public record against the policies of the South African government. Distinguished attorneys placed their services at the disposal of the defendants and such men as Alan Paton, Arthur W. Blaxall and Ambrose Reeves, Anglican Bishop of Johannesburg, publicly stated their opposition to the government's position.

Boycott and the Peaceful "Riot"

What is of more interest, however, is the fact of continuing protest actions by Africans on a local scale during this period, despite the government's success in virtually hamstringing the national resistance organizations. Perhaps the most noteworthy campaign was a bus boycott by Africans in the Alexandra district of Johannesburg, which began on January 7, 1957, in protest against a rise in fares. Significantly, it was not an action against *apartheid* nor was it directed against the government, but againt a privately owned transit company. Nevertheless, mass organized protest action by blacks against a white-owned public facility could not but pose an implied threat to *apartheid* institutions, as government reaction clearly indicated.

Beginning in Alexandra, where Dan Mokonyane organized the People's Transport Action Committee, and spreading to half a dozen other townships, the movement involved some 60,000 Africans who chose to walk rather than pay the higher fares. Some of them walked as much as eighteen miles a day in addition to putting in their hard day's work. According to an American observer, "hundreds of motorists gave daily lifts to weary boycotters; for many Johannesburg whites it was their first human contact with Africans, outside of the master-servant relation." [19]

Although the English-language press viewed the boycott sympathetically, the Minister of Transport, Ben Shoeman, charged on January 16: "The boycott has political motives. It is a trial of strength by the African National Congress. If they want a showdown, they will get it." [20]

The police were given orders to crush the boycott and began a "blitz" against the lift-giving motorists. Cars were stopped and searched and the drivers' names taken down, and as a result many were intimidated into "minding their own business."

Even more harassed, however, were the walkers. One day over a hundred were arrested for crossing an intersection against the light. Some Africans rode bicycles; police deflated their tires and confiscated the valves. African hostels in Johannesburg were raided night after night to catch Africans bunking with friends (without official permission to stay the night) in order to spare themselves two stretches of the grueling hike. In all, during the boycott, there were 14,000 arrests, most of them for violations of the pass laws.

The boycott lasted twelve weeks and was suspended when the Chamber of Commerce negotiated a working compromise, pending an investigation, with the Joint Boycott Committee that had by then been set up with Alfred Nzo as secretary. A final settlement was reached when Shoeman introduced a bill in Parliament doubling the levy on employers to subsidize African transport and thus holding the fares at their previous rate.

The victory for the Africans was implicitly political as well as economic, inasmuch as the government's resort to police measures had given the campaign a political character. Walter Sisulu, a banned ANC leader, said as much afterward: "The bus boycott has raised the political consciousness of the people and has brought about a great solidarity and unity among them." [21] Soon afterward, the ANC launched a wide economic boycott of Nationalist-controlled firms and their products. For a time this tactic enjoyed a certain degree of success and was joined by sympathizers in Great Britain and elsewhere. Efforts to develop economic pressure, internally or on the world market, were not sufficient, however, to cause the government of South Africa to alter its policies. One of the difficulties inherent in a wide-scale boycott, as Luthuli pointed out, is that "it is not easy to avoid injury to the wrong man's pocket, and we have never been callously indiscriminate in our attitudes." [22]

One segment of the long-term, wide-range boycott was a three-month boycott against potatoes grown by convict labor in Eastern Transvaal and elsewhere. Originally conceived as a one-month protest, this gesture struck a responsive chord in the African community. Although it meant hardship for the consumer, since potatoes were the staple of the impoverished Africans' diet, it also meant a vivid rebuke to the whole pass-law system: it was through infractions of the pass laws that labor was obtained for the farm jails where a sizable proportion of the potato crop was grown. At the same time, the act of self-denial served as a gesture of solidarity with the convicts themselves, who had to dig the potatoes with bare fingers, under the lash of an overseer, in bestial conditions of temporary slavery. The "potato boycott" was successful in that it glutted the market with unsold potatoes; and despite the combined efforts of government, merchants and farmers to break it, it held fast until officially called off by Luthuli. It was also successful in that it contributed to the morale of the Africans, giving them a sense of their own moral power. But it did not bring amelioration in the conditions on the farms, nor did it weaken the pass system.

Indeed the pass system, long applied to African men, was extended to women in 1956. This action brought about a massive demonstration in which black women from every corner of the country took part. Some of them had to travel as far as a thousand miles to reach the capital city, Pretoria, where the demonstration was held. Numbers of white women, organized in the Black Sash Movement, demonstrated in sympathy with their black sisters. In 1957 there were demonstrations in rural areas on this same issue. A South African attorney describes the "riot" in Lichtenburg: "At a meeting there was a disturbance as a result whereof the police fired at the people and killed a number of residents. A number of people were arrested and charged with public violence. They were all acquitted . . . and the magistrate blamed the police publicly for what had transpired." [23] There were subsequent disturbances in Nelspruit and Zeerust, where women either refused to take out pass books or burned them if they already had them, and there were police shootings and arrests.

In 1958 the demonstrations by women reached a high pitch, beyond the organizational powers of the Congress Women's League to control them. This led to mass action in Johannesburg that resulted in more than 2,000 arrests.

In Natal in 1959 a deputation of women from the township of Cato Manor slept in an open field for two nights and planted themselves on the city hall steps in Durban in order to gain an interview with the mayor to protest against injustices in housing. The mayor, says Luthuli, "did try to do something, but it was too little and too late." [24] As demonstrations spread, there were outbreaks of violence, notably the destruction of municipal beer halls and the burning of Bantu Education Schools. The pattern was apparently not unlike that which the government used to dampen the defiance campaign of 1950: destructive acts committed by hooligans or agents provocateurs followed by police brutality directed against the freedom movement or even against innocent bystanders. In Pietermaritzburg, bystanders, including elderly Hindu women, were beaten by police who launched a baton charge against a picket line of African women from the countryside. In nearby Sobantu Village, where schools were burned, the police wantonly shot and killed two African men who had been nowhere near the burning schools. In Camperdown, another rural area near Pietermaritzburg, a group of African women marched with white flags to present their demands to the native commissioner. The police confronted them, ordered them to disperse and then, before waiting for them to obey the order, charged with clubs flying. In another area, Ixopo, when the order to disperse was given, the women fell to their knees and began to pray. The police did not know what to do.

The aftermath of the Cato Manor disturbances was to become an ominous prelude to tragedy. Early in 1960 the police were conducting pass raids at least three times a week there. This fact, coupled with the forced removal of residents to a new "native location" in which they were deprived of certain rights that they had formerly enjoyed, made for a tense situation. Then a trivial incident triggered mob violence that took the lives of nine policemen on a routine raid.

The Pan-African Congress and the Sharpeville Massacre

Throughout its history the African National Congress looked to a multiracial solution within South Africa. Inasmuch as its philosophy has been articulated by Christians such as Luthuli, Matthews and others, it has stressed reconciliation and nonviolence. "As long as our patience can be made to hold out," wrote Luthuli, "we shall not jeopardize the South Africa of tomorrow by precipitating violence today." [25] For some time, however, dating back to the defiance campaign of 1950, there had been developing a so-called "Africanist" wing within the ANC. This faction increasingly identified itself with the ongoing struggle of black Africans throughout the continent against white colonial rule. In a word, the "Africanists" tended to see themselves as a South African part of a continentwide movement which elsewhere was establishing new independent states. This definition necessarily skimps the complexities of the situation. But broadly speaking it was this emphasis which culminated in the formation of the Pan-African Congress in 1958, under the leadership of thirty-three-year-old Robert Mangaliso Sobukwe.

At a time when the ANC had already begun preparations for a new campaign against the pass laws, Sobukwe seized the initiative and on March 21, 1960, launched a campaign in the name of the Pan-African Congress. The year 1963 was specified as the date by which South Africa was to be free—that is, under black rule. Rejecting cooperation with Indian and other groups, the PAC's manifesto nevertheless called for "absolute nonviolence" and proclaimed as its mission the leading of "the vital, breathing and dynamic youth of our land . . . not to death, but to the life abundant." [26] At the time of its writing, Sobukwe claimed a membership of 30,000, and entire branches of the ANC were said to be seceding to the new movement.

Charging Luthuli with overcautiousness and with being too much under "white influence," Sobukwe said: "We will send our leaders to jail first. That is where our leaders belong—in front." [27] True to his word, on the appointed day Sobukwe led a group of sixty nonviolent resisters to the police station in Orlando township and demanded to be arrested for violating the pass laws. They were. Simultaneously, in Langa and Nyanga locations near Capetown, crowds numbering thousands demanded arrest. "At Langa, Philip Kgosana turned back 30,-000 demonstrators and thus avoided bloodshed, and at Nyanga the whole demonstration degenerated into prolonged riot and arson," wrote Luthuli.[28] Kgosana was a twenty-one-year-old Pan-Africanist, one of the last black students admitted to the University of Capetown before the encroachment of *apartheid* there. This courageous youth was the leader of the procession. Here is his own account of what happened in Langa:

The senior officer in charge of the police refused to arrest me. He wanted to know who would control the demonstrators while I was in jail. I told him that our demonstration was opposed to any form of violence. The police then wanted to know what our plans were. I told them we were marching to the police station where we wanted to be locked up for being without our passes. The senior officer told me that if we went anywhere near the police station he would defend the station to the last bullet and to the last drop of blood.

As I am against violence, I asked my people to disperse. I told the officer I would withhold my labor and I asked him to withhold his bullets. I then picketed the police station, and kept the demonstrators away from the police station.[29]

A police captain later testified that he heard Kgosana say repeatedly to the crowd: "I will not allow the police to be attacked. I will protect them with my life." [30]

Simultaneously in Sharpeville, thirty miles from Johannesburg, on the morning of March 21 a crowd of some 7,000 Africans (nearly half the location's population) massed at the gate as part of the Pan-Africanist nonviolent demonstration. Police were on the scene and tried to disperse the crowd with tear-gas bombs. The orderly, disciplined crowd fell back thirty paces but did not disperse. Armored cars were brought up and military aircraft were used in an attempt to intimidate them.

After several hours of this, a few Africans broke discipline and began to throw stones at the police. Without a word of warning and without firing a warning shot, the police opened fire on the crowd. According to an official report, 476 bullets were fired. Sixty-seven African men, women and children were killed and many others wounded.[31]

Later that day in Langa wild disorder broke out. Police killed three people and that night mobs set fire to schools, churches, a library and administration buildings, all symbolic of white rule. Thousands from both Langa and Nyanga stayed home from work on March 22 and those who did not were approached by Pan-Africanists who told them to quit. According to Norman Phillips of the *Toronto Star*, "Irresponsible elements joined in, uninvited, and one gang known as 'The Spoilers' was reported in Capetown intimidating Africans still at work." [32]

On March 24 the police invaded Langa and tried to force Africans to go to work, but by noon Capetown was virtually deserted by its black work force. On March 25 Kgosana led a procession of 1,500 pass-less men from Langa to the police station in Capetown and demanded their arrest. The police chief turned them away and they went home in orderly fashion.

On March 30 the government of South Africa decreed a state of emergency, authorizing arrests without warrant or charge. Philip Kgosana hurriedly assembled a protest march of thirty thousand Africans from Langa and Nyanga, and led them, thirty abreast, through the streets of Capetown. As they entered the city, Kgosana halted the crowd and said, "I appeal to you for nonviolence. We must avoid bloodshed at all costs." [33] Then he led the crowd to the police station, demanded the release of the arrested Pan-African leaders and voiced a protest against the police molestations of March 24. He secured a promise from the city's police chief that a small deputation led by Kgosana would be given an opportunity to present their grievances to the minister of justice. Thereupon Kgosana dispersed the marchers—this while truckloads of armed police rolled along the streets and armored cars formed a cordon around Parliament.

That night, under cover of darkness, thousands of troops were sent out to Langa and Nyanga, forming a cordon of steel around the two locations. Kgosana was called in for the promised meeting but was arrested under the Emergency Regulations.

The Africans continued their strike. On April 4 the government unleashed a reign of terror. White bystanders jammed the switchboards of the Capetown newspapers, trying to tell of widespread unprovoked attacks by police on Africans. Clergymen, university professors and others were slapped or beaten with whips. C. F. Regnier, president of the Cape Chamber of Industries, was so disturbed that he went to the chief of police, Colonel I. P. S. Terblanche, and pleaded with him to stop the assaults.

But the situation was even worse in Nyanga. This is Norman Phillips' account:

At 11 A.M. police squads were turned loose inside the location with orders to whip every male African they encountered. They broke into houses to flog men in their beds. Terrified, screaming wives and children watched their husbands being dragged out into the streets.

Whips and batons ruled Nyanga. The hospital clinic was closed down, leaving only one doctor to minister to the wounded. . . . As further punishment, water supplies to the surrounding locations were cut off. . . .

Four Africans were wounded on Monday. At least five, including a seven-year-old child, were injured by police bullets on Tuesday. Fourteen Anglican clergymen appealed to the Government to restrain its use of force. . . .

For sheer sadism, the closest comparison to what happened at Nyanga was when the Gestapo sealed off the Warsaw ghetto and began to annihilate it. Had Nyanga fought back, it too would have been wiped out; but the Africans employed non-aggressive tactics that puzzled the police.[34]

After four days of this the police climaxed their reign of terror by taking 1,525 of Nyanga's people to a police station for screening. Of these they detained 162.

The response of Albert Luthuli and the African National Congress to the Sharpeville massacre was a call for a national day of mourning on March 28, when all people were urged to stay at home and pray. Many Pan-Africanists were among those who honored this appeal. Two days earlier, Luthuli publicly burned his pass and called upon other Africans to do likewise. It was ostensibly in response to this action that the government proclaimed an emergency empowering magistrates and commissioned officers to prohibit public meetings and processions. Under the Emergency Regulations some 1,900 people of all races were arrested without charges or trial and held for three or four months, including two attorneys engaged by the Anglican Bishop of Johannesburg, Ambrose Reeves, to prepare evidence for the Sharpeville Commission of Inquiry. An additional 20,000 Africans were detained on charges of vagrancy. Luthuli was arrested in the home of some white friends, who were also taken into custody, as were a number of Anglican priests. Like many of his countrymen, Luthuli was slapped and reviled by white jailers. After five months in prison he was banned to his home for five years—with a brief suspension in 1961 to permit him to go to Sweden to receive the Nobel Peace Prize for his steadfast adherence to Christian nonviolence.

The Defeat of the Nonviolent Movement

The state of emergency was lifted at the time of Luthuli's release from prison in August 1960, but worse developments were in store. As for the nonviolent movement, its back was broken by Sharpeville and its aftermath. Many of the thousands arrested emerged from the jails convinced that the nonviolent methods of ANC were leading nowhere. A decade of struggle thus ended with heightened tensions and a grim outlook for the future.

It would be easy to say (and it has been said often) that the nonviolent movement was defeated by sheer force and violence. To some extent this is true, but it is nevertheless strange that such a movement, representing seventy-seven per cent of the country's population, could be utterly crushed in a decade. A candid assessment cannot absolve the ANC itself of a share of blame for its defeat.

Although it became a mass organization on the eve of the defiance campaign, the ANC's membership never totaled more than 100,000 by its own estimates—one per cent of the black population. Of this number, only 8,000 volunteers engaged in direct action. And even with this broadening of the membership base, its policies continued to be made by a leadership that had originally constituted itself more as a body speaking to the white power structure than as one arising from the masses.

Add to this a weak and cumbersome organizational structure, based on local branches varying in size from a handful to 15,000 members, virtual absence of any full-time professional staff, and insufficient finances for normal travel, publications and other expenses, and we begin to marvel that the ANC was able to make the impact it did. The simple lack of membership rolls and bookkeeping explains more than the economic poverty of the members (whose dues were less than forty cents a year), since the Congress had no way of knowing who had paid.

Congruent with this pattern was the ANC's general lack of strategy. Edward Feit, in his acute study for the London Institute of Race Relations, has stated it well:

Greater willingness to participate, even to accept losses of wages, might have been developed, had the objects of each campaign been presented simply to African workers and had they been convinced that these objects could be attained. This was not possible, for the leaders themselves were not sure of where they were leading. They knew their destination, but not how to get there. Unanimity existed in the knowledge of the most distant goal . . . but attainable short-term aims were lacking.[35]

The rest is epilogue, consisting mainly of new government repressions countered by sporadic violence from extremists and valiant but ineffectual verbal gestures from ANC leaders. The first outburst was a well-organized regional rebellion in Pondoland in December 1960. In April 1961 Nelson Mandela became the first ANC leader to go underground, and from somewhere in hiding he organized and led a partly successful stay-at-home strike to coincide with the proclamation of the Republic of South Africa in May. It was "partly successful" in that it happened at all, but it had no effect on the government. In December a secret organization, Umkonto We Sizwe—"Spear of the Nation"—derailed trains and set off bomb explosions in what it described in a leaflet as the beginning of full-scale sabotage, asserting that the patience of black Africans was coming to an end.

The promise of sabotage was not fulfilled, but the government used it as a pretext for the passage of the Sabotage Act in June 1962. This law provided severe punishments, including death, for any form of public protest. Under its drastic provisions even newspapers were prohibited from publishing anything said by any man who had been banned from attending public meetings. A month before it became law, Patrick Baron, Dean of Johannesburg Cathedral, asserted that it would be the duty of every true Christian to disobey it. Black Sash women who demonstrated against it on May 23 were assaulted by Nationalist youths.

With passage of the Sabotage Act, both ANC and Pan-African Congress were outlawed. Hundreds of members of the latter formed themselves into a terrorist organization called Poqo—"We Stand Alone"—which on November 29, 1962, raided the police station in Paarl, near Capetown, killing two white people. Five of the raiders were shot and 346 suspects were arrested. Later raids in the Transkei took a further toll of dead and injured, including both whites and blacks hacked to death. According to testimony before a Commission of Inquiry, one informer was beheaded in his sleep. Other victims were soaked with gasoline and set on fire.

In August 1962 Nelson Mandela and Walter Sisulu, former ANC general secretary, were arrested. Tried under the Sabotage Act, Mandela was sentenced on November 7 to five years in prison. Of those arrested in the Paarl raid, three were executed and 62 others were given prison terms ranging from twelve to twenty-five years. Hundreds of other Poqo suspects were arrested for terrorist activities elsewhere (350 in the Transkei alone), and these were not the only ones nor the last ones. Those arrested ranged from Arthur W. Blaxall, a white minister and former secretary of the Christian Council of South

Africa, to teams of saboteurs intercepted on their return from training abroad.

Despite all efforts, including a United Nations resolution of November 6, 1962, to boycott South Africa, white racism continued to hold its ground. Nelson Mandela, before his arrest, voiced a question that was in the minds of many when he addressed a Pan-African conference in Addis Ababa in February 1962: "Can a government bent on using the utmost force to crush the freedom struggle be forever countered by peaceful and nonviolent means?" The answer given by nearly half of a group of middle-class black Africans sixteen months later, in an opinion poll published by the South African Institute of Race Relations, was an unequivocal "No!" They looked to the banned Pan-African Congress rather than to the ANC for a solution of the problem through the overthrow of the government.

Undisclosed numbers of ANC supporters had long been organized into small underground cells as outlined in what is known as the "M Plan" developed by Mandela during the defiance campaign of 1952. Whether they or the avowedly terrorist organizations would one day act to unseat the rule of white supremacy, no one could say. Possibly aided by the newly independent African nations, almost certainly with armed force, it seemed inevitable to everyone that a major and bloody upheaval lay ahead, though some continued to hope for a miracle. It was clear that nonviolence had tragically failed, and if it had any further part to play on the South African scene it would be only as a tactical prelude to a violent holocaust.

REFERENCES IN CHAPTER 18

1   Albert Luthuli: *Let My People Go* (New York: McGraw-Hill Book Co., 1962), p. 91.
2   *Ibid.*, p. 92.

 3 *Ibid.*, p. 93.
 4 *Ibid.*, p. 109.
 5 Leo Kuper: *Passive Resistance in South Africa* (New Haven: Yale University Press, 1957), p. 101.
 6 Full text appears as Appendix C in *ibid., q.v.,* p. 251.
 7 *Ibid.*, p. 253f.
 8 *Ibid.*, p. 102.
 9 Full text appears as Appendix B in *ibid.,* p. 238.
10 Quoted in Luthuli, *op. cit.,* p. 116.
11 Luthuli, *op. cit.,* p. 117.
12 Kuper, *op. cit.,* p. 117.
13 Quoted in *ibid.*
14 Quoted in *ibid.,* pp. 130-131.
15 Quoted in *ibid.,* p. 138.
16 Luthuli, *op. cit.,* p. 127.
17 Quoted in Kuper, p. 145.
18 For full text see Appendix B in Luthuli, *op. cit.,* pp. 239-243.
19 Mary-Louise Hooper: "The Johannesburg Bus Boycott" in *Africa Today* (New York), November-December 1957, p. 14.
20 Quoted in *ibid.*
21 Quoted in *ibid.,* p. 16.
22 Luthuli, *op. cit.,* p. 217.
23 *Christian Action Newsletter* (London), Summer 1961, p. 13.
24 Luthuli, *op. cit.,* p. 217.
25 *Ibid.*, p. 219f.
26 Quoted in Norman Phillips: *The Tragedy of Apartheid* (New York: David McKay Co., Inc., 1960), p. 60.
27 *Ibid.*, p. 61.
28 Luthuli, *op. cit.,* p. 222.
29 Quoted in Phillips, *op. cit.,* p. 163.
30 *Ibid.*
31 For a full account, see Ambrose Reeves: *The Shooting at Sharpeville* (Boston: Houghton Mifflin Co., 1961).
32 Phillips, *op. cit.,* p. 164.
33 Quoted in *ibid.,* p. 165.
34 *Ibid.*, p. 171f.
35 Edward Feit: *South Africa: The Dynamics of the African National Congress* (London: Oxford, 1962), p. 65. Feit's study amply documents the above critique of Congress' shortcomings.

19

Ghana: The Positive Action
Campaign of 1950

During the same period when nonwhites in South Africa were embarking upon their defiance campaign, the first in a series of many painful struggles, black Africans in the British crown colony of the Gold Coast were on the eve of a lightning-swift campaign that resulted in complete independence within a very short time.

The Gold Coast on the eve of its independence was strikingly different from South Africa in certain ways. A small, compact country with a population of 4,500,000, all but 0.2 per cent of its people were indigenous black Africans, fifteen to twenty-five per cent literate and thirty per cent Christian. Most of the latter were concentrated in the coastal areas which were also occupied by no more than four thousand British settlers with no appreciable property such as that of the white South Africans. Here the social issues were not complex, if indeed they could be said to exist at all. The struggle for independence turned almost entirely on the question of political administration: how soon and in what manner would the government of the colony be transferred from the hands of the British Colonial Office to those of the Africans themselves? To state the issue so simply is not to suggest that the Africans' own efforts to achieve self-government did no more than to hasten an inevitable eventuality. Without these efforts the British might have procrastinated for decades. The point, rather, is that once this clearly seen goal was realized there were no other considerations that were likely to upset it.

The story of the Gold Coast's road to independence is very largely the story of Kwame Nkrumah and the Convention People's Party. Born in 1909 in a small village, the son of a goldsmith, he received his early education at Roman Catholic mission schools. At the age of twenty-six he came to the United States, where he worked his way through Lincoln University, earning degrees in theology and science as well as a B.A. and M.A. A classmate there described him as a man of set purpose, "sober, reserved and conscientious, as well as brilliant." [1] After serving briefly as an instructor at Lincoln—and experiencing American-style racial discrimination—he went to London, where he lived for a number of years and studied at the London School of Economics.

During Nkrumah's stay in England, a Pan-African Congress (not to be confused with the South African body) was held in Manchester in October 1945, and the thirty-six-year-old graduate student attended and helped to formulate its strategy and tactics. "The delegates," writes George Padmore, "endorsed the doctrine of Pan-African socialism based upon the Gandhian tactics of nonviolent noncooperation." [2] From England Nkrumah kept in close contact with developments in the Gold Coast until two years later, when J. B. Danquah, president of the United Gold Coast Convention, invited him to become secretary of this, the colony's chief political organization.

Nkrumah Assumes Leadership

Nkrumah arrived on December 16, 1947, and set to work immediately. Hardly had his work begun, however, when a national crisis occurred. On February 28, 1948, a peaceful demonstration of unarmed African ex-servicemen set out on a march from Accra to the suburban residence of the British governor to present him with a petition of grievances. Ordered by police to halt, they refused and the police opened fire, killing two and wounding five of the Africans. When news of the incident spread, rioting broke out in several towns and lasted for days, with twenty-nine deaths and 237 other casualties before it was over.

Prior to the riots there had been a month-long boycott of shopkeepers, which in fact had been terminated on the very day the riots broke out. Neither of these events was the work of the UGCC, which had been engaged in agitation for constitutional reform. Nkrumah, however, had the presence of mind to turn the crisis to the account of the movement. On February 29 in the midst of the rioting he cabled to the Colonial Office in London: "People demand self-government immediately. Send commission supervise formation constituent assembly. Urgent." [3] He also took time to send copies of the cable to *The New York Times,* the Associated Negro Press (a Chicago syndicate serving many Negro newspapers), the Moscow weekly *Novoe Vremya* (which was also published in English, German, French and other editions for world distribution) and eight or nine other key publicity media throughout the world.

To curb the riots the governor assumed emergency powers and on March 13 exiled Danquah, Nkrumah and other UGCC leaders. Nkrumah was sent off to a remote village in the north of the colony, without trial or formal accusation. As a result of an investigation of the underlying causes of the disturbances, however, the governor set up an all-African committee of forty tribal chiefs, conservative politicians and others to draft a new constitution. This body, the so-called Coussey Commission, issued a report which was adopted with some modifications by the Colonial Office as a basis for gradual, guided self-government and for the first general election in Gold Coast history.

Dissatisfied with this solution, Nkrumah, who had meanwhile been released from exile, pressed for a more radical alternative. He precipitated a split within the UGCC, out of which emerged the Convention People's Party on June 12, 1949, with Nkrumah at its head—just eighteen months after his arrival from England. In August, Nkrumah and a team of nine co-workers embarked on a countrywide tour to present the CPP's program to the people.

They gained wide support quickly and on November 20, 1949, a month after the Coussey Report was issued, the CPP called a constituent assembly such as Nkrumah had earlier demanded of the Colonial Office. The assembly was attended by more than 80,000 representatives of over fifty groups, including cooperatives, labor unions, farm groups, educational, cultural, women's and youth organizations. This body rejected the Coussey Report, specifically its provisions for British cabinet ministers in the key posts of justice, finance, external affairs and defense; its designation of the voting age at twenty-five; and its provision for a number of appointive seats in the legislature in addition to the elective ones. Taking a leaf from India's recent history, the assembly demanded that "the people of the Gold Coast be granted immediate self-government, that is, dominion status," and drew up a memorandum outlining the structure of government, both central and local, which they wanted embodied in the new constitution. Nkrumah also asked for a round-table conference with the British officials, but they remained committed to the Coussey Report and refused to meet with him or with other CPP leaders, or otherwise to recognize the assembly.

Nkrumah gave the British a little more than three weeks to respond and when they did not, says Padmore,

After repeated requests for a round-table conference with British officials, Dr. Nkrumah . . . informed the Governor on December 15, 1949 . . . that the CPP would embark upon a campaign of "Positive Action," based upon Gandhi's philosophy of nonviolent noncooperation, and would continue with it until such time as the British Government conceded the right of the Gold Coast people to convene their Constituent Assembly.[4]

On the same date, in a front-page editorial in the CPP newspaper, the *Accra Evening News,* Nkrumah instructed the nation to prepare. "Remember," he stressed, "the strike is on the basis of perfect nonviolence. There shall be no looting or burning of houses or rioting or damage or disturbances of any sort. Nonviolence is our creed." [5]

It had not always been Nkrumah's creed, nor was it ever to become a matter of absolute religious conviction for him. In his autobiography Nkrumah indicates how widely eclectic his outlook was. Coming from a Roman Catholic background, as an adult he described himself as a "nondenominational Christian" and a Marxist, while admitting to such widely divergent influences as those of Lenin, Hitler and Gandhi, to mention only a few. Always alert to currents within the struggle for independence throughout the colonial world, Nkrumah was particularly attentive to the developments in India. The final phase of the Indian struggle coincided almost exactly with Nkrumah's own active entry into political life. By all available accounts nonviolence had won a tremendous victory in India at the very time he was taking the helm of the UGCC, and he could well discount the impact of the Hindu-Muslim massacres, since there was no analogous problem in his own country. In his autobiography Nkrumah discloses his thinking on the matter:

At first I could not understand how Gandhi's philosophy of nonviolence could possibly be effective. It seemed to me to be utterly feeble and without hope of success. The solution of the colonial problem, as I saw it at that time, lay in armed rebellion. How is it possible, I asked myself, for a revolution to succeed without arms and ammunition? After months of studying Gandhi's policy and watching the effect it had, I began to see that, when backed by a strong political organization, it could be the solution to the colonial problem. In Jawaharlal Nehru's rise to power I recognized the success of one who, pledged to Socialism, was able to interpret Gandhi's philosophy in practical terms.[6]

We see here no sense of saintly or utopian purpose, no philosophy of redemptive suffering, but a strongly pragmatic evaluation in which the pivotal terms are "effective," "practical," "success"—in the clearly down-to-earth usage of the trained political scientist. Nkrumah made it clear that his conception of nonviolence was entirely expedient and did not imply the abandonment of armed force once the leaders of a nonviolent insurrection obtained a monopoly of such force by taking control of the government. Speaking from the vantage point of experience, he distinguishes two stages in the independence struggle:

First there is the period of "positive action"—a combination of nonviolent methods with effective and disciplined political action. At this stage open conflict with the existing colonial regime is inevitable and this is a test of strength for the organization. Since it is marked by nonviolence and since the forces of might are on the side of the colonial power, there is little chance of complete success in this period.

The second stage is one of "tactical action," a sort of contest of wits.[7]

Already CPP organizers had gone out from the assembly to prepare the people throughout the country for the first stage of civil resistance or "positive action," and now the stage was set for a showdown. The government had earlier tried cracking down on critics of its policies, as if to test the strength of the resistance movement. Three CPP journalists and the secretary of the Ex-Servicemen's Union were imprisoned on charges of sedition and as a result of articles he published Nkrumah was fined £300 for contempt of court. The sum was quickly raised by CPP volunteer women who collected the money in small change from thousands of passersby in the streets. The latter event boosted the morale of the CPP workers and contributed to the massive turnout for the assembly in November.

Now the government apparently yielded. Hoping to forestall the threatened positive action campaign, government officials agreed to a conference with CPP leaders, which began on January 5, 1950. At the meeting, the British told Nkrumah that they were studying his proposals and asked him to postpone positive action. They then announced on the radio that an agreement had been reached. Nkrumah broke off the negotiations when he learned of this and on the same day, January

8, at 5:00 P.M., he called a mass meeting at the West End Arena. "There I declared to the people," he afterward wrote, "that . . . a general strike should begin from midnight. The response of the people was spontaneous. The political and social revolution of Ghana had started." [8] The timing of this sequence of events is sufficient to suggest the efficiency and popular strength of a political organization geared to move into action on so wide a scale on such short notice.

Nkrumah's speech on that occasion reveals a good deal about the personality of the man as well as the dynamics of the movement he led, and is particularly valuable for its immediacy, unadorned by the benefits of hindsight. Here is the working definition of Nkrumah's method as given in verbatim extracts from the speech of January 8:

The term Positive Action has been erroneously and maliciously publicized, no doubt by the imperialists and their concealed agents-provocateurs and stooges. These political renegades, enemies of the Convention People's Party and for that matter of Ghana's freedom, have diabolically publicized that the CPP's program of positive action means riot, looting and disturbances, in a word, violence.

There are two ways to achieve self-government: either by armed revolution and violent overthrow of the existing regime, or by constitutional and legitimate nonviolent methods. In other words: either by armed might or by moral pressure. . . . We believe that we can achieve self-government even now by constitutional means without resort to any violence.

By Positive Action we mean the adoption of all legitimate and constitutional means by which we can cripple the forces of Imperialism in this country. The weapons of Positive Action are: (1) Legitimate political agitation; (2) Newspaper and educational campaigns; and (3) as a last resort, the constitutional application of strikes, boycotts and noncooperation based on the principle of absolute nonviolence.

But as regards the final stage of positive action, namely, nationwide nonviolent sit-down-at-home strikes, boycotts and noncooperation, we shall not call them into play until all the avenues of our political endeavors of attaining self-government have been closed.[9]

Immediately after the speech, Nkrumah rushed to other key cities—Cape Coast, Sekondi and Tarkwa—formally declaring the onset of positive action in each of them, while CPP organizers spread the word to other areas.

The next morning, from 7:00 A.M., the effectiveness of the strike was greatly in evidence. As Richard Wright describes it,

not a train ran; no one went to work; buses and transportation trucks stood still. The nationalist leaders agreed to the functioning of essential services: water, electricity, health, medical care, etc. For twenty-one days, despite threats of dismissal of workers from jobs, numerous warnings and curfews, and the full evocation of the emergency powers of the Governor, positive action continued.[10]

The Battle of Communications

Although the campaign immediately took hold and held fast, it threatened to falter on the second day as a result of radio broadcasts by the government. Seeking to create division among the strikers, local radio announcers in each section of the country were telling their listeners that people in the other sections had already gone back to work. This bit of psychological warfare might have caused people in Accra, for example, to go back to work, thinking that it was pointless to hold out since the campaign had collapsed everywhere else. And by causing people in Sekondi, Kumasi and Saltpond to act likewise, the fictitious collapse could be made real.

Seeing this, Nkrumah called another mass meeting at the Arena on January 11, where he spoke for two hours to a huge crowd. "At the end of it," Nkrumah reports, "no Government propaganda machine could have succeeded in pacifying them or controlling them. Their blood was fired and they wanted justice." [11]

At 7:00 P.M. on the same day, the governor proclaimed a state of emergency and imposed a curfew. The nonviolent battle was joined. Nkrumah adds details to the picture already given above:

The whole economic life of the country was at a standstill. Public meetings were forbidden and all party letters were opened and censored. The *Evening News,* the Cape Coast *Daily Mail* and the Sekondi *Morning Telegraph* fanned the flame by exhorting the workers to stand firm and to continue Positive Action. Then the office of the *Evening News* was raided and closed down by the police and the newspaper was banned. The same was the fate of my other two newspapers.[12]

The editors of the newspapers were jailed, as were a score of key CPP leaders, including Nkrumah. There was incidental brutality by the British, who for example took Nkrumah's personal servant and some companions to the police station and beat them, but on the whole they acted with restraint matching that of the Africans. Only one serious incident marred the campaign—an outburst on January 17, at the height of the campaign, when ex-servicemen staged a march to Christiansborg. There was a violent clash in which two policemen were killed. Nkrumah did not halt the campaign on this account and at his trial he disclaimed responsibility for this unauthorized occurrence.

When arrested, Nkrumah offered no resistance and none was made on his behalf. Anticipating this event, he had made it clear to his followers throughout the country that "it was important that they should keep calm and make no demonstration of any kind." [13]

Nkrumah and his colleagues were tried and convicted for "inciting others to take part in an illegal strike," and received prison sentences ranging from six months to two years.

Positive action was over now, but the solidarity it had demonstrated was now channeled to electoral activity within the framework of the elections promised in the Coussey Report. When elections for the town councils took place in Accra, Cape Coast and Kumasi, the condemned CPP won majorities in all three cities. In April 1950 Kimla Agbeli Gbedemah, one of the jailed CPP leaders, was released from prison. Taking charge of the party as acting chairman, he proceeded to organize it for the forthcoming general elections, receiving directives smuggled out of prison from the other leaders. When the elections were held on February 8, 1951, less than a year after the positive action campaign, the CPP swept the country, winning thirty-five out of thirty-eight seats.

The British, seeing how things stood, were gracious enough to release the CPP leaders who had remained in prison until this time. They literally went from their prison cells into government posts. The governmental structure contained all the defects that they had protested against, but under Nkrumah's leadership these were worked out as the Gold Coast moved by rapid stages toward full self-government and independence, which was proclaimed on March 6, 1957, with Nkrumah as prime minister of the new nation of Ghana. The nonviolent "positive action" campaign was not the sole factor in bringing this result, but it provided strong impetus to hasten the day, and powerful leverage for political action both through the election and in the parliamentary maneuvering that followed. Though not used again, its potential gave substance to CPP moves within the government.

The aftermath of victory, however, saw tragic departures from the spirit of nonviolence. Most of the men who brought Nkrumah to power were purged and either driven into exile or imprisoned under a detention law whereby Nkrumah arrogated to his government the right to hold anyone in jail for as long as twelve years without charges. In September 1961 Kimla Gbedemah, one of Nkrumah's oldest and closest political associates, was ousted as finance minister. He fortunately fled to Togo, for a month later a law was passed which decreed the death penalty for political offenses. Even after amnesties of some 300 political prisoners in May and June 1962, an estimated 200 to 700 remained behind bars, and to their number were added scores of new suspects during a series of attempts to assassinate Nkrumah in August and September of that year. In one district an estimated 2,000 people were arrested, while homes were looted and pillaged and women raped by Nkrumah's troops. In neighboring Togo there were 3,800 refugees from Ghana, most of them political. Capping the process, the CPP, now clearly Nkrumah's personal instrument, used its overwhelming preponderance of votes successively to install him as prime minister for life, to establish a one-party system of government, and to abolish the ballot in favor of voting by acclamation.

Despite these ominous trends, Nkrumah remained apparently a popular leader and life in Ghana was not unbearable for the average citizen. Yet as Cecil Northcott observed: "In gaining its freedom from imperialists Ghana seems to have lost its independence to an African fascism" in which Nkrumah had become "an astute demagogue-dictator, who is busy creating an image of himself as 'father and founder.'" [14] Nkrumah had tried to mix Gandhi and Hitler. The spirit of the latter had won.

REFERENCES IN CHAPTER 19

1 Quoted in John Gunther, *Inside Africa* (New York: Harper & Brothers, 1955), p. 799.
2 George Padmore: *The Gold Coast Revolution* (London: Dobson, 1953), p. 61f.
3 Quoted in Gunther, *op. cit.*, p. 801.
4 Padmore, *op. cit.*, p. 79.
5 Quoted in Bankole Timothy: *Kwame Nkrumah: His Rise to Power* (London: Allen and Unwin, 1955), p. 97.
6 Kwame Nkrumah: *Ghana: An Autobiography* (New York: Thomas Nelson & Sons, 1957), p. xiv.
7 *Ibid.*, p. xv.
8 *Ibid.*, p. 117.
9 Quoted in Timothy, *op. cit.*, pp. 97-100 passim.
10 Richard Wright: *Black Power* (New York: Harper & Brothers, 1954), p. 95.
11 Nkrumah, *op. cit.*, p. 118.
12 *Ibid.*
13 *Ibid.*, p. 122.
14 Cecil Northcott: "New Gods in Ghana" in *The Christian Century*, November 23, 1960, p. 1367.

20

Nonviolence in the Southern United States Since 1955

A full history of nonviolence in the struggle for racial equality in the United States would probably begin with 1942, when the first component of the Congress of Racial Equality conducted its first sit-in at a Chicago restaurant. It would go on to document the historic Journey of Reconciliation of 1947 in which a group of Negroes and whites led by two secretaries of the Fellowship of Reconciliation, George M. Houser and Bayard Rustin, carried out the first integrated "freedom ride" across the Upper South. But it was not until the Montgomery bus boycott of 1956 and the numerous campaigns following it that nonviolence began to accelerate toward a major, national impact. It is beyond the scope of this book to chronicle each of the proliferating campaigns throughout the country or even in the South, but it is useful to trace the broad outlines and briefly to examine the key events in some detail.

The Montgomery Bus Boycott of 1956

The first sustained mass-scale nonviolent campaign began in December 1955 in Montgomery, Alabama. Earlier the same year five Negro women and two children were arrested and one man was shot to death for disobeying a bus driver's order. It was not unusual for the latter to compel pregnant Negro women to yield their seats to white teenagers, to curse some Negro women and molest others. For many months the Negro community had been smarting under these abuses.

Early in the evening on December 1, a number of white passengers boarded a city bus and, as usual, the driver asked four Negroes to give up their seats. Three did so, but a fourth, Mrs. Rosa Parks, refused. She was arrested and released in bond, with her trial set for the following Monday, December 5.

A mild-mannered seamstress at a department store, this forty-two-year-old woman was well known and highly respected, and news of the incident spread quickly among the city's 50,000 Negro citizens. In the barrooms, hoodlums decided it was time to "beat the hell out of a few bus drivers," and they began sharpening their switchblade knives, readying their pistols and collecting an arsenal of spiked sticks and baseball bats. When word of these preparations reached a number of the community's Negro ministers, they parleyed and decided that some alternative had to be found, and quickly, to avert a riot. A flurry of telephone calls ensued, in the course of which the Women's Political Council hit upon the idea of a boycott. They suggested it to E. D. Nixon, head of the Montgomery local of the Brotherhood of Sleeping Car Porters, the man who had posted Mrs. Parks' bond. Nixon responded enthusiastically. Next morning he phoned two young Baptist ministers, Ralph D. Abernathy and Martin Luther King Jr., who in turn called other ministers and arranged for a meeting at King's church that evening. Nixon and some others began circulating a mimeographed leaflet urging a boycott. By 7:30, when the meeting began, it had already been widely distributed.

In addition to ministers there were physicians, lawyers, schoolteachers, businessmen and union officials at the meeting, representing the leaders of the Negro community. After a brief devotional period the chairman, L. Roy Bennett, president of the Interdenominational Ministerial Alliance, took the floor and proposed a one-day boycott of the buses. After a lively discussion the group agreed to issue a call for both a boycott and a mass meeting to consider further action.

Early the next morning, Saturday, the mimeograph machine

at King's Dexter Avenue Baptist Church was turning out leaflets. By 11:00 A.M. some 7,000 of them were being distributed throughout the Negro community. Meanwhile, the local newspaper, *The Montgomery Advertiser,* had received one of Nixon's leaflets and published it on the front page, unwittingly augmenting the tedious hand-to-hand distribution.

A subcommittee contacted the city's Negro taxicab companies, which agreed to place their 210 taxis at the disposal of the boycott, charging riders the equivalent of their normal bus fare. On Sunday morning the call was sounded from every Negro pulpit. By the afternoon, in one way or another, virtually everyone knew of the boycott scheduled for the next day.

Monday came. Mrs. Parks was tried, found guilty and fined ten dollars plus four dollars costs. She appealed the decision. The boycott took hold with extraordinary effectiveness. Not more than a handful of Negroes rode the buses even during the peak of traffic. Many buses that would normally have been crammed were empty, and many others carried only white passengers. Thousands of Negroes rode in taxis and in car pools. Thousands more walked, a few as far as ten miles. A cautious estimate was that the boycott was eighty per cent effective, a fact that was disquieting to city officials and alarming to Montgomery City Lines, seventy per cent of whose passengers were Negroes.

On Monday evening, some 5,000 Negroes joined in the mass meeting at Holt Street Baptist Church, fired with enthusiasm. Earlier in the day the leadership group had met and founded the Montgomery Improvement Association, with Martin Luther King—to his great surprise—as president. They decided to draft a list of grievances and continue the boycott until they were met. One man later proposed that this decision be reconsidered. The boycott, so successful as a one-day affair, he said, might fizzle out after a few days. "This argument was so convincing," wrote King later, "that we almost resolved to end the protest. But we finally agreed to let the mass meeting . . . be our guide." [1]

The mood of the mass meeting ruled out any hesitation. There was clamor for the boycott to continue. And it not only continued but it grew, holding a level of ninety-five per cent effectiveness for a whole year. Carl T. Rowan, then a reporter for the *Minneapolis Star,* noted other remarkable results: "The Negro ministers . . . had achieved the most unbelievable by pulling the hoodlums out of the crap games and honky-tonks into the churches, where they sang hymns, gave money, shouted amen and wept over the powerful speeches." [2] For months, all classes of people thronged the churches several evenings each week to receive spiritual sustenance and practical instruction for the ongoing struggle. During the day, one might see a Negro doctor's wife offering a ride in her shiny Cadillac to a group of domestic workers, or even an occasional white driver stopping to pick up a Negro. Letters to the editors of local newspapers, written by white people, weighed five to one in sympathy with the boycott.

The campaign was nonviolent throughout. What kept it so? Where did the idea come from? Martin Luther King had heard of Gandhi, but it took some time for the message to penetrate. Even after the boycott was under way, he yielded to his friends' suggestion that he apply for a permit to carry a pistol for self-defense.

The first explicit reference to nonviolence that arose in the context of the campaign came from a white librarian, Juliette Morgan. In a letter published in the segregationist *Montgomery Advertiser* on December 12, 1955, she compared the Negroes' boycott to Gandhi's dramatic salt march of 1930. Unpublicized, however, was the arrival of two men who were to exert an inestimable influence on King's thinking. One was Glenn E. Smiley, a white Methodist minister from Texas, field secretary of the Fellowship of Reconciliation. The other was Bayard Rustin, a Negro Quaker and one of the most courageous men in the annals of nonviolence, who was to serve as a special advisor to King for the next several years.

King was not an immediate success as head of the Montgomery Improvement Association. Failing to achieve an agreement after several meetings with city officials and bus company representatives, the young minister even offered to resign, but was prevented by a unanimous vote of confidence by the MIA's executive board. The vote proved well-founded when the segregationists turned from verbal sparring to rougher tactics.

On January 21 the city commissioners issued a press release for publication the next day, stating that they had reached a settlement and that the boycott was over. In Minneapolis, Carl Rowan saw the advance text when it came in on the Associated Press wire. Incredulous, he phoned King to verify it. As it turned out, the Montgomery officials had duped three Negro ministers, not members of the MIA, into attending a meeting with them and had then issued the statement. King immediately alerted his fellow ministers, and they set out on a Saturday-night tour of the Negro night clubs and taverns to warn the people there. The next morning, from every Negro pulpit came a repudiation of the bogus agreement, effectively countering the newspaper account. The city fathers' scheme fell flat, and the boycott held firm.

Next the segregationists tried intimidation. They arrested drivers in the Negro car pool for minor or trumped-up traffic violations and threatened to arrest waiting riders for vagrancy. King and other leaders were among those taken to jail for "speeding." They also received obscene and insulting, often threatening letters and telephone calls. King alone sometimes got as many as forty a day.

On January 30 a bomb was exploded on the porch of King's home. Hundreds of angry Negroes gathered at the scene, many of them armed and talking of "shooting it out" with the police, who had arrived before them with the mayor and police commissioner. It was the first serious test of nonviolence under provocation. Fortunately no one had been injured in the blast, but King could easily have yielded to the prevailing mood. Silence alone could have triggered a riot.

"Now let's not become panicky," he said, and the crowd

hushed to listen. "If you have weapons, take them home; if you do not have them, please do not seek to get them. We cannot solve this problem through retaliatory violence. . . . We must love our white brothers no matter what they do to us. We must make them know that we love them. Jesus still cries out in words that echo across the centuries: 'Love your enemies; bless them that curse you; pray for them that despitefully use you.' This is what we must live by. We must meet hate with love."

Two nights later a stick of dynamite was exploded on E. D. Nixon's lawn. Again a large crowd gathered but remained nonviolent. A third bombing struck the home of Robert Graetz, white Lutheran pastor of an all-Negro congregation, who was an active MIA member. Miraculously, in all of these explosions no one was hurt, and the terrorists did not succeed in provoking retaliation or breaking the spirit of the boycott. The strain was great, however, and King felt anger welling up in him when he thought of the viciousness of those who might have killed his wife and baby daughter.

On February 22, more than ninety Negroes, including twenty-four ministers, were indicted under an almost forgotten labor law of 1921 outlawing boycotts. They demanded separate trials. No one tried to evade arrest. King's trial was the first, held March 19-22. Though convicted, he appealed and the verdict was eventually reversed.

In May, the MIA asked attorneys of the National Association for the Advancement of Colored People to file a suit on its behalf in the U.S. District Court to overturn the city ordinances which maintained segregation on the buses. The boycott continued for seven months more, as the litigation made its way up to the Supreme Court. Finally, on December 1, 1956, a decree was issued upholding the MIA's plea. The boycott was ended and Negroes resumed riding the buses.

It is widely believed that the year-long boycott resulted in desegregating the Montgomery city buses. Actually it was the court order that did so, to the extent that desegregation occurred at all. It might also be supposed that the ordeal of passive resistance assured harmony at the end and ushered in a new era in race relations in Montgomery. The facts are less heartening. Long after the court decree, few Negroes actually exercised their right to sit anywhere in the buses. Closer to the event, three white men beat a teenage Negro girl as she got off a bus. A shotgun blast was fired into the front door of King's home. Snipers fired at buses, wounding one Negro woman in the leg. On January 10, 1957, four Negro churches and the homes of two ministers were dynamited. Then violence subsided. But as late as August 1962 the MIA newsletter observed that the buses were "not entirely integrated" and cited instances of continued intimidation of Negro passengers.

The enthusiasm and unity of the nonviolent movement rapidly ebbed. King's stature as a local leader declined. According to his biographer, L. D. Reddick, his colleagues "began to question his judgment, to mention his shortcomings. . . . The people had turned, not *against* King, but to some extent away from him." [3]

The MIA declined, too, playing a modest and restricted role in subsequent years and scoring such gains as the hiring of a few Negro bus drivers on exclusively Negro routes. After the boycott of 1956 it no longer functioned as the leadership group for a mass movement, though it continued to be the chief means of communication with the white power structure of the city.

The real importance of the Montgomery bus boycott does not consist in its purported achievement of a local objective. Though it failed there, it had important repercussions. First, the sheer fact of mass unity shattered the myth that Negroes approved of their inferior status under segregation. It set in motion the concept of the "new Negro" and pricked the slumbering consciences of millions of Americans. Second, it sparked similar boycotts in Birmingham, Tallahassee and elsewhere, bringing out new local organizations patterned on the MIA and a new leadership of ministers such as Fred L. Shuttlesworth and C. K. Steele. Third, the publicity emanating from Montgomery spurred scores of Southern cities to desegregate their buses even before the court ruling. Fourth, though diminished at home, Martin Luther King's stature was greatly enlarged on the national level, and he became the acknowledged head of a rapidly growing movement led by Negro ministers, the Southern Christian Leadership Conference.

Finally, nobody noticed the fact that the bus boycott had not brought victory. There had been a boycott and then there had been victory. Here was a powerful legend that would inspire others to authentic victories based wholly or largely on nonviolence.

From a purely strategic standpoint, the Montgomery campaign first sought to attain its objective through passive resistance, then shifted to a legal strategy in which such resistance played no part. Even though it continued, it had no discernible effect on the course of events.

Since the outcome was finally the desired one, there is little point in criticizing what was done. But there were possible alternatives. One was to terminate the boycott and endure the experience of segregation until the Supreme Court ruling was issued. Another was to move from passive resistance to nonviolent direct action. This course of action might have been most promising when the U.S. District Court ruled in favor of the MIA, although it could have been undertaken even earlier. It would have meant going to jail for doing what Mrs. Parks had done instead of going to jail for boycotting the buses—in other words, invading segregationist territory and contesting it directly. Many tactics might have been added to either of the strategic alternatives but were not. The next phase was to see a variety of them in use on a wide scale, with direct action forming the strategic backbone.

The Sit-Ins

In January 1960 a freshman at Shaw University in Greensboro, North Carolina, read a "comic book," *The Montgomery Story,* published by the Fellowship of Reconciliation and widely distributed on Negro college campuses in the South. On February 1, he and three classmates decided to try out its principles and went to a local Woolworth store. They sat down at the lunch counter, which was reserved for white customers. Although refused service, they continued to sit. Day after day they returned with increasing numbers and sat at the counter.

Soon they were joined by white students from Greensboro College for Women. Elsewhere, students at Negro colleges throughout the South heard of the Greensboro sit-in and flocked to nearby lunch counters to start their own. Sometimes they too were joined by white allies. Here and there, the growing movement centered around groups that had attended seminars and workshops conducted by Glenn Smiley and others. Copies of Richard Gregg's *The Power of Nonviolence* were sought out and studied. Dozens of these had been given to Negro college libraries by Smiley on his visits there. Thousands of copies of the FOR leaflet, *How to Practice Nonviolence,* and the leaflet, *CORE Rules for Action,* found their way into the students' hands. Many of the students were not primed at all, however, and knew about nonviolence only by word of mouth.

In some places there was disorder. In Portsmouth, Virginia, for example, Negro high-school students rioted in response to provocation from whites, bringing CORE field secretary Gordon Carey in on an emergency mission to instruct them in nonviolence. For a time the FOR had a three-man team at work, together with volunteers, touring communities where sit-ins were in progress. The team included Glenn Smiley and regional secretaries James M. Lawson Jr. and Charles C. Walker. Their work was closed out as local and regional organizations sprang up, while CORE blossomed into a major nationwide body with many new local chapters and field secretaries in the South, recruited from the student ranks. Under the aegis of the Southern Christian Leadership Conference, sit-in leaders themselves launched a new organization, the Student Nonviolent Coordinating Committee. All of these organizations provided full- or part-time staff to instruct local groups in nonviolent conduct, tactics and strategy, thus curbing or forestalling much of the violence that might otherwise have occurred.

Abundant local leadership was doubtless more crucial to the rapid spread of the nonviolent sit-ins. Typical of many was the situation as it developed in Raleigh, North Carolina, where students from two campuses joined to form the Shaw-St. Augustine's Student Movement during the first week of the demonstrations. One of the leaders, Glenford E. Mitchell, tells how the movement was organized. He points out that, while on some campuses the elected president of the student body readily took charge, in Raleigh and elsewhere the leadership emerged on the spot "by natural selection."

The nine-member Intelligence Committee—five from Shaw and four from St. Augustine's—planned all the strategy with the aid of its subsidiary committees: the Group Movement Committee, which directed the movement of the students on the streets so as to avoid congestion and to effect proper placing of students in or about the stores; the Steering Committee, which studied the day-to-day conditions on the scene and made recommendations such as the best way and the best time to move; the Negotiating Committee, a stand-by committee which consisted of students who represented the schools at Mayor's committee meetings; and the Coordinating Committee, whose members later became representatives to the Student Nonviolent Coordinating Committee. The Intelligence Committee was approved by both student bodies.[4]

At first, says Mitchell, daily mass meetings were held for morale and information, with prayers, speeches and singing, after which the intelligence committee (what would more often be called an executive committee) met to make preparations for the following day's activities. In doing so, they made it a practice to keep talking until they were able to arrive at unanimous decisions. "We had learned early in the movement that to keep the students together we had to be unified as a committee at all times." This in turn made for solidarity among the mass of students, who "always responded in unison and with complete acceptance." [5]

At Claflin College in Orangeburg, South Carolina, students grouped themselves into classes of forty, each spending three or four days studying and discussing Martin Luther King's account of the Montgomery bus boycott, *Stride Toward Freedom,* and the *CORE Rules for Action.* "In these sessions," wrote a student leader, "we emphasized adherence to nonviolence and discussed various situations which might provoke violence. Could each of us trust our God and our temper enough not to strike back even if kicked, slapped or spit upon?" [6]

From those who felt ready, forty cadres were picked for the first demonstration in Orangeburg. Action plans were then charted, taking into consideration every detail: the number and position of the entrances to the store, the number of lunch-counter stools, the exact number of minutes required to walk from the campus to the store by various routes.

The sequence of events in the Orangeburg campaign is largely representative of the sit-ins as a whole. At 10:45 A.M. on February 25 the cadres started out in groups of three or four, each with a designated leader, walking by different routes timed to arrive simultaneously at the store. The first fifteen students then entered and seated themselves at the lunch counter. After fifteen minutes the management posted a sign there, "Closed in the Interest of Public Safety." The students left and were replaced by a second wave of twenty, each of whom sat until the seats were removed.

The next day they returned and stood several rows deep along the seatless counter. Subsequently the store would not let more than two Negroes enter the store at one time.

On March 1, a thousand students marched through the streets with placards saying "All Sit or All Stand," "Segregation Is Obsolete" and "Down with Jim Crow." There were no disorders, but the lunch counters were shut down for two weeks. In the interval the students formed a statewide movement and launched a boycott against stores that had lunch counters at which Negroes were not served.

On March 14 the lunch counters reopened. The students planned another mass march to be followed by resumption of the sit-in on the next day. The march began in below-freezing cold. They did not get far before they encountered police with tear-gas bombs and fire hoses, which were used indiscriminately against the young Negroes. Many were knocked down and all were drenched. Over 500 were arrested, of whom 150 were taken to jail. Some 350 others, soaked and shivering, were jammed into an open-air stockade, where they sang hymns and said prayers. After a few hours they were released in ten dollars bond. Trials began the next day, a few students at a time, and all were convicted of disturbing the peace. For some time to come, the Orangeburg campaign was effectively thwarted.

There were variations on this pattern, hinging to some extent on the activities of friendly or hostile whites other than the police. In Tallahassee, white CORE members bought food and passed it to their Negro companions. In Jacksonville, Florida, a mob armed with axe handles and baseball bats descended upon the sit-ins. In Dallas, fifty-eight white students at Southern Methodist University joined two Negro classmates in a sit-in at a drugstore and were sprayed with insecticide.

In North Carolina, where the sit-ins had originated, white and Negro ministerial associations joined in appeals to businessmen. In Raleigh the Catholic Interracial Council issued a statement of support and the local Fellowship of Southern Churchmen circulated a petition among white Christians indicating the signers' support of stores "which decide to reopen their lunch counters on a nondiscriminatory basis." In Durham the Baptist Student Union of North Carolina College pledged a boycott of stores to "remain in force until unequal policies are terminated." With such responses it is not surprising that victory came quickly in this state. In New Orleans, by contrast, bitter resistance met the sit-ins. Only after two years and more than 300 arrests were negotiations begun, leading to the sudden opening of lunch counters to Negroes at fifteen stores on September 12, 1962. At the other extreme were such communities as Houston and San Antonio, Texas, where variety stores hastened to desegregate their lunch counters before demonstrations even occurred, wishing to avoid the disturbances that had happened elsewhere. In the first two months, sit-ins had spread to fifty Southern cities, with more to come, and some had already yielded.

If Orangeburg offers a good example of planning, probably Nashville is more typical of the characteristic detail. Here, soon after the Montgomery bus boycott, a number of Negro ministers organized the Nashville Christian Leadership Council, one of the strongest local affiliates of SCLC. For years they conducted workshops in nonviolence as well as fruitless negotiations for the desegregation of lunch counters. The organizational instrument was ready for the challenge of Greensboro when it came.

On February 13, students from Fisk and Vanderbilt began their sit-in, harassed by white troublemakers. A Methodist editor on the scene described their conduct:

When called names, they keep quiet. When hit, they do not strike back. Even when hostile white youth pull hair and snuff out burning cigarettes on the backs of Negro girls, the girls do not retaliate. They pray and take what comes, in dignity.[7]

On the first day, seventy-nine students were arrested and convicted of disorderly conduct. For two months thereafter the sit-ins continued, augmented toward the end of March by an economic boycott. On April 12 a mass march encountered white toughs with baseball bats, and a near-riot ensued, whereupon local merchants agreed to negotiate. On May 10, six lunch counters were opened on a desegregated basis, with others to follow. Three years later, a new campaign was launched to open cafeterias to Negroes, and victory came only after riots in which several persons were injured.

Two predominant facts emerge from an over-all assessment of the sit-ins. First, settlement almost invariably occurred through direct negotiations rather than by court rulings. Second, opponents were seldom if ever won over to the side of justice as a result of voluntary suffering or Christian love on the part of the demonstrators. The key factor was economic leverage, and closely related to this was the merchants' desire for stability and civil order. A marginal factor of varying importance was the basic attitude of the white community: hostile, neutral or sympathetic.

Merrill Proudfoot, a white Presbyterian minister, found himself among the leaders of a six-week sit-in in Knoxville, Tennessee, which he documented in a highly instructive book, *Diary of a Sit-In*. The abuse and mistreatment the demonstrators experienced were similar to those of Nashville and elsewhere. They were pushed, hot coffee was spilled on them and they were sprayed with insecticides. One day white high-school boys were heckling him. They poured Coca-Cola on his head and began striking him in the face. When they started to pull him from his booth, a "neutral" white man intervened and told the youths to get out. A sentimental interpretation would focus solely on this act of decency. But Proudfoot observed that nonviolence had a polarizing effect; it "caused this 'neutral' to declare himself for decency and order" but also "brings out the bully in those who are inclined to be bullies." [8] Moreover, the intervention of a "decent neutral" can no more be considered a token of strategic success than a display of decency by a determined opponent, though certainly these qualities are to be welcomed.

Both Mitchell and Proudfoot agree on the effectiveness of the economic factor. In Raleigh a three-pronged strategy evolved pragmatically: first, the sit-in; second, picketing as a means of garnering sympathy. The third grew out of the second:

After a week of continuous educational picketing we learned that business at variety stores was suffering a loss of some eighteen per cent. Our new knowledge provided us with a new weapon—the economic boycott. The wording of signs then assumed a new slant. At Easter we appeared with such signs as "Wear last year's Easter bonnets!" [9]

Proudfoot notes that when sit-ins occurred during mealtime they added to the economic drain of the boycott, as did the generally unsettled condition of the shopping district. Many prospective customers refrained from buying, not because they sympathized with the integrationists but because they did not want to get mixed up in what was going on. As a result, the stores "decided they risked greater losses by not desegregating than by desegregating. This is *the one decisive reason* for the speedy success of the movement." [10]

Attitudes do change, but more often they do so as an accommodation to a new situation of order and stability rather than in response to the process of change itself. And they change unevenly. In Proudfoot's Knoxville three years later, as in Nashville and Greensboro, sit-ins had to be waged once again to win new objectives even as an interracial exchange program of children was getting under way. Gang violence may increase at the same time that politicians become more conciliatory.

Although the sit-ins did not go far toward ending racial segregation, they did register tangible gains. More important, they set in motion a large-scale ongoing movement that was to have continuing repercussions. They consolidated the leadership of Martin Luther King and others who were committed to nonviolence. And the nonviolent content of the campaigns added mightily to the stature of the Negro, dramatizing clearly the righteousness of the cause of integration. The calm courage and endurance of the demonstrators contrasted sharply with the ugly image of their opponents, whose underhanded tactics jolted the public's sense of fair play. Particularly among white students, liberals and churchmen, dormant consciences were stirred.

The Freedom Rides of 1961

As 1960 was pre-eminently the year of the sit-ins, 1961 was the year of freedom rides which "put the sit-ins on the road." Conceived by CORE members along lines similar to the 1947 Journey of Reconciliation, the initial freedom ride set out from Washington, D.C., on May 4, heading for New Orleans. Its participants were six pairs of white and Negro cadres, most of the latter drawn from the student sit-ins. Together with a white CORE observer they were to travel through Virginia, the Carolinas, Georgia, Alabama and Mississippi aboard Greyhound and Trailways interstate buses. At each stop they tested the facilities, entering segregated waiting rooms and seeking service at segregated lunch counters. In some instances both members of a pair entered together, in others the Negro went to the white facility while his white teammate went to the facility marked "colored."

The journey was largely uneventful until the freedom riders reached Rock Hill, South Carolina. Here for more than a year, lunch-counter sit-ins had been held repeatedly both by local students and by cadres of the Student Nonviolent Coordinating Committee from many parts of the South, who were subjected to vicious harassment and jailings. A score of hoodlums were on hand when the freedom riders' bus arrived. When Negro divinity student John Lewis approached the white waiting room he was assaulted by two of them. Three others began pummeling his white teammate, Albert Bigelow, a former U.S. Navy commander. Neither of them offered any resistance. Only when another CORE member, Genevieve Hughes, was pushed to the ground did police intervene.

Most of the stops en route to Atlanta were without incident, but the next leg of the trip was a harrowing one. When the Greyhound bus arrived at Anniston, Alabama, it was attacked by an angry mob armed with iron bars. They smashed windows, punctured tires and set fire to the bus with an incendiary bomb. Some of the freedom riders were beaten as they emerged from the smoke-filled bus before police arrived and tardily dispersed the mob. After the injured were treated at the hospital, they were taken to Birmingham in automobiles sent by the Rev. Fred L. Shuttlesworth. FBI agents later arrested nine local residents, who were brought to trial, but some were acquitted and charges against the others were dropped. None were punished.

When the Trailways bus arrived an hour later, eight of the hoodlums boarded it. They forced all the CORE members to the rear, kicking and beating them. When veteran CORE activist Jim Peck and Walter Bergman, a retired college professor, remonstrated with their assailants they were knocked to the floor of the bus.

In two hours the bus pulled into the Birmingham terminal. Another mob of white men was waiting for them. Negro student Charles Person and his white teammate Jim Peck were the first to leave the bus. As soon as they entered the white wating room they were grabbed bodily and pushed into an alley, where five of them set upon Person and six began beating Peck. Police did not appear until both had been beaten unconscious. Person survived with a gash on the back of his head and a swollen face. Peck's face and head required fifty-three stitches at the hospital.

Plans to resume the ride the next day were thwarted by the refusal of bus drivers to take them. Rather than become embroiled in a prolonged campaign in Birmingham, they decided to fly to New Orleans since a rally had already been arranged for their arrival there.

The bus burning at Anniston and the savage beating of Jim Peck were widely reported, and newspapers throughout the country took editorial note of the fact that unarmed men of ostensible good will had been attacked without striking back. Sidney Smyer, president of the Birmingham Chamber of Commerce, returning six weeks later from a tour of the Far East, said that his city had lost much prestige as a result of this violence.

In Nashville, a group of students from the sit-in movement resolved to carry on the freedom ride from Birmingham to New Orleans. They started out on May 18, the day after the CORE group landed in New Orleans. Although they were arrested by Alabama state police and returned to the Tennessee border, they went back, made their way to Birmingham and, after an all-night vigil at the bus terminal, succeeded in finding a driver who would transport them to Montgomery.

When they arrived, they were greeted by a surly mob numbering hundreds of people who had been called together by the Ku Klux Klan. The freedom riders were mauled, kicked and slugged as they left the bus. James Zwerg, a white member of the group, was cornered by sixteen Klansmen, beaten unconscious and left lying in the street for an hour before an ambulance took him to the hospital. Others were rescued by members of the Montgomery Improvement Association, whose cars were waiting for them. Police appeared belatedly but were unable to control the mob. In the ensuing riot, one Negro (not a freedom rider) was soaked with kerosene and set on fire. Finally the police resorted to tear gas to disperse the racists.

Sporadic violence continued through the day. In the evening the Federal Government stepped in when it became evident that the Governor of Alabama was unwilling to protect the freedom riders. Four hundred U.S. marshals were rushed to Montgomery, with another 266 following the next morning. Governor John Patterson, an arch-segregationist, insisted that they were not needed and even threatened to arrest them if they violated any local laws.

Even as he was saying this, local radio stations were broadcasting the news that Montgomery Negroes led by Martin Luther King, who had returned from his new home in Atlanta, were planning a mass rally for the freedom riders at First Baptist Church. Carloads of white men from the rural areas began to converge on Montgomery, moving toward the church. Some 3,000 persons were besieged inside. The U.S. marshals attempted to turn back the mob, which succeeded in smashing some windows and injuring at least one person inside. Before the evening was over, Governor Patterson called out the National Guard and dispersed the mob.

Diane Nash, a Roman Catholic freedom rider, described the mood of the beleaguered Negroes:

In the dire danger in which we were that night, no one expressed anything except concern for freedom. . . . We stayed there until dawn and everyone was naturally tired, but no one said so. . . . I don't think I've ever seen a group of people band together as the crowd in the church did that night.[11]

The following morning, joined by three members of the first freedom ride and five New Orleans CORE members, the Nashville group resumed its journey. Before their departure, they ate together at the terminal restaurant without incident. There were now twenty-seven freedom riders in two buses, accompanied by a large escort of National Guard troops and highway patrolmen. They drove to Jackson, Mississippi, without making the usual rest stops. Instead of a mob, they were met by city police who arrested them as soon as they tried to integrate the terminal facilities. Brought quickly to trial and convicted of disturbing the peace, they chose to go to jail rather than pay fines.

The two initial freedom rides were soon followed by many more. The first was a group of ten men from colleges and seminaries in Connecticut, led by William Sloane Coffin Jr., chaplain of Yale University. When they arrived in Montgomery they spent an evening trying to persuade Justice Department officials to arrange guarantees with state authorities that facilities would be integrated at the end of a "cooling-off period" called for by U.S. Attorney General Robert F. Kennedy. This cooling-off period meant, in effect, a temporary return to the segregated status quo, backed up with a court order barring the activities of freedom riders in Montgomery for ten days. "Why should Negroes always be asked to make the concessions?" asked the Connecticut group. "Why not allow free, unhampered travel during the moratorium period, allowing the white community to become accustomed to it? Or, if there are to be no freedom rides for a while, assure their right to resume freely at some mutually agreeable fixed date." [12]

Unable to obtain such assurances, the group proceeded to the bus terminal and were arrested at the lunch counter as they drank coffee with four Negro ministers.

Another freedom ride involved two Jewish rabbis and eight Negro and white Christian ministers, including Ralph Lord Roy and Robert McAfee Brown. This group went to Tallahassee under CORE auspices, while another which included officials of the United Auto Workers terminated in St. Petersburg and Ocala, Florida.

There were others as well, going to a variety of destinations, but the greatest number focused on Jackson, Mississippi. Most of them arrived by bus, but some came by air or rail. By mid-August over three hundred had been arrested. The last major event in the freedom ride chronicle was the arrest on September 13 of fifteen Episcopal priests who were on an interracial prayer pilgrimage from New Orleans to Chicago.

Nine days later the Interstate Commerce Commission issued new regulations to secure the right of integrated travel. Beginning on November 1, interstate buses were required to display a sign: "Seating aboard this vehicle without regard to race, color, creed or national origin, by order of the Interstate Commerce Commission." The same statement was printed on all interstate bus tickets the following year. Terminals servicing interstate buses were required to post similar signs.

CORE test teams found that compliance with the ICC regulations was widespread and included Birmingham and Anniston, though pockets of resistance continued elsewhere and were met with Federal Court injunctions or renewed freedom rides, not always successfully.

Unlike the sit-ins, the freedom rides exerted virtually no economic pressure. Indeed it is difficult to speak of strategy or tactics at all in a meaningful sense when participants only sit in waiting rooms or at lunch counters. The key fact of the freedom rides was what has been called "nonviolent insistence" —simple individual action undergirded by nonviolent conduct under provocation or attack. The pressure exerted was almost solely moral and indirect. The first freedom ride, building on the climate already created by the sit-ins, stung the consciences of others who formed subsequent freedom rides. The cumulative pressure of them all acted to compel the federal authorities to take the steps that followed. In all of this the involvement of well-known and respected church leaders was an intangible but relevant factor. In the Episcopal priests' pilgrimage were Malcolm Boyd, a writer and chaplain at Wayne State University, and Robert L. Pierson, assistant to the director of the American Church Union and son-in-law of Governor Nelson A. Rockefeller of New York. Regardless of their attitude toward the issue at stake, Federal officials did not want the embarrassment of appearing to condone the mistreatment of such men, once the latter showed that they would not be deterred by anything short of decisive action. In this respect, names may have compensated for lack of numbers.

This is not to deny the moral impact arising even when participants were "unknown." But it is a fact that the mere arrest of the Yale chaplain and the Governor's son-in-law had wide repercussions, while the brutal beating of James Zwerg went virtually unnoticed. In the press, the assault on Jim Peck, white, was dramatized and the fate of Charles Person, Negro, was barely mentioned. And a large part of the reason for dramatizing the Peck beating undoubtedly was the fact that it was the first event of its kind. It was not enough, by itself, to bring about the ICC regulations, though it evidently was enough to swell the ranks of the freedom rides.

The testimony of John Maguire is relevant here. Born in Montgomery, he was professor of religion at Wesleyan University. He credited the freedom rides with accelerating the process of desegregation as well as his own move from benign neutrality to a positive, articulate position:

> For us who went on the freedom rides there has resulted an identification and empathy with Negroes that we never knew before, and the realization that just such a sense of identification by our national leaders will be necessary if they are to understand this group on the move, and sense the heart of this worldwide social revolution. The freedom rides have dramatized this need and profoundly affected the lives of everyone involved.[13]

Robert McAfee Brown, then professor of systematic theology at Union Theological Seminary, corroborated this view from his experience on the freedom ride to Tallahassee. He cited the rides generally as a "creative alternative to violence" which expressed solidarity with Negroes as well as strengthening the hand of white liberals in the South who, without necessarily expressing overt approval of this tactic, could "perhaps pick up and build upon whatever a freedom ride may have done to loosen segregation patterns in their own towns." [14]

One immediate outgrowth of the 1961 freedom rides was the 1962 Freedom Highways campaign launched by CORE to open Howard Johnson restaurants and other accommodations to interracial use. Again there were arrests and abuses such as the use of insecticides and ammonia against the nonviolent cadres, but by the end of the year all but eighteen out of 297 company-operated Howard Johnson restaurants were desegregated by negotiations without court action. This success in turn led to a new strategy, the "freedom task force" of CORE field workers and trained volunteers, concentrating on public accommodations in a number of cities, beginning in

1963 with communities located near the major highways where CORE had been working.

Other organizations such as SCLC, SNCC and the NAACP took a similar turn, often coupling such campaigns with drives to secure the right to vote for disfranchised Negroes, particularly in Mississippi, Alabama and Georgia. Although civil-rights activities increased in the Upper South and spread to the North and West, the most significant development was the onset of numerous campaigns in the Deep South. Rather than attempt a survey, two major contrasting campaigns have been chosen for detailed scrutiny, partly because of their historic importance for the over-all struggle in the United States but also because the detailed information that is available can compensate somewhat for the more general accounts presented elsewhere in this CASEBOOK. It is simply not feasible to do for, say, Debrecen in 1859, what we can do in the studies that follow.

The Albany Movement of 1962

Albany is a city in southwest Georgia. About a third of its 56,000 inhabitants are Negroes. It is the birthplace of the noted composer, Wallingford Riegger, and the site of Albany State College for Negroes, with a student enrollment of 650. Like many Deep South towns, it had maintained rigid patterns of white domination since the post-Reconstruction period, typified in the derogatory reporting of news of the Negro community in James Gray's daily *Albany Herald*.

For years, local Negroes endured the situation, but with the advent of the sit-ins there were stirrings of discontent. In January 1961 a group of Negro ministers wrote to the editor of the *Herald*, politely requesting that he stop degrading them in print. They were told in an editorial to mind their own business. As if to underline the point, white hoodlums threw stones at the homes of three of the ministers. Police did nothing to apprehend them, and subsequent appeals to Mayor Asa D. Kelley went unheeded.

In July, SNCC field secretaries arrived to scout the possibility of a voter-education project for Albany and the surrounding rural areas, sponsored by the Field Foundation, SCLC and the American Missionary Association, an instrumentality of the United Church of Christ. By October the project was begun, but the SNCC workers did not confine their efforts to it. Two of them tested integration at the bus terminal when the ICC regulations went into effect on November 1, and were ordered to leave.

Soon afterward, one of the Negro community's leading citizens, Dr. William G. Anderson, brought together a number of local organizations to form the Albany Movement for a concerted campaign to improve the status of the city's Negroes. Founded on November 17, the Movement embraced the Ministerial Alliance, the Federation of Women's Clubs, the Negro Voter League, SNCC, the local NAACP branch and NAACP Youth Council and the Criterion Club, one of the South's oldest organizations of professional men. Again, requests for talks with the mayor were denied.

Its first direct-action project came on November 25, when three youths and two adults sought service at the bus station dining room. They were arrested. Moreover, there was an upsurge of sporadic incidents. Negro college girls were molested, and there were cases of arson and vandalism.

It was in this atmosphere, on December 10, that eight freedom riders arrived by train from Atlanta and were joined by Albany Negroes and SNCC workers at the station. They were jailed. When they were brought to trial two days later, 400 Negro high-school and college students marched in protest and were arrested when they refused to disperse. For two more days, with dwindling numbers, the marches continued, and the total number of those arrested rose to 560, of whom 300 chose to remain in jail, hoping thereby to exert further pressure by encumbering the city officials with the problem of logistics which this would involve.

It seemed momentarily that a victory had been won. Police released 118 juvenile prisoners, and the mayor set up a biracial commission which had been requested by the ministers' group and again by the Albany Movement. The Movement suspended further demonstrations as negotiations began, late on December 14. The talks quickly reached an impasse and were broken off. Martin Luther King arrived the next day, and he and Dr. Anderson led a protest march in which they and 250 others were arrested. Negotiations were resumed and the city commission finally agreed to desegregate bus and train terminals and to hear the Negro community's grievances. A truce was established pending the election of a new commission on January 11, and the Movement agreed to abstain from mass demonstrations until after that date.

The Movement did not wait before initiating other types of nonviolent action. Marion S. Page, the Movement's executive secretary, made a special trip to Columbus to do his family's Christmas shopping, and many others followed suit. In January an organized selective-buying campaign was begun to persuade merchants to hire Negro sales clerks and open lunch counters, and indirectly to exert pressure on city officials to abolish segregation laws. No serious attempt was made to confer with businessmen either before or during this campaign. Ranging from fifty per cent to seventy-five per cent effectiveness, its effect was negligible since Negroes did not comprise a sizable market, and retailers did not figure importantly in the political power structure.

It was easier to get effectiveness in a boycott of the city buses, since ninety per cent of the passengers were Negroes. By the end of December the bus company agreed to desegregate and to hire at least one Negro driver, but the Movement held out for a written guarantee from the city commissioners promising not to hinder these moves. When this was refused, the Movement rejected the bus company's offer. The continued boycott led to cessation of the company's operations early in February.

January 11 came and there was no change. Instead of resuming mass action, the Movement concentrated on its selective-buying campaign and SNCC workers devoted their efforts to voter education. In February, Martin Luther King and the others, including Ralph D. Abernathy, were convicted for their part in the December protest, but they were not sentenced until July 10. Thus nearly seven months passed without mass demonstrations and without significant progress.

Sentenced to forty-five days at hard labor, King and Abernathy decided not to appeal but to serve their sentences as a form of moral protest. This gesture brought new demonstrations. On July 11, thirty-six Negroes were arrested for marching or picketing. The next day, King and Abernathy were released when, according to the police, "an unidentified, well-dressed Negro" paid their fines.

For the next few days there were mass meetings, attended by more than a thousand Negroes each evening. King and the Albany leaders insisted that negotiations be reopened. Mayor Kelley replied that he would not negotiate with "lawbreakers." Throughout the week, singly or in small groups, Negroes tested parks, libraries and other facilities, seeking service but avoiding arrest by leaving when ordered to do so. As preparations were being made for mass action, the city officials sought to forestall it by obtaining an injunction by a Federal district judge prohibiting boycotts, picketing and speeches promoting racial demonstrations. Instead of halting the Movement, however, this triggered a series of three public demonstrations on July 21 in which 161 persons were arrested, while Movement lawyers went into court to obtain a stay of the injunction, which was granted on July 23.

Many Negroes took this to mean that there would be no arrests. They were infuriated when forty members of a prayer pilgrimage to city hall were arrested the next day. A crowd of 2,000 massed in the Negro district and when 170 police moved in to disperse them, bottles and rocks were thrown, injuring two officers. Despite the wish of many Movement leaders to press forward, Martin Luther King stepped in and called a halt to further demonstrations, declaring a "Day of Penitence" on which nonviolent cadres visited Negro poolrooms, taverns and restaurants, preaching the need for discipline in the struggle. For the rest of the week, action was confined to prayer vigils of ten to thirty persons. Anderson and King led the first one and were arrested, as were the groups that followed. Toward the end of the week, a new tactic was introduced. When arrested, cadres "went limp," refusing to walk or stand, compelling the police to carry them bodily to jail.

During this period, Albany's police chief, Laurie Pritchett, had found an answer to the tactic of filling the jails, sending arrested Negroes to the jails in surrounding counties. Conditions there were worse than in Albany. In Terrell County, for example, Negroes outnumbered whites two to one, but whites held onto political power with a voting strength that outnumbered the Negroes fifty-eight to one—dangerous territory for integrationists. There were many incidents of violence against SNCC workers in the area as well as against those whom Pritchett exported. On July 23 the wife of real-estate agent Slater King, vice-president of the Albany Movement, was knocked down and kicked while attempting to deliver packages to prisoners in the Mitchell County jail at Leesburg. Mrs. King was five months pregnant and later had a miscarriage. Her brother-in-law, attorney C. B. King, was struck with a cane by D. C. Campbell, sheriff of Dougherty County, when he went to arrange medical care for William Hansen, a white SNCC field secretary who was badly beaten by fellow prisoners when police told them he was a "nigger-lover."

These and other incidents of violence, together with the repeated jailing of Martin Luther King, impelled a group of Negro and white ministers and rabbis in the North to plan a motorcade to Washington to seek White House intervention. At the same time a bipartisan group of ten U.S. Senators urged the Department of Justice to take "all possible steps" on behalf of those arrested in Albany. On August 1, President John F. Kennedy said publicly that he could not understand the unwillingness of Albany officials to negotiate.

When the prayer-vigil trial of Martin Luther King and his associates was held on August 10, a group of thirty-five Northern ministers and rabbis was present in the courtroom. One of them wrote: "The trial was a farce. The judge had his opinion and judgment written out when he came into the court." [15] King and the others were given suspended sentences. Upon their release, small-scale testing tactics were used. Small biracial teams went to three public parks and two libraries. Instead of arresting them, officials closed these facilities. The pools remained closed until months later, when one of them was sold to James Gray and reopened for whites only. Seats were removed from the libraries and the checkout desk was opened on a desegregated basis.

Election time was drawing near, and the Movement gave new emphasis to voter registration. In the rural areas, SNCC workers encountered increased harassment as they labored to enroll Negro voters. Their meetings in country churches were invaded by white officials. They were threatened or beaten and local Negroes were intimidated. White-supremacy candidates openly encouraged these acts. At dawn on August 15, Shady Grove Baptist Church in Leesburg was dynamited by terrorists.

On the same day the Albany City Commission met and promptly adjourned after refusing to consider proposals made by the Movement. The Northern ministers and rabbis left the day after, taking with them a vivid impression of conditions in southwest Georgia. Before they departed, they were asked to organize another and larger pilgrimage. This they did. In ten days eighty men and women from Chicago and the Northeast arrived in Albany. After a briefing session at Bethel A.M.E. Church, seventy-five of them agreed to risk arrest. Going in groups of five, they assembled before the city hall for a two-hour prayer vigil. After brief scripture readings, they were ordered to disperse and then hauled off to jail, where some of them fasted for thirty-six hours. Most of them then posted bail and returned to their homes. A few remained in jail for a week.

The pilgrimage focused national attention on Albany once more and stimulated sympathy within the religious bodies to which the pilgrims belonged. The ten rabbis in the group were given scrolls by the American Jewish Congress for their "courage, devotion to liberty and fulfillment of the teachings of our prophets." Their gesture of solidarity heartened the Negroes of Albany, but it had no discernible positive effect on the whites. Even as they were ending their fast, night riders in Lee County fired volleys of rifle bullets into the homes of four Negro families. And soon after the last of them left on September 3, there were more outrages. In Terrell County a white SNCC worker was wounded in the arm by a night rider's shotgun blast. In little more than a week, three more Negro Baptist churches were destroyed. One of them was rebuilt by the white citizens of Terrell County. Funds were collected by several agencies to enable SCLC to rebuild the others, including Shady Grove, but white vandals with a bulldozer knocked down the walls of one of them a year later, before it was even completed.

With the departure of the Northern clergymen, the Albany Movement declined. It had little to show for its efforts except bruises. Although it continued to stage demonstrations from time to time, it made no headway the following year. The pathos of the situation is suggested by the events of May 1963. In three weeks, May 7-27, some 120 people were arrested, sixteen of whom vowed to fast "until there is some indication of a total solution to the racial problem here in Albany." This gesture had no effect but to exhibit a capacity for bluffing. Unable to muster more than a hundred demonstrators, Dr. Anderson announced on May 10 that Martin Luther King had been asked to come. "Then the sparks will begin to fly—in a nonviolent way, of course." But King did not come. A month later, Anderson moved to Detroit to begin a residency in surgery, turning over the presidency of the Movement to Slater King.

The Albany Movement, said one observer, "was successful only if the goal was to go to jail." In part, its failure was due to the skill of Police Chief Pritchett, who won fame as an expert in quelling "racial disturbances," and to the stubbornness of city officials. The inaction of Federal authorities was also a factor. But of greater concern to us is the strategic failure of the Movement itself.

One episode not already mentioned is the attempt at school integration. On September 3, Dr. Anderson announced at a mass meeting that an attempt would be made to integrate the schools. The next day, he took his fourteen-year-old daughter and thirteen others to Albany Senior High School, while four children were taken to two junior high schools in the same manner. After talking with the principals, who refused to register the students, the Negro parents applied to the superintendent of schools, also without result. Dr. Anderson thereupon threatened to sue. Seven months later, on April 8, 1963, the suit was filed, bringing a Federal Court order in July for the county school board to submit a desegregation plan.

Most of the Albany Movement's actions were hastily conceived, shortsighted, overambitious. The Movement relied too much on the inspiration of the moment. It had no definite plan or advance schedule, no provision for alternative moves. No serious attempt was made to evaluate different actions or to synchronize them. Each time a major thrust was made, it was pinned to the same blind hope that it would bring a sweeping solution. The bus boycott is an excellent example of the kind of error to which the Movement was prone. Here was the weakest point in the opponent's system, and the bus company's offer provided an opportunity for nonviolent direct action—boarding the buses on an integrated basis and either scoring an immediate victory or, if police intervened, attacking the segregation ordinances in the courts. This opportunity was simply thrown away, probably because the Albany leaders were trying to do, and surpass, what they thought had been done in Montgomery.

Virtually no approaches were made to white leaders or masses except at the least accessible point—the mayor and police chief.

Professor Howard Zinn of Spelman College in Atlanta concisely summed up the Movement's defects in a valuable study for the Southern Regional Council:

Sometimes there has been a tendency simply to repeat old actions under new circumstances. The movement delayed legal action, for instance, which might have been initiated last winter [1961-62], and continued to depend mainly on demonstrations, instead of linking the two. There has been a failure to create and handle skillfully a set of differentiated tactics for different situations. The problem of desegregating Albany facilities involves various parties: some situations call for action by the city commission; some for decision by the Federal Courts; some for agreement with private businessmen. Moreover, there are advantages to singling out a particular goal and concentrating on it. This is an approach not only tactically sound for Negro protest but also creates a climate favorable to a negotiated solution. The community is presented with a specific, concrete demand rather than a quilt of grievances and demands which smothers the always limited ability of societies to think rationally about their faults.[16]

Rectifying such faults is not easy for a movement that has squandered its potential. After a series of defeats it is, for example, hard to persuade members of teenage gangs to give up their knives, and the use of those knives under stress will sabotage the efforts of the few nonviolent cadres that can be counted on. In Albany, defeat brought division and apathy concerning nonviolence and the Movement, while at the same time whetting the Negro community's bitterness and frustration, conjuring up new goals even farther-reaching than the old. As one observer stated, "If anything, the Negroes' ambitions have grown in ratio to the decline of their hopes." [17]

Birmingham 1963

To a great extent, what was learned from the failure in Albany was used in scoring an important victory in Birmingham, a city ten times larger and ranking among the ugliest in its racial attitudes. Unsolved bombings of Negro homes were not uncommon, nor was unprovoked police brutality under the administration of Eugene "Bull" Connor, commissioner of public safety. It seemed hardly a promising location for a breakthrough, but Martin Luther King was determined to achieve gains here that would recoup prestige lost at Albany.

Birmingham's own nonviolent movement began in 1956 when the Rev. Fred L. Shuttlesworth launched a bus boycott on the Montgomery pattern and founded the Alabama Christian Movement for Human Rights. Although the boycott did not reach mass proportions, it led to a suit that integrated the Birmingham bus lines. In subsequent years, Shuttlesworth made repeated forays against segregation. At one time in July 1961 he was under indictment in six criminal cases for breaking Jim Crow laws and was involved in a dozen civil cases.

In March 1962, Shuttlesworth launched a campaign to end segregation in hiring practices and at lunch counters of downtown Birmingham stores. There were brief demonstrations and a continuous boycott which inflicted serious economic losses on merchants. In September, when he announced an imminent renewal of demonstrations, white businessmen agreed to negotiate. As a first step toward meeting the Negroes' demands, they even removed the "white" and "colored" signs from drinking fountains and rest rooms. But as a result of pressure from city hall they reneged and suspended the talks.

In November a referendum was held which abolished the commission form of government and called for the election of a mayor and city council. Partly at the urging of white moderates, Shuttlesworth and his movement deferred further demonstrations until after the final run-off election on April 2, 1963, when moderate Albert Boutwell defeated Bull Connor in the contest for the mayoralty. Seven weeks were to pass, however, before Boutwell could take office, pending a court ruling, since Connor filed suit to retain the old system until 1965, the end of the term for which he and his colleagues had been elected.

After the run-off, Shuttlesworth saw no reason for further delay. Boutwell gave no assurance of change, and the businessmen took no steps to integrate. SCLC leaders were called on for help, and on April 3 picketing and sit-ins began, involving some thirty Negroes. Twenty of them were arrested at Britt's Department Store. Others at Woolworth's, Loveman's and elsewhere found the lunch counters closed when they appeared.

Martin Luther King arrived and addressed a rally of 500 Negroes that evening: "We are heading for freedom land and nothing is going to stop us. We are going to make Birmingham the center of antidiscrimination activity in the nation. I have come to stay until something is done."

As sit-ins continued, a new tactic was added on April 6, a protest march to city hall led by Shuttlesworth, in which forty-two Negroes were arrested. The next day the Rev. John T. Porter and the Rev. A. D. King, Martin's brother, led a contingent of twenty-six to kneel in prayer there. They refused to disperse and were taken to jail as some 500 Negro bystanders looked on. Some of the policemen had police dogs on leashes and did not hesitate to torment bystanders with them. When one of the latter slashed at a dog with a knife, six policemen pounced on him and disarmed him. Only the efforts of SCLC staff members kept a riot from breaking out.

On Good Friday, April 12, Shuttlesworth, King and Abernathy led a group of fifty hymn-singing Negroes out of Sixth Avenue Baptist Church toward city hall. Five police vans awaited them en route, and they were hustled into them and driven to jail. It was Dr. King's thirteenth arrest. When he was jailed in 1960 during a sit-in at Rich's Department Store in Atlanta, presidential candidate John F. Kennedy had interceded for him. Again in 1962 President Kennedy told Justice

Department officials to keep him informed of King's well-being in the Albany jail. Now the President alerted Assistant Attorney General Burke Marshall to keep an eye on the Birmingham situation.

On Easter Sunday, small groups of Negroes sought admittance to six white churches. At First Baptist and First Presbyterian they were cordially received. At First Christian, two women were denied entry but were escorted to the parish house by four elders, who tried to explain their situation and prayed with them. Elsewhere, Negroes were turned away. At Sixth Avenue Presbyterian, SCLC Youth Secretary Bernard Lee walked halfway up the steps with two women. An usher blocked the door and said: "Go to the colored church. White people built this church and white people worship here."

Later in the day at Thurgood C.M.E. Church, after a worship service, the Rev. A. D. King emerged in his pulpit robe, Bible in hand, leading a procession of twenty-eight Negroes. They intended to march to the city jail and pray for his imprisoned brother and some 150 other cadres now being held. They did not get far before they were arrested. As they waited for the police vans, a crowd of about 2,000 Negroes gathered, protesting angrily against the arrests. After the prisoners were taken away, police seized a jeering woman and wrestled with her as she resisted arrest. A number of rocks were thrown from the rear ranks of the throng, smashing a police car's windshield. SCLC leaders remonstrated with the people in the crowd, imploring them to be nonviolent. Policemen moved in and one of them broke his nightstick on a young Negro's head. For ten minutes a serious riot threatened. Police reinforcements arrived and many of the Negroes drifted away as others followed SCLC cadres into Thurgood Church for another long service.

These incidents began to provoke responses, both locally and nationally. A group of eight Birmingham clergymen, including the two who had admitted Negro visitors at Easter, issued a statement characterizing the campaign as "unwise and untimely," and commending the police for their restraint in keeping order. To this, Martin Luther King replied in a long letter from his jail cell. Widely reprinted, it stated in part:

I don't believe you would have so warmly commended the police force if you had seen its angry violent dogs literally biting six unarmed, nonviolent Negroes. I don't believe you would so quickly commend the policemen if you would observe their ugly and inhuman treatment of Negroes here in the city jail . . . if you would observe them, as they did on two occasions, refuse to give us food because we wanted to sing our grace together.[18]

Soon after the arrest of Abernathy and King, telegrams were sent to the President and the Attorney General, especially deploring the use of police dogs. Among the signers were prominent churchmen, literary figures, labor leaders and actors. Behind the scenes in Birmingham, small groups of Negro and white ministers began meeting. Through them, contact was established between representatives of SCLC, the Alabama Council on Human Relations, local merchants and Mayor-elect Boutwell. Together they began to sketch a program to meet the Negroes' demands, but the store owners hesitated to implement it without clear support from the larger business community, including Birmingham's industrialists.

On April 20, as daily arrests continued in the face of a sweeping injunction against demonstrations, King and Abernathy had themselves released from jail in $300 cash bonds in order to consult with their strategy committee. It was decided to organize Birmingham's Negro school children for a massive nonviolent assault on segregation, a tactic that had earlier been used in Statesville and Durham, North Carolina.

For over a week, SCLC cadres visited classrooms and school libraries, recruiting students. When principals called police, the cadres left and returned when the police were gone. The response was overwhelming; students flocked in large numbers to pledge themselves to nonviolence and receive training for action, which was conducted in a number of Negro churches. By Thursday, May 2, some 6,000 children were organized and ready to march, and detailed arrangements were made to feed them at the churches where they assembled.

Shortly after noon, King and other leaders at Sixteenth Street Baptist Church addressed the first group of 300 children, ranging from six to sixteen years old. They divided into smaller groups and, joining hands and singing "We Shall Overcome," the first thirty-eight marched forth as a throng of some 400 Negro spectators cheered. They were arrested two blocks from the church. For four hours thereafter, successive waves of children marched out to be arrested, and others arrived at the church to wait their turn.

Three groups managed to reach the downtown shopping area and one was arrested only fifteen feet from the city hall steps. Marchers were given directions by older youths with walkie-talkies. Excellent discipline was maintained; when police approached, the youngsters fell to their knees and started to pray. In all, 959 children and ten adults, including A. D. King, were arrested on this day.

Another 250 were arrested on Friday. Although a thousand jammed the Sixteenth Street Church, only half of them got out before police barred the exits. Fire hoses, which had been held ready on Thursday, were now turned on with a pressure of fifty to one hundred pounds. Torrents of water knocked many of the children to the ground and literally ripped the T-shirt from one youth's back as he sprawled on the pavement. The dogs were also brought out and released into the crowds. Five Negroes were bitten and many more were savagely menaced. "The police made no effort to restrain them," said the Rev. Andrew J. Young, leader of SCLC's action workshop. "It was almost as if they were trying to incite a riot."

Despite these provocations, the Negro bystanders, few of whom had received training in nonviolent conduct, remained unusually well disciplined until a state police investigator deliberately swerved his car into the crowd. This brought a shower of rocks and bottles from a cluster of Negroes on a nearby rooftop, which injured a news photographer and two firemen manning hoses. In retaliation the hoses were turned on the crowd.

Alarmed by these events, Burke Marshall arrived in Birmingham on Saturday to confer with both Martin Luther King and the white businessmen. Demonstrations continued and for half an hour unruly elements in the crowd hurled rocks and bottles at the firemen when the hoses were turned on. James Bevel, an SCLC secretary, borrowed a policeman's bull-horn amplifier and called to the crowd: "Everybody get off this corner. If you're not going to demonstrate in a nonviolent manner, then leave." Soon after the crowd cleared, further demonstrations were called off until Monday. Bevel saw a number of knives and pistols in the hands of Negro spectators and feared that bloodshed might occur.

On Sunday, small groups of Negroes again sought admittance to white churches. They gained entry to four and were turned away from seventeen others. Late in the afternoon a mass meeting was held at New Pilgrim Baptist Church. Lined up outside were fifty policemen and a fire truck with water pressure cranked up to 700 pounds. A little before sunset the crowd of about two thousand Negroes came out and faced the police. They knelt in silence as one of the ministers prayed solemnly: "Let them turn their water on. Let them use their dogs. We are not leaving. Forgive them, O Lord."

Perhaps for a moment this touched something in Bull Connor, for he let the Negroes cross the police line and spend fifteen minutes in a small park near the city jail, where they prayed and sang hymns within hearing of the hundreds of demonstrators inside. Afterward, they returned to the church, where it was announced that the children would definitely march on Monday.

At 1:00 P.M., May 6, comedian Dick Gregory led the first contingent of nineteen marchers from Sixteenth Street Baptist Church. They were quickly arrested. Then, as on Thursday, wave after wave of them went out. The last group, a little over an hour later, was led by Barbara Deming, a writer for *The Nation*. More than 200 others drifted rather than marched to the downtown area, where they assembled and began picketing the stores. About a thousand Negroes were arrested, half of them adults. Fire hoses were present but not used, and again SCLC cadres remonstrated with a large crowd to remain calm. Only one incident occurred. When police attempted to force a woman off the sidewalk, she resisted. Five policemen wrestled her to the pavement and one of them pinned her down with his knee in her neck. An angered Negro man ripped the shirt of one of the officers and tried to slip his revolver from its holster. Both of the Negroes were arrested. At this moment a riot could have erupted but for the cadres' exhortations.

Since his arrival on Saturday, Burke Marshall met repeatedly with Negro and white leaders, while from Washington Attorney General Robert F. Kennedy, Secretary of the Treasury Douglas Dillon and Defense Secretary Robert McNamara made dozens of telephone calls to businessmen and industrialists, pressing for a speedy settlement. Believing that not enough was being done, Dean Eugene V. Rostow of Yale Law School volunteered his services by phoning Roger Blough, chairman of the board of United States Steel. A graduate of the law school, Blough agreed to call his associates in Birmingham and impress them with the national importance of reaching an agreement. By Tuesday morning, Marshall was strongly urging the Birmingham businessmen to accede to the Negroes' demands, and they were listening to him.

The jails by now were overflowing. According to the *Birmingham News,* the children were treated gently. But the reports that came to SCLC told a different story. All the girls were examined for venereal disease, like common criminals. Those who requested aspirin were given laxatives. When they complained to newspapermen, their complaints went unreported and they were made to scrub the halls with toothbrushes and steel wool as punishment. One day 800 children under sixteen were kept in the jail yard for four hours in pouring rain. Those who protested were placed in solitary confinement. Dick Gregory was beaten three times, and he was not the only one.

Yet none of them showed fear. Many, after being released on bail, marched and were jailed again.

Partly because of the congested conditions of the jails, police resorted to new tactics on Tuesday. When 500 children began marching from the church at noon, police broke up their formations and dispersed them without making arrests. Inside the church, the Rev. James Bevel said: "If they're not going to arrest our marchers, we'll charge downtown, right in the face of the white people." They streamed out by the hundreds, heading toward the business district by different zigzag routes, joined by others on the streets as they went, until more than 3,000 of them converged on the downtown area. Groups of them trooped in and out of stores, singing "Ain't gonna let nobody turn me 'round" and "I'm on my way to freedom land." After this brief foray—the first "sing-in"—they dispersed, returned to the church, regrouped and again streamed downtown. According to one SCLC staff member, this had a considerable effect on the white businessmen.

When they returned a second time, city police augmented by fifty sheriff's officers in steel helmets with guns and nightsticks cordoned off an eight-block area to bar a third raid. Many demonstrators were herded into the park across from the church, where together with bystanders they formed a crowd of about 2,000. Contrary to nonviolent discipline, they taunted the police: "Bring on the dogs! Bring on the water!" Jets of water smashed into the crowd, forcing them back. Neon signs and shop windows were shattered by the force of the blasts. Fred Shuttlesworth was knocked flat and taken away in an ambulance. Negroes broke up paving blocks and hurled them at the police. For an hour and a half they fought, as SCLC cadres pleaded with the Negroes to abandon violence. The final skirmish, ironically, was fought on the church steps, where retreating Negroes threw their last rocks and the hoses cracked stained-glass windows and flooded the basement. In the lull that followed, Negro leaders reiterated their pleas: "Go home. You are not helping our cause." Finally the remnant of the crowd dissolved. Some forty Negroes were arrested. At least a dozen people were injured, including three policemen.

This episode played into Bull Connor's hands. At his request the Governor ordered 250 state troopers sent into the city. Given their reputation for racist brutality and given the rising Negro temper, the stage was being set for a bloodbath. The negotiators became anxious to reach agreement before it came, and they worked far into the night, deciding at last on a tentative accord. A one-day truce was to be called while details were worked out.

During the truce, downtown Birmingham bristled like an armed camp, with some 750 city, county and state police, firemen with hoses, an armored car with tear-gas guns, and the police dogs. Several thousand Negroes massed in churches near the downtown area, ready to march if the truce was broken.

They were ready again on Thursday morning in even greater force. There were 1,200 law officers at Kelly Ingram Park and ominous reports of increased activity by the Ku Klux Klan and other racist organizations. That morning, May 9, the agreement was confirmed and the truce extended. A Negro and a white lawyer worked out the exact terms that night.

The next morning, all of the 790 prisoners who remained in jail were released on bail. A total of $237,000 for this purpose was contributed by the United Auto Workers, the National Maritime Union and other groups. In the afternoon, Martin Luther King announced the four-point settlement. It provided for: 1) desegregation of lunch counters, rest rooms, fitting rooms and drinking fountains in all downtown stores within ninety days; 2) placement of Negroes in previously all-white clerical and sales positions, through upgrading or hiring, within sixty days; 3) release of prisoners, which by now had been accomplished; and 4) firm establishment of permanent communication between white and Negro leaders. "This is the most significant victory for justice we've ever seen in the Deep South," said King, beaming. But he added a sober note:

This is the time that we must evince calm, dignity and wise restraint. Emotion must not run wild. Violence must not come from any of us. . . . As we stand on the verge of using public facilities heretofore closed to us, we must not be overbearing and haughty in spirit. We must move now from protest to reconciliation.

Though less enthusiastic, Sidney W. Smyer, chairman of the white merchants' negotiating committee, called upon all of Birmingham's people to be calm and accept the pact. When white extremists urged that he encourage new violence as a pretext for repudiating the agreement, he publicly voiced "unalterable opposition" to this viewpoint. The thirst for revenge did not die so quickly, however. On Saturday night, after a Ku Klux Klan rally on the outskirts of town, a dynamite blast ripped the front part of A. D. King's home in suburban Ensley, and half an hour later another explosion tore a hole in the side of the A. G. Gaston Motel, which served as SCLC headquarters in the city.

Large crowds of Negroes milled about both places. Fortunately A. D. King was at home and unhurt. Although a few hotheads threw rocks and let the air out of the tires of police cars that had arrived, King quickly calmed and dispersed the gathering.

Near the motel the atmosphere was more volatile. Men flocked there from saloons in the nearby Negro slum area, some of them shouting angrily: "Let's get Bull Connor!" Police, firemen and members of a Negro civil-defense unit were also on the scene. SCLC executive secretary Wyatt Walker pleaded with the crowd: "Please, please move back. Throwing rocks won't help. This is no good. Please go home. It does no good to lose your heads."

"Tell it to Bull Connor," they roared. "This is what nonviolence gets you."

The rioting had begun to subside when, at 1:10 A.M., Colonel Al Lingo and his state troopers arrived. They piled out of their cars with machine guns, shotguns and unsheathed bayonets, and began to club and jab Negroes indiscriminately.

Walker's wife was struck in the head with a gun butt and taken to the hospital. Birmingham Police Chief Jamie Moore quickly intervened: "Wait, wait a minute now, you're going to get somebody killed with those guns."

"I damn sure will if I have to," Lingo retorted. But after further urging, he and his troopers got back into their cars, where they sat and watched the fighting.

The mob smashed police-car windows and slashed the tires. They set fire to a motorcycle and tried in vain to overturn a patrol wagon. In the melee, city police acted with restraint. One patrolman was knifed and others were punched, as were the Negro civil-defense men, but they did not resort to shooting. At one point, Chief Inspector William J. Haley was struck in the forehead with a brick, and an infuriated policeman started toward the crowd with a shotgun, knocking A. D. King out of the way with the butt as he went. But a police lieutenant grabbed him and ordered him back.

Enraged Negroes broke into three white-owned grocery stores, looted them and set them on fire, then stoned firemen who attempted to extinguish the blaze. Unchecked, the flames spread to adjoining Negro homes. Half an hour later, Negro civil-defense worker Sylvester Norris drove a fire truck through the barrage of stones, enabling the firemen to go into action.

By 3:40 A.M. the combined forces of white police and firemen and Negro CD workers and SCLC cadres brought the riot to an end. The pivotal event was perhaps an encounter between A. D. King and the drunken leader of the mob. King tried to talk to the man, who was cursing him as an Uncle Tom, when someone whispered to the man and he said: "You Dr. King? You been to jail? Your home got bombed?" King said he was, and the man turned to the crowd. "This is our leader," he told them. "He say you go home, you go home." Although obviously drunk, said King, the man's control over the crowd was amazing.

After the drunken mob dispersed, the state troopers went after Negroes who had taken no part in the riot, clubbing old men and women sitting on their porches and forcing them indoors.

When daybreak came it was Sunday, Mother's Day. In the night's rioting an estimated fifty persons had been injured. Miraculously, no one was killed. Property damage was conservatively assessed at $41,775. In Washington, President Kennedy issued a statement in which he said:

The Birmingham agreement was and is a fair and just accord. . . . It was a tribute to the process of peaceful negotiation and to the good faith of both parties. The Federal Government will not permit it to be sabotaged. . . .

I call upon all the citizens of Birmingham . . . to realize that violence only breeds more violence. . . . There must be no repetition of last night's incidents by any group.

Martin Luther King was in Atlanta during the riot. He returned to Birmingham and on Monday set out on a pilgrimage of the Negro pool halls, accompanied by several aides. They entered the first one. Playing stopped and a number of others came in from the street to listen. King spoke of Saturday night's ravages and Abernathy asked them to pledge themselves to nonviolence, then led them in singing "We Shall Overcome," using a pool cue as a baton. They moved to another pool hall and did likewise. As they left, one of the players nodded toward the state troopers in the street and muttered: "I ain't gonna take none of that damn stuff." Others tagged along as the SCLC leaders headed for another pool hall. The procession now numbered about 100. They did not get far, however, before state troopers with carbines compelled them to disperse, ordered onlookers back into stores and houses and made King's group return to the Gaston Motel. With 700 state troopers in the city, it was as if martial law had been imposed. Police Chief Moore was privately known to be unhappy about their presence, fearing that they might provoke a new riot.

After a few tense days marked by minor, scattered incidents, Birmingham began to settle down. On May 23, scarcely two weeks after the riot, the Alabama Supreme Court unanimously upheld Mayor Boutwell's election, and five days later the new city council authorized the formation of a biracial Committee on Community Affairs, in accordance with the pact. Waiting for tensions to ease, the resolution was not publicized for six weeks, when invitations were sent out. Only three persons declined, and on July 16 some 200 leading citizens, Negro and white, made their way through clusters of protesting Klansmen to enter city hall and register as members of the committee. By the following month, each of the provisions of the May agreement had been implemented. As a further gesture of good faith, the city opened its golf courses on an integrated basis, although they were not included in the pact.

Racist Counterattack: The Church Bombing

The Birmingham campaign was not perfect. It did not usher in a golden age, nor did it even initiate an upswing of unbroken progress. Bull Connor, Governor Wallace, the Ku Klux Klan and other die-hards were not suddenly converted to integration. Scarcely four months after the bombing of the Gaston Motel, four Negro children were killed and twenty injured in the first of a new series of terroristic acts. The children were attending a Bible class at Sixteenth Street Baptist Church, the very bastion of nonviolent action in the May campaign. It was not the first bombing, nor would it be the last in Birmingham. There had been some fifty unsolved bombings prior to 1963, and in the wake of the church bombing there were more, as well as shootings, arson and other depradations.

The church bombing followed the first steps in integrating the city's schools. It occurred as demagogues, including the Governor, urged defiance of the Federal Courts which had ordered these steps. It is outside our purpose here to detail all the facts. It is sufficient to note the impact of the tragedy, which posed a crisis for nonviolence. The instantaneous reaction of hundreds of Birmingham Negroes was understandable. They vented their panic and frustration by spilling into the streets and pelting police and firemen with rocks until the church's pastor, the Rev. J. H. Cross, pleaded with them to disperse. It was a blind lashing out at those who for many years had symbolized that same enemy from whose ranks the bombers undoubtedly came. At the same time, the attitude of city officials, though not repentant, was at least regretful. Mayor Boutwell offered his cooperation to Federal investigators, but he did so without conferring with Negro leaders. One noted Birmingham attorney, Charles Morgan, in an impassioned speech to the Young Men's Business Association, excoriated the mayor, the police and white ministers as well as the white population of the city: "Every person in this community who has in any way contributed during the past several years to the popularity of hatred is at least as guilty as, or more than, the demented fool who threw that bomb."

Some good might eventuate from such soul-searching—and from the shock felt by many complacent citizens in the South and throughout the nation. But of more concern here is the reaction of many Negro leaders, typified in this statement by Dr. Gardner Taylor, an influential figure in the Progressive Baptist Convention: "That incredible act forces a re-examination by serious Christians of the entire doctrine of nonviolence except as a tactical approach in selected situations." Writer John O. Killens said more pointedly that he doubted that nonviolence offered the way out in the civil-rights struggle and asserted the right of Negroes to defend themselves with weapons. "As a tactic, nonviolence has been successful, but as a philosophy we need to get rid of it."

Louis E. Lomax, author of *The Negro Revolt*, was present at a memorial service for the four dead children when Killens spoke. "The time is coming," Lomax said, "when the Negro must arm himself to defend his home." Also present was Christopher McNair, whose only child was one of those killed. With the authority of experience, he said: "Such an effort would be fruitless. I'm not for that. What good would Denise have done with a machine gun in her hands?"

Nonviolence, it must be admitted, has no solution for bombs set off by unknown persons. Neither do pistols or shotguns in citizens' homes. And certainly the way to deal with a frenzied, rock-throwing mob, however righteous its anger, is not to urge more lethal weapons upon it—especially when their victims are sure to be indiscriminately chosen. What is required is neither a blind acceptance of nonviolence as a cure-all, nor the exasperated abandonment of nonviolence because it does not always work miracles, but a clear-sighted understanding of its possibilities and limitations in each situation. It is a hard fact, unaltered by all the bombings, riots and shootings, that in May nonviolence achieved stated objectives in a very brief span of time, objectives that were probably unattainable in any other way, certainly not by mob violence. Undoubtedly the capacity for violence, glimpsed in the incipient riots at the height of the May demonstrations, played a part in expediting a settlement. But any display of this potential could be effective only as it also showed the power of the SCLC leaders to curb it. The lesson is clear. Nonviolence can be effective when it is used skillfully. It does not require perfection, nor does it produce perfection. It does call for discipline, courage and restraint in the face of adversity, as well as good strategy. And in the pivotal Birmingham campaign of May 1963 it had all these attributes, winning out against fire hoses, police dogs and in-grained racist attitudes.

REFERENCES IN CHAPTER 20

1 Martin Luther King Jr.: *Stride Toward Freedom* (New York: Harper & Brothers, 1958), p. 58.
2 Carl T. Rowan: *Go South to Sorrow* (New York: Random House, 1957), p. 119.
3 L. D. Reddick: *Crusader Without Violence* (New York: Harper & Brothers, 1959), p. 178.

4   Glenford E. Mitchell: "College Students Take Over" in Mitchell and Peace, eds.: *The Angry Black South* (New York: Corinth Books, Inc., 1962), p. 79f. See also Louis E. Lomax: *The Negro Revolt* (New York: Harper & Brothers, 1962), pp. 121-146.

5   *Ibid.,* p. 80f.

6   Thomas Gaither: news report in *Community* (Chicago), June 1960, p. 4.

7   Jameson Jones: "Issues in the Sit-Ins" in *Motive* (Nashville), May 1960.

8   Merrill Proudfoot: *Diary of a Sit-In* (Chapel Hill: University of North Carolina Press, 1962), p. 94.

9   Mitchell, *op. cit.,* p. 87f.

10 Proudfoot, *op. cit.,* p. 185.

11 Diane Nash: "Inside the Sit-Ins and Freedom Rides" in Mathew H. Ahmann, ed.: *The New Negro* (Notre Dame: Fides Publishers, Inc., 1961), p. 55.

12 John David Maguire: "When Moderation Demands Taking Sides" in *Christianity and Crisis,* June 26, 1961, p. 115.

13 *Ibid.,* p. 116.

14 Robert McAfee Brown in *Presbyterian Life,* August 1, 1961.

15 Ralph Lord Roy: "Albany Diary" in *The New York Amsterdam News,* September 8, 1962.

16 Howard Zinn: *Albany* (Atlanta: Southern Regional Council, 1962), p. 19. See also Wyatt Tee Walker: "Achievement in Albany" in *New South* (Atlanta), June 1963.

17 Reese Cleghorn: "Epilogue in Albany" in *The New Republic* (Washington), July 20, 1963, p. 17.

18 Martin Luther King Jr.: *Letter from Birmingham City Jail* (Valley Forge, Pa.: American Baptist Convention, 1963), p. 13.

21

Episodes of Spontaneous Nonviolence

Throughout history from earliest times, man has shown his capacity for revolt and resistance, frequently reckless and bloody. Sometimes he has also shown a capacity for restraint that has enabled him to voice his protest through direct action short of violence, actually refraining from bloodshed in circumstances that made it difficult to do so, yet without any guiding principle or plan of nonviolence.

In the Russian Revolution

In his monumental *History of the Russian Revolution,* Leon Trotsky tells of a remarkable encounter between a crowd of 2,500 striking industrial workers and a troop of Cossacks, the most ruthless and reliable of the tsarist armed forces for conducting anti-Semitic pogroms, quelling peasant uprisings and breaking strikes. The date is February 24, 1917, the second of the five days of mass demonstrations that preceded the seizure of power by the revolutionists. On this day, some 90,000 workers were out on strike, marching in the streets. Trotsky's source of information was Kayurov, a strike leader who participated in the incident described here.

The mass of 2,500 workers from the Erikson mill in the Vyborg district of Petrograd had marched to Sampsonevsky Prospekt, where they encountered the Cossacks. First the officers streamed through the crowd. Normally, the rank-and-file horsemen would have galloped after them, fanning out and wielding their knouts or sabers as they came.

But the horsemen, cautiously, in a long ribbon, rode through the corridor just made by the officers. "Some of them smiled," Kayurov recalls, "and one of them gave the workers a good wink." This wink was not without meaning. The workers were emboldened with a friendly, not hostile, kind of assurance, and slightly infected the Cossacks with it. The one who winked found imitators. In spite of renewed efforts from the officers, the Cossacks, without openly breaking discipline, failed to force the crowd to disperse, but flowed through it in streams. This was repeated three or four times and brought the two sides even closer together. Individual Cossacks began to reply to the workers' questions and even to enter into momentary conversation with them. Of discipline there remained but a thin transparent shell that threatened to break through any second. The officers hastened to separate their patrol from the workers and, abandoning the idea of dispersing them, lined the Cossacks out across the street as a barrier to prevent the demonstrators from getting to the center. But even this did not help: standing stock-still in perfect discipline, the Cossacks did not hinder the workers from "diving" under their horses. The revolution does not choose its paths: it made its first steps toward victory under the belly of a Cossack's horse.[1]

This incident was not typical. Kayurov's group was unarmed and made no attempt to provoke violence, though elsewhere in the city twenty-eight policemen were beaten by workers on the same day and the day before. And the next day, with the ranks of the strikers swollen to 240,000, shooting began. Perhaps even more remarkable than the episode above was another in which Kayurov appealed to the Cossacks to defend the workers against the mounted police. Cap in hand, he turned to them: "Brothers—Cossacks, help the workers in a struggle for their peaceable demands." [2]

"The Cossacks glanced at each other in some special way," Kayurov continues, "and we were hardly out of the way before they rushed into the fight." And a few minutes later, near the station gate, the crowd were tossing in their arms a Cossack who, before their eyes, had slaughtered a police inspector with his saber.[3]

Women strikers went up to infantrymen, boldly taking hold of their rifles and pleading: "Put down your bayonets—join us." On many occasions they did so, or at least broke ranks to permit the workers to pass.

Trotsky holds no brief for nonviolence, certainly, and he calls these episodes "more symptomatic than substantial," forming a prelude to a decisive clash of armed force, but nevertheless of key importance for winning support on the side of the insurgents.

It is not properly within the scope of nonviolence, of course, to encourage anyone to kill on our behalf. What is to the point is that, within history, it has happened repeatedly that unarmed men such as Kayurov—not a pacifist but a Bolshevik—have succeeded in appealing to their enemies, getting them either to stand aside neutrally or to defect to the other side, throwing down their weapons or handing them over or using them against the oppressor. As Trotsky, the great revolutionary theorist, points out, "The whole history of street fights and revolutionary victories swarms with such improvisations. But they are drowned without a trace in the abyss of great events." [4] In fact, few historians trouble to record these incidents in many cases. Of the Petrograd events, for example, Sukhanov says only that "fugitive meetings were held in the main streets and were dispersed by Cossacks and mounted police—but without any energy or zeal and after lengthy delays." [5] Trotsky, for his own reasons, stands alone among the major historians of the Russian Revolution in giving more than this cursory account.

Other Episodes: Hungary 1849, France 1871, Algeria 1962

If it was important to Trotsky to record these minor episodes as symptoms of the revolutionary situation, it was of interest to Arthur Griffith as a proponent of passive resistance in the early days of the Sinn Fein resistance organization in Ireland to ferret out a similar episode that occurred during the Hungarian Revolution of 1849.[6]

A mob had lynched the Austrian Lord Lieutenant on his arrival in Budapest, and Lajos Kossuth was installed as president. To quell the revolt, the Austrian Grenadier Guards were sent from Vienna, but they refused to march. The Kaiser ordered the National Guard to fire on the recalcitrant Grenadiers, but they refused to do so and joined the latter in mutiny against the crown, cheering for Kossuth and for liberty. This was only a brief interlude, easily forgotten in the subsequent history of the Austrian and Hungarian revolutions and eclipsed by the military and political struggles that ensued.

Much the same occurred in Paris on March 18, 1871, when troops sent to suppress demonstrations in Montmartre refused to fire and fraternized with the insurgents—a prelude to the short-lived Paris Commune.

On August 31, 1962, a crowd of 20,000 workers thronged the streets of Algiers to forestall a threatened civil war between rival Algerian government factions, soon after the end of a bloody and bitter seven-year war for independence from France. Fighting had already begun and many persons had been killed, when the General Union of Algerian Workers threatened a general strike. In one district, union leaders declared:

Go out into the streets and shout your anger in front of the tanks and the armored cars. In front of the machine guns you will stand up, armed with your courage alone, to stop those who want to unleash civil war. Seven years of bloodshed is enough.[7]

On the border between two rival districts (*willayas*), reported the *Manchester Guardian,*

The soldiers of the two Willayas faced one another; but . . . on the insistence of the local villagers first the men, then the officers shook hands and laid aside their arms.[8]

At Boghari and elsewhere, the populace formed a human barrier against the troops, shouting: "No more bloodshed!" As a result the rival factions quickly declared a cease-fire which led to a political settlement.

A fact of key importance in the Algerian episode is that it occurred after the end of a long and exhausting war in which both of the now rival factions and the intervening peacemakers were all united against the French *colons*. In a different way, war weariness also helped to bring together the rank-and-file Cossacks and the Petrograd workers. This did not forestall bloodshed, but it contributed to a weighting of the workers' side of the scales which made the democratic February insurrection swift and successful. It is a moot question whether, without the dramatic and spontaneously nonviolent appeal for "no more bloodshed," the strife between the Algerian factions might have developed into a devastating civil war such as that which ravaged Russia after the Bolshevik seizure of power, some nine months after the brief democratic revolution. In any case this is not the place to examine the complexities of Russian history. But in evaluating the Algerian situation it is well to remember its parallel in Asia: the protracted struggle against the French in Indo-China, which was followed by years of guerrilla warfare in Vietnam and Laos, independent states that were carved out of the former French Indo-China.

The East German Revolt of 1953

June 17, 1953, is a memorable date in the annals of man's struggle for freedom. It is also a date that figures, if somewhat ambiguously, in the history of nonviolent direct action. This was the date on which workers throughout Soviet-occupied East Germany rose up and very nearly overthrew the totalitarian regime under which they lived. "The very fact that this great uprising could and did take place," said West Berlin's Mayor Ernst Reuter, "proves to the world that the totalitarian machine is not infallible or omnipotent, that it has its weaknesses, and that if the free world only had the political imagination to match the human courage which the enslaved world is ready to show, then the days of the Iron Curtain in Central Europe would be numbered." [9]

The people who revolted had lived under totalitarian rule for twenty years—twelve under Hitler and eight under Stalin and Ulbricht. One analyst, referring to those whose peaceful strike triggered the revolt, has stated:

The building workers of Berlin and the steel workers of Hennigsdorf were known for their support of revolutionary actions during the pre-Nazi era, 1918-1933. They were strongholds of the Communist movement in Berlin during that period. Under the Nazis they defied the regime whenever possible.[10]

Many of the other leaders of the strikes that spread throughout East Germany were former members of the banned Social Democratic Party, who maintained ties with their party in West Germany, in effect operating in the East Zone as an underground. M. S. Handler of *The New York Times* called the uprising "a masterpiece of direct action. . . . The rapidity and simultaneity of the strikes throughout East Germany indicated the extent of the ramifications of the underground organization." [11] In less than a week the revolt spread to 350 towns and villages, involving millions of people estimated at half the entire working population and including people of all social strata. According to Stefan Brant:

Irrespective of origin, character, sex, social and professional ties or age, millions of individuals acted as one, obeying the same signals, striving to reach the same goal and formulating the same program. . . .[12]

As Melvin J. Lasky, editor of *Der Monat,* pointed out, this was "an objective revolutionary situation" right out of the Marxist lexicon. "The notion of the general strike sprang to the minds of millions with a spontaneity that went beyond Sorel's fondest hopes." [13]

Georges Sorel, proponent of violent revolt, was not the East

Germans' only ideologue, however. Rainer Hildebrandt says that Gerald Wagner, a radio editor who managed to help spread the word of the uprising from the RIAS transmitter in West Berlin, "believed with Gandhi that the most moral resistance was the most demoralizing to the adversary." [14] However imperfect or indirect, this was a motif widely attested by observers and reporters, as epitomized in this sample by Norbert Muhlen:

Often the demonstrators went first to the prisons to ask for the release of political prisoners; only when their requests were refused did they storm the prisons and free the inmates. . . .

Yet in every case they refrained from taking the weapons of the disarmed guards and police for themselves. In the first place, they wanted to avoid bloodshed—a revolutionary pacifism unheard of in history. In the second place, they assumed . . . that if order were maintained, the Soviet occupying power would stand by neutrally.[15]

Naïve as the latter assumption may seem, it was not without some substance. Lasky, for example, saw East Berliners haul down the red flag on top of the Brandenburg Gate and destroy the Soviet bookshop on the Alexanderplatz while Soviet troops looked on indifferently.[16] Hildebrandt tells of two Soviet Army lieutenants who cast their lot with the struggle for liberty. One of them, a Lieutenant Gregoriev, fled to West Berlin after the revolt collapsed; the other, Lieutenant Rakit Kastanov, was executed.[17] Both expected, as did many others, that the revolt would succeed and spread to the USSR. Exact information in detail is hard to find, but by June 28 at least thirty-two men had been executed by Red Army firing squads for siding with the revolt, and these included Volkspolizei (East German militia or "people's police") who had been sent to help suppress the revolt and had instead torn off their uniforms and turned over their weapons to the insurgent workers. So widespread were the defections of German troops that the Soviet authorities moved to demobilize the East German Army (Bereitschaften) and reorganize it. Hundreds of its officers, reported C. L. Sulzberger, were "reduced in rank or court-martialed." [18] In Goerlitz, on the Polish border, thousands of German demonstrators greeted Polish tanks that were sent in to disperse them. An Associated Press correspondent who witnessed the encounter reported:

The senior Polish officer stepped out of his tank, faced the Germans —and saluted. "I don't fire on German workers," he said. The Germans returned his salute.

When the Russians saw the Poles were not going to resist the Germans, they ordered the Polish troops back across the border and sent in Russian tanks.[19]

Throughout East Germany, efforts were made by revolt leaders to restrain their followers from resorting to violence, even under provocation, or at least not to initiate violence. The case of Friedrich Schorn, leader of the insurgents at East Germany's largest chemical plant, the Leunawerke near Leipzig, is indicative. Addressing the workers, Schorn, an accountant at the plant, said: "This isn't a matter of just Leuna. It's a matter of every German in the Soviet Zone. Everything is at stake. But violence isn't the answer. If we overrun the plant and wreck the machinery, we'll only have to rebuild it later. Let's keep order." [20] When factory guards handed over their weapons, Schorn gave orders that they were not to be used but locked in a storeroom.

From the plant, the workers marched to Merseburg. When Volkspolizei tried to block their path, the workers laughed and shouted: "Out of the way! Stand aside or join us!" Two or three of them doffed their caps and tunics and joined the ranks of the marchers.

They arrived at the Uhlandsplatz in Merseburg, where Schorn addressed a crowd of some 70,000 or more strikers from factories in the vicinity, together with their wives and children. When Soviet troops advanced on the square, Schorn asked the crowd to remain calm, telling them once more that violence would get them nowhere. At first they heeded him, but soon long pent-up emotions got the upper hand. As Schorn told Joseph Wechsberg,

Some began to shout abuse at the Russians and a few spat on their trucks. I knew that things would get out of hand if we stayed there much longer. I stepped back to talk the matter over with the other strike leaders, and they agreed that we had better break it up.[21]

Turning to the crowd again, he told the strikers to return to their factories but not to resume work. "The people reacted well," reports Wechsberg. "They formed columns and marched off in perfect discipline." [22]

Upon arrival at the Leunawerke, Schorn found Soviet troops in charge. The next night, strike leaders were arrested in their homes, but Schorn had not gone home and thus was able to flee to West Berlin. Even with a heavy Soviet guard and without leaders, however, the Leuna workers continued sitdown strikes for weeks.

As late as February 6, 1954, there continued to be widespread resistance, punctuated with outbursts of vocal protest demanding free elections, from workers throughout East Germany. At the Leunawerke, for example, at a compulsory Communist propaganda meeting to promote the Molotov proposal for German reunification, the workers shouted in unison: "We want free elections first!" In Brandenburg, high-school students were given the Molotov plan as their discussion topic for the day, but they refused to discuss it. There were similar actions in all the major centers of the June revolt, resulting in the formation of a special auxiliary police force made up of picked Communist party members.

As recently as August 1962 the West German newspaper *Bild Zeitung* quoted refugees as saying that there was "deep unrest" in East Germany. In several towns placards appeared, lettered "We want more to eat and we have not forgotten June 17." In Mühlhausen, Soviet tanks were again brought in when metalworkers went on strike to protest food shortages and high work norms. In Eisenach someone painted a rope around the neck of Walter Ulbricht in a huge public portrait. Thus the spirit of resistance continued to flicker long after actual revolt had died out.

In the first two or three days of the 1953 revolt, the insurgents came within an ace of seizing control of the country. In a number of towns, the workers went so far as to take charge of the local administration. H. F. Stille argues persuasively that "without the last-minute intervention of the Russian tank division [on June 18], the workers would have seized party and government headquarters with little chance of escape for the SED [East German Communist] leaders." [23] So widespread was the uprising that the SED's central committee complained that large numbers of party members were doing nothing to suppress it. "Tens of thousands of them sit in their offices, write some papers or other and simply wait," it reported.[24]

Three factors appear to account for the failure of the revolt. First, the intervention of Soviet tanks. Second, the failure of the West to aid the East German workers (U.S. officials obstructed efforts by RIAS to broadcast a call for a general strike). Third, the failure of the insurgents either to obtain and use sufficient armed force to repulse the Soviet tanks or to maintain a nonviolent discipline that might have disarmed the Soviet tankmen.

It is the last of these points that of course concerns us in this study. We have already seen that it was possible in this Stalinist country to begin and to sustain a massive resistance. We have seen that it was possible to neutralize or win over armed opponents in the police and the army and even in the Polish and some Soviet forces. And we have seen that discipline was maintained and orders obeyed—up to a point. This point is where we begin to enter the area of clear-cut nonviolence. Despite generally good organization, the East German workers had no deep-going understanding or resolve to stay nonviolent. In many cases they displayed great courage. As Stille says: "The workers did not run away when the guns of the Russian tanks were turning against them. They faced them with desperate courage and iron discipline. Politically conscious workers advised their colleagues not to engage in an open and unequal fight with the Russian forces." [25] But in all except a few instances this advice was not heeded.

Ella Sarre was an instructor in the Freie Deutsche Jugend, the Communist youth organization, who sided with the revolt. Her story is typical of many of the clashes:

> A Russian officer stood atop one tank and amiably waved the crowd aside. A hail of stones answered him. Ella was unhappy; she spoke some Russian and would have liked to tell the officer that the workers did not hate him, only his tank—but no parley was possible in the roar of a battle that saw tanks fought with stones and crowbars. [26]

We may admire this reckless courage and audacity, but in realistic terms stones and crowbars and shouted abuse are no match for military armor. Stefan Brant says that "eighteen Soviet officers and men were executed after June 17 for refusing to obey orders." [27] He also observes that even among Soviet tank groups that were not in habitual contact with the Germans but completely isolated in Soviet bases, there were several instances in which the Russians "showed great reluctance to open fire on the strikers." [28] There is no way of estimating the total number of Russian soldiers who acted in ways favorable to the workers, for example, by firing as ordered but aiming to miss. Certainly the total must have been far more than the eighteen who were executed; more even than those like Lieutenant Gregoriev, who escaped, or others who presumably were imprisoned rather than shot. Considering all the factors militating against such defections—the isolation, the stones and crowbars—it is noteworthy that there were so many who acted in this way. And it is certainly cogent to assume that there would have been substantially more if the East German workers had been trained in nonviolence, ready to lose as many lives as they did lose, but as a price for establishing rapport with the majority of Soviet troops who evidently did not know what to think and were stoned instead of persuaded. There was a demonstrated potential, and it was thrown away each time a rock was cast.

If the nonviolent alternative had failed, as well it might have, the outcome could hardly have been worse than the disaster which history records.

Budapest 1956

A few days after the East German revolt began, leaders of the Hungarian Workers Party (Communist) were summoned to Moscow and warned that unless they adopted reforms they faced the prospect of a similar uprising. On their return, they installed Imre Nagy, a Communist moderate, as premier, only to unseat him and expel him from the party two years later.

In Poland, too, currents set in motion by the impact of the East German uprising led to a revolt centered on the city of Poznan—and to a wiser response from Moscow, which replaced Poland's Stalinist government with that of the popular moderate, Wladyslaw Gomulka. This in turn led a group of Hungarian Communist intellectuals to band together as the Petöfi Circle and press for Nagy's reinstatement.

On October 13, 1956, Nagy's party membership was restored, whereupon the Petöfi Circle stepped up its clamor for his return to the premiership, culminating on Monday, October 22, in "an unprecedented series of mass meetings in Budapest's colleges and universities" [29] and a silent demonstration outside the Polish embassy. The university students drew up a list of fourteen demands, including immediate evacuation of all Soviet armed forces, general elections "by universal, secret ballot" and "complete recognition of freedom of opinion and expression." [30] During the night, mimeographed leaflets stating these demands were posted throughout the city and a mass demonstration was set for 3:00 P.M. the next day.

At 12:53 P.M. on October 23 the Communist government broadcast a communiqué forbidding the demonstration, but backed down an hour later when the students refused to abandon their plans. The effect of the ban, while it was in force, was to spur the demonstrators on and add to their ranks thousands of workers who had not earlier planned to join in, as well as 800 cadets from Petöfi Military Academy. Through the afternoon and early evening they covered a lot of ground, rallying at the Petöfi monument not far from the Radio Building, moving across the Danube to the Jozsef Bem statue and back over to Lajos Kossuth Square, facing the Parliament Buildings. By this time the crowd numbered between 150,000 and 200,000 marchers. They called for Nagy, and after some delay he appeared and tried to calm them. Part of the crowd, which continued to grow, split off and marched to the Stalin Memorial where, with ropes, acetylene torches and tractors, they toppled the huge statue of the Soviet tyrant. Another group of students went to the Radio Building, seeking to have their Fourteen Demands broadcast. The door was barred to them, and when they tried to force their way in, tear gas was used against them by the Communist security police or AVH, who were on guard there.

It is not clear how the order to open fire came to be given, but on the evening of October 23 AVH men began shooting at demonstrators in several parts of the city. Almost immediately there were defections from the Hungarian Army. These and munitions workers passed arms to insurgents who formed themselves into units of Freedom Fighters. Shooting between AVH detachments and Freedom Fighters raged through the night and were to continue for a week.

It was in such an atmosphere, on the morning of October 24, that tens of thousands of students, factory workers and white-collar employees marched down the boulevards to the Parliament Buildings, resuming their demonstrations. Along the way, they were joined by Soviet tanks. "The throng showed no hostility toward the soldiers who manned them," says Meray. "On the contrary, they began to fraternize with them." [31] They explained their cause, their goal of liberty and independence, and the Soviet soldiers listened and smiled, and allowed the Hungarian youths to climb aboard the tanks and plant Hungarian flags on them.

Peter Fryer, who went to Hungary as a correspondent for the London *Daily Worker* and returned as an anti-Communist, continues the narrative:

Entering Parliament Square they met another Soviet tank which had been sent to fire on them, and this tank, too, turned and joined the demonstration. In the Square were three more Soviet tanks and two armored cars. The crowd went right up to them and began to talk with the soldiers.[32]

These reports are corroborated by John MacCormac of *The New York Times,* who said that in front of the Astoria Hotel the Russian soldiers "shouted that they did not want to fire on unarmed Hungarian workers," [33] and by Endre Marton of the Associated Press, who observed that the fraternizing students and soldiers "were smiling uneasily." [34]

An AVH officer appeared and ordered the crowd to disperse. He threatened them, and the crowd responded with a torrent of abuse: "Pig! Assassin! Down with the AVH!"

These epithets may have been well-aimed, but were they well-timed? From the roof of the Ministry of Agriculture, across the street, the AVH troops opened fire on the crowd. Presumably some of the fraternizers were still sitting on Russian tanks. In any case, as Meray reports,

The Russians, not knowing who the men were who had fired into the square . . . thought they had been ambushed—that the fraternal appeals and embraces to which they had been subjected were aimed at disarming their vigilance and laying them open to a surprise attack at the moment when they least expected it. Accordingly, they fired mainly at the AVH, but also into the crowd of demonstrators.

The square was soon strewn with the dead and wounded. According to many witnesses, the dead alone must have numbered between 170 and 180.[35]

Consistently, the AVH forces comprised the mainstay of Hungarian Stalinism. In Budapest they were increasingly backed up by Soviet armor. But even here, under provocative and ambiguous conditions not calculated to encourage fraternization, the noted Italian orchestra conductor, Mario Rossi, who left Budapest on October 26, said: "All eye-witnesses agree absolutely that Russian troops as well as Hungarians joined the insurgents." [36] One such eye-witness, Andor Heller, reported this incident:

A few blocks from us there is a bridge. As I came by, several Freedom Fighters, together with some bystanders, were near one end of it. A Red Army tank was rumbling up, but instead of firing, the driver, a young Ukrainian, stuck his head out and waved. He stopped alongside our boys, jumped down and walked away. Three of the Freedom Fighters got in and moved off toward firing in the center of the city. [37]

This event and others like it were all the more remarkable since the Hungarians had no pretensions of nonviolence. In Budapest after October 24, few attempts at fraternization were made. More often, Hungarian youths approached tanks with Molotov cocktails or paving stones, seeking to disable the vehicle and kill its driver rather than to win both for the cause.

That side of the struggle is well-known—the savagery of the AVH, the heavy reliance of the Freedom Fighters on guerrilla tactics and the frequent excesses of the Soviet troops. But this pattern applied chiefly to Budapest and a few other places, such as Magyaróvár, where 5,000 unarmed demonstrators were the targets of machine guns and hand grenades wielded by AVH men, who killed eighty-five and wounded an unknown number of the townspeople. Although refraining from initiating violence, the people soon turned to the Hungarian Army barracks for weapons and stormed the AVH headquarters. AVH Lieutenant Jozsef Stefko, who had given the order to fire and had been wounded in the fighting, was tracked down in his hospital, brought out on a stretcher, and kicked and trampled to death.

Elsewhere there was little AVH strength, hence little provocation for incidents bringing Freedom Fighters and Soviet troops into conflict. In Györ, for example, on October 27 "there was a strong concentration of Soviet troops, who did not attack the insurgents, not even to defend themselves when demonstrators pelted them with stones." [38] A broadcast over Radio Vienna relayed information from the liberated city of Miskolc:

Radio Miskolc has called on the Hungarian authorities to grant political asylum to all Soviet soldiers who left their units during the last few days and sided with the Freedom Fighters, adding that there were many Soviet soldiers who would claim political asylum if granted it.[39]

By October 28, Soviet tanks commanded all key points in Budapest but the Freedom Fighters were in control in virtually all the rest of the country and with the accession of seven divisions that had held back until now, the Hungarian Army was clearly on their side. Political events were keeping pace, for Nagy had formed a government that included two non-Communists and now promised reforms, including dissolution of the AVH. Given the demonstrated unreliability of the Soviet garrisons outside the capital, the USSR deemed it wise to pull its forces out of Budapest. They began their withdrawal on October 29 and completed it on October 31.

Meanwhile, Nagy declared that the Freedom Fighters were to become the new national guard. Social Democratic, Smallholders and Peasant Party newspapers resumed publication for the first time since 1945 and Jozsef Cardinal Mindszenty was released from prison. For the next four days, Hungary was free. So definite was the fact that Free Petöfi Radio announced that "members of a Soviet battalion in the Gyongyos area have handed their arms over to the civilian population, stating that they do not wish to fight the Hungarian people." [40] Cardinal Mindszenty commented on the fact that "very many Russian soldiers" had been among those who fought against the old Stalinist regime.

The revolution appeared to be clearly victorious. Pending free elections, Nagy formed a new government made up of three Communists, eight representatives of parties formerly banned, and one independent.

Then at dawn on Sunday, November 4, the Soviet Union invaded Hungary with 6,000 tanks and 200,000 troops that had reportedly been secretly shifted to the Hungarian border from Soviet Central Asia. They struck instantly into Budapest, where the free radio gave its last frantic SOS alarm at 8:00 A.M. and then fell silent, speaking again at 5:00 P.M., no longer free.

Throughout the country and in isolated strongholds within the capital, the Hungarians maintained a brave but hopeless battle against the invaders. On November 9 the last of the free radio stations was silenced, and with the collapse of the Csepel Island stronghold in Budapest, large-scale fighting was over. Untold thousands of Hungarian youths were deported to the USSR. General Pal Maleter, leader of the Freedom Fighters, was lured to a parley with Soviet generals and taken prisoner, to be executed along with other leaders of free Hungary. Nagy was abducted, spirited out of the country and held in Rumania until June 15, 1958, when he was executed after a purported secret trial which probably never occurred at all. Others met a similar fate.

Moscow did not seek to reimpose the severe Stalinist regime of Matyas Rakosi, however, but installed as its puppet the moderate Janos Kadar, who had been a member of Nagy's Communist cabinet and a man who had been jailed along with Nagy during the height of Stalinist oppression. To Kadar was given the task of doing what Nagy had been supposed to do—institute reforms while keeping Hungary firmly under Communist control.

With the collapse of armed resistance, Hungarian workers held fast for weeks to the general strike they had begun on October 24-25. In Budapest in early November, appeals framed in tricolored stripes appeared on walls. A typical text, written about November 10, was this one: "Because enemy action is mainly causing the civilian population to suffer, it is necessary to put an end to desperate armed resistance. It is necessary to follow a course of passive, moral resistance." [41]

Such resistance was impossible to maintain for a protracted period on the economic plane. After five weeks, the workers' general strike ebbed to seventy per cent effectiveness, gradually declining to a sporadic level by the turn of the year. The Hungarian writers, who had sparked the revolt, maintained a silence that lasted for more than a year. In January, François Fejto wrote:

This strike still continues. One seeks in vain the signature of any reputed writer in all the official newspapers and periodicals. The voluminous Christmas issue of *Nepszabadsag* was published without a single article or poem or story by any known living writer.[42]

Eventually, most of the Petőfi Circle men who neither fled to the West nor were executed made their peace with the Kadar regime. Several who were imprisoned were released on parole in March 1960. Among them was Tibor Dery, who maintained his silence for six years and never recanted. His first story published since the uprising appeared in the fall of 1962. It described the last days of a Hungarian professor who decided to escape after the revolt of 1956 was crushed, but changed his mind within sight of the Austrian frontier. Tired, the professor sits down and freezes to death.

During August and September 1962 the Kadar government carried out a purge of Stalinists that included the expulsion from the Communist party of Rakosi, Gerö and others whom the 1956 revolt had unseated, and in 1963 Cardinal Mindszenty was enabled to step out of the U.S. Embassy, where he had taken refuge during the Soviet invasion. Thus, gradually, in six or seven years, Kadar moved to restore much of what had been won in as many days under Nagy.

Taking a shorter perspective on the Hungarian revolution, Professor Hugh Seton-Watson drew these lessons from it:

The Hungarians have showed us that a united nation can unseat a totalitarian regime in two days.

The second lesson is that the forces which led the revolution were precisely those on which the regime had counted for support. . . .

The third factor of course is the Hungarian army . . . built since 1947. . . .

Intellectual youth, workers and army joined in the Hungarian revolution. The rest of the nation . . . were of course behind them. Only the security police were against, and they were quickly overcome.[43]

Conclusion, or Beginning?

What, if anything, is the relevance of nonviolent action to Hungary's struggle for freedom? First, as a matter of record, it is important to note with Seton-Watson that the unsuspected possibility was actualized of marshaling one-sixth of the population of the capital city in demonstrations that were initially peaceful. In addition, we have seen the extent to which, even amid confusion and gunfire or stone-throwing, occupation troops showed a potential for moral conversion either to solidarity with the insurgents or to effective neutrality. These facts alone are of sufficient weight to warrant the inclusion of this episode in our study.

From here on, we have no further answers but a number of speculations that might be fruitful. One thing seems certain: with training and discipline in nonviolent conduct, the Freedom Fighters could have won considerably more Soviet troops to their side. More problematical is the question of the justly hated AVH forces. It is hard to imagine their being won over. Yet it was in fact impossible to win them at all, or to neutralize them, by venting verbal hatred on them, let alone shooting. Probably the possibilities of success in this direction would have hinged in part on a slower tempo for the whole course of events and a more restricted range of immediate goals. Given the Soviet acceptance of Poznan and Gomulka, there is reason to think that the perfidious onslaught of November 4 could have been avoided if Nagy had been permitted to consolidate earlier gains before moving to the extreme of leaving the Soviet bloc, with all that this implied, including the panic it must have induced in Moscow.

In short, it is a fact of history that the four days of freedom which Hungary obtained through a mixture of moral suasion and armed struggle were only part of a process that led through the Soviets' ruthless attack on November 4 to its culmination in the Kadar reforms of 1962, at great cost in human lives. Nonviolence could not have brought freedom—lasting freedom—in two days or in ten days any more than armed revolt. What was in fact accomplished might have been gained sooner and at less cost by consciously adhering, despite the AVH, to the peaceful demonstrations of October 22-23 and capitalizing on the losses suffered from the AVH, making a moral appeal to Nagy to call them to heel, or seeking support from the Soviet troops.

It is easy to speculate from the distant perspective of a six-year retrospect, when none of the options are open. Given all the many complex circumstances, none of the events that came to pass could have been anticipated and adequately provided for. This is true not only of Hungary but of all the historic episodes we have studied, in this and other categories. The past is past; let the dead bury their dead. It remains for us the living to extract from it the historical generalities of possibility and limitation to flesh out the bones of theory and thus equip ourselves as best we can to face the tasks that confront us in our own time and place. Among the conditions that will determine the history that we will make are these lessons from the past, and our assimilation of them.

REFERENCES IN CHAPTER 21

1 Leon Trotsky: *The History of the Russian Revolution* (New York: Simon and Schuster, Inc., 1932), Vol. 1, p. 105.
2 *Ibid.*, p. 108.
3 *Ibid.*
4 *Ibid.*

5   N. N. Sukhanov: *The Russian Revolution 1917* (London: Oxford, 1955), p. 6.
6   See Arthur Griffith: *The Resurrection of Hungary* (Dublin: Duffy and Co., 1904), p. 27.
7   Quoted in *Peace News* (London), September 7, 1962.
8   September 1, 1962.
9   Ernst Reuter: "The Berlin Revolt" in *The New Leader,* June 29, 1953, p. 2.
10 H. F. Stille: "The East German Workers' Revolt" in *The New International,* May-June 1953, p. 141.
11 *The New York Times,* June 20, 1953.
12 Stefan Brant: *The East German Rising* (London: Thames and Hudson, 1953), p. 193.
13 Melvin J. Lasky: "Germany's 'June Days' " in *The New Leader,* July 6, 1953, p. 7.
14 Rainer Hildebrandt: *The Explosion* (Boston: Little, Brown & Co., 1955), p. 50.
15 Norbert Muhlen: "The People Speak in a People's Democracy" in *The Reporter,* September 1, 1953, p. 14.
16 See Lasky, *op. cit.,* p. 7.
17 See Hildebrandt: *op. cit.,* pp. 139-145.
18 *The New York Times,* July 4, 1953.
19 Don Doane, Associated Press dispatch datelined Berlin, June 22, 1953.
20 Quoted in Joseph Wechsberg: "A Reporter in Germany" in *The New Yorker,* August 29, 1953, p. 38.
21 *Ibid.,* p. 49.
22 *Ibid.,* p. 50.
23 Stille, *op. cit.,* p. 141.
24 Quoted in Gaston Coblentz, dispatch from Berlin dated June 22, in *New York Herald Tribune,* June 23, 1953.
25 Stille, *op. cit.,* p. 141.
26 Hildebrandt, *op. cit.,* p. 103.
27 Brant, *op. cit.,* p. 151.
28 *Ibid.*
29 Tibor Meray: *Thirteen Days That Shook the Kremlin* (New York: Frederick A. Praeger, Inc., 1959), p. 65.
30 Full text in *ibid.,* p. 77.
31 *Ibid.,* p. 109f.
32 Peter Fryer: *Hungarian Tragedy* (London: Dobson, 1956), p. 46.
33 *The New York Times,* October 27, 1953.
34 Associated Press dispatch dated October 25, 1953.
35 Meray, *op. cit.,* p. 110f.
36 Dispatch from Torino, Italy, in *News Chronicle* (London), October 29, 1953. Quoted in Melvin J. Lasky, ed.: *The Hungarian Revolution* (New York: Frederick A. Praeger, Inc., 1957), p. 90.
37 Andor Heller: *No More Comrades* (Chicago: Henry Regnery Co., 1957), p. 70.
38 Dispatch from Nickelsdorf in *Neue Zürcher Zeitung,* October 29, 1956, quoted in Lasky, *op. cit.,* p. 102.
39 Quoted in Lasky, *op. cit.,* p. 102.
40 Quoted in *ibid.,* p. 223
41 Quoted by Viktor Woroszylski in *France Observateur,* January 3, 1957.

42   Francois Fejto in *France Observateur,* January 24, 1957. Quoted in Lasky, *op. cit.,* p. 304.
43   Hugh Seton-Watson: "Eruption in East Europe" in *Commentary,* December 1956, p. 521f. (Copyright is held by the American Jewish Committee.)

Glossary

Agapaic. From Greek verb *agapaon,* "to love"—adjectival coinage signifying *agapē* (q.v.).

Agapē. New Testament Greek word for "active love."

Ahimsa. Sanskrit word for Hindu concept of nonharm, translated by Gandhi as "nonviolence."

ANC. African National Congress.

Cadre. Person acting under a discipline, e.g., of nonviolent conduct.

Civil disobedience. Deliberate refusal to comply with laws considered unjust, or with laws enacted by an unjust government.

Civil resistance. Strategic application of civil disobedience.

CORE. Congress of Racial Equality.

CPP. Convention People's Party (Ghana).

Defiance campaign. South African application of civil disobedience.

Direct action. Social action exerting direct pressure as distinguished from political, legislative, judicial or other types of indirect action.

FOR. Fellowship of Reconciliation.

Force. Action, armed or otherwise, usually employing proportionate restraint under law.

NAACP. National Association for the Advancement of Colored People.

Noncooperation. A form of passive resistance.

Nonresistance. A type of nonviolence which does not overtly resist but combats evil with agapaic love.

Nonviolence. A generic category of actions and attitudes that deliberately abstain from using force and violence in situations to which they might be applied.

Nonviolent direct action. A type of nonviolence which usually operates assertively, by making incursions into disputed areas, as exemplified by the sit-in.

PAC. Pan-African Congress (South Africa).

Passive resistance. A type of nonviolence which acts by noncooperation, withdrawal, etc.

Positive action. Nkrumah's term for passive resistance.

Satyagraha. Gandhi's concept of nonviolent action, often translated as "soul force" or "the power of truth."

Satyagrahi. One who uses *satyagraha;* a Gandhian cadre.

Shanti sena. Peace army as conceived by Gandhi, Bhave and others.

SCLC. Southern Christian Leadership Conference.

SNCC. Student Nonviolent Coordinating Committee.

Unviolent. Term used to designate acts which do not happen to be violent, as contrasted with those that employ nonviolence.

Violence. Illegitimate or disproportionate harmful acts or attitudes.

Bibliography

The following is a brief, select list of books for further study.

Those included are largely theoretical, though some contain historical cases which have been omitted from this book. As noted, some of these books contain one or more chapters that are of interest; some may be read in their entirety. The immense Gandhian literature is represented by only a few titles; a more extensive list will be found in Mayer, listed below. For documentation of historical episodes presented in this book, see the chapter footnotes.

BALLOU, ADIN: *Christian Non-Resistance* (Philadelphia: McKim, 1846). The impact of Ballou's idea of "moral resistance" on Tolstoy and Gandhi did much to condition Twentieth-Century conceptions of nonviolence. Of scholarly historical interest— not for the general reader.

BONDURANT, JOAN V.: *Conquest of Violence* (Princeton University Press, 1958). A sympathetic and careful analysis of Gandhian *satyagraha,* with studies of five key Indian campaigns.

BONHOEFFER, DIETRICH: *The Cost of Discipleship* (New York: The Macmillan Co., 1960). The chapters on "Revenge" and "The Enemy" are highly pertinent to an understanding of nonviolent conduct for Christians.

CAPITINI, ALDO: *La Nonviolenza, Oggi* (Milano: Comunità, 1962). A general study along pacifist-Gandhian lines with appendixes documenting noncooperation under the Mussolini regime, Italian peace marches in 1960 and 1961, etc.

CASE, CLARENCE MARSH: *Non-Violent Coercion* (New York: Century Co., 1923). A pioneer sociological study that evaluates techniques of nonviolence and presents a useful brief history of religious nonresistance, conscientious objection and Gandhi's early campaigns.

CORMAN, LOUIS: *La Non-Violence* (Paris: Stock, 1949). Of chief interest are the chapters on Gandhi and Christianity, nonviolence in daily life and in the education of children. By a noted psychologist.

GALTUNG, JOHAN: *Forsvar Uten Militærwesen* (Oslo, Folkereisning Mot Krig, c. 1959). A pacifist booklet which includes a useful chapter on nonviolent national defense. By a noted social scientist.

GANDHI, MOHANDAS K.: *Nonviolent Resistance* (New York: Schocken, Books, 1962). A collection of newspaper articles from *Young India* and *Harijan,* rooted in the Indian struggle, which represents the best of Gandhi's thinking on questions of theory. Also published in India under the title *Satyagraha.*

GREGG, RICHARD B.: *The Power of Nonviolence* (Nyack, N.Y.: Fellowship Publications, 1959). Second revised edition of a book that has had considerable influence since it first appeared in 1934. The chapter on "moral jiu-jitsu" is of particular interest.

HERSHBERGER, GUY F.: *War, Peace and Nonresistance* (Scottdale, Pa.: Herald Press, 1944). A cogent presentation of Christian nonresistance as distinguished from modern pacifism and nonviolent resistance.

KING, MARTIN LUTHER, JR.: *Strength to Love* (New York: Harper & Row, 1963). The autobiographical essay, "Pilgrimage to Nonviolence," and sermons on "Love in Action" and "Loving Your Enemies" are especially valuable but by no means the only chapters worth reading.

KUPER, LEO: *Passive Resistance in South Africa* (New Haven: Yale University Press, 1957). The chapter on "The Sociological Nature of Passive Resistance" is of primary importance for theory.

LAKEY, GEORGE RUSSELL: *The Sociological Mechanisms of Nonviolent Action* (Philadelphia: University of Pennsylvania, unpublished M.A. thesis, 1962). A study which builds on the work of Case and Gregg and adds much detail from subsequent scholarship.

LEWIS, JOHN: *The Case Against Pacifism* (London: Allen & Unwin, 1940). A Marxist critique which embodies a healthy corrective for sentimental interpretations of purportedly nonviolent historical episodes.

LIGT, BARTHÉLEMY DE: *The Conquest of Violence* (New York: E. P. Dutton & Co., Inc., 1938). Highly propagandistic and largely outdated, this book nevertheless includes a chapter on "Lessons of History" which can serve as a basis for research. Not all of his examples will withstand scrutiny.

MAYER, PETER, ed.: *The Nonviolent Tradition* (New York: Orion Press, 1964). An anthology of writings on peace rather than nonviolence, it nevertheless contains some interesting material and an extensive bibliography.

MAYR, KASPAR: *Der Andere Weg* (Nürnberg, Germany: Glock und Lutz, 1957). An exposition of Christian pacifism which includes insights about nonviolence.

MITCHELL, GLENFORD E., and PEACE, WILLIAM H., III, eds.: *The Angry Black South* (New York: Corinth Books, Inc., 1962). The chapter on "Nonviolence" by Robert Brookins Gore, a seasoned cadre, is well worth study.

MURTY, K. S., and BOUQUET, A. C.: *Studies in the Problems of Peace* (New York: Asia Books, 1960). The chapter on "The Philosophies of Ahimsa and Forgiveness" embodies useful information as well as a penetrating critique of nonviolence.

MUSTE, A. J.: *Nonviolence in an Aggressive World* (New York: Harper & Brothers, 1940). A discussion of the relevance of nonviolence to the political and economic situation of the United States before World War II, with emphasis on labor struggles.

NANDA, B. R.: *Mahatma Gandhi* (Boston: Beacon Press, Inc., 1958). Probably the best brief biography of Gandhi as a leader on the socio-political scene.

RAMSEY, PAUL: *Christian Ethics and the Sit-In* (New York: Association Press, 1961). A conservatively oriented brief critique of some of the principles of nonviolence, with special attention to civil disobedience.

RÉGAMEY, PIE: *Non-Violence et Conscience Chrétienne* (Paris: Cerf, 1958). An incisive theological study from a largely

Thomistic perspective, which includes a detailed and balanced inquiry into a variety of questions posed by nonviolence.

SHARP, GENE: *The Politics of Nonviolent Action* (unpublished book manuscript). A monumental study of the techniques and dynamics of nonviolence with particular reference to its relationship to political power. The author is a sociologist at Oxford University who has done important studies such as *Gandhi Wields the Weapon of Moral Power* and *Gandhi Faces the Storm* (Ahmedabad: Navajivan).

SIBLEY, MULFORD Q., ed.: *The Quiet Battle* (Garden City, N.Y.: Doubleday & Co., Anchor Books, 1963). An anthology of classic texts on nonviolence, including documentation of several historic episodes, chosen by a noted political scientist.

TENDULKAR, D. G.: *Mahatma* (Bombay: Jhaveri & Tendulkar, 1954). This eight-volume biography is the most comprehensive study of Gandhi's career and includes an extensive bibliography.

TROCMÉ, ANDRÉ: *Jésus-Christ et la Révolution Non Violente* (Geneva: Labor et Fides, 1961). A biblical study which examines the teachings of Jesus in their historical context, contrasting them with the way of the Zealots and other sects and arguing persuasively for the relevance of Christian nonviolence to social struggle. By a French Reformed pastor.

WEINBERG, ARTHUR and LILA, eds.: *Instead of Violence* (New York: Grossman, 1963). Although chiefly an anthology of writings on peace, this book also includes brief pieces on nonviolence, from Lao-tzu to Danilo Dolci.

WOLFF, OTTO: *Mahatma und Christus* (Berlin: Lettner, 1955). A thorough-going and generally critical study of Gandhi's life, character and teachings. By a German Evangelical theologian.

WRIGHT, QUINCY, et. al., eds.: *Preventing World War Three* (New York: Simon & Schuster, Inc., 1963). The chapter by Arne Naess on "Nonmilitary Defense" is highly relevant.

Index

M. K. GANDHI
COLLECTED WRITINGS ON
NON-VIOLENT RESISTANCE *(Satyagraha)*

The gathering storm of new social forces and aspirations in America today has turned fresh attention to Gandhi's ideas on non-violence. That Gandhi draws in part on Emerson and Thoreau gives him a further relevance to the American scene. But the system of massive resistance which he pioneered is broad in its application and many-sided in form. The self-training which he describes in these pages has welded inert groups into powerful social movements. Gandhi himself does not claim finality for his methods; he traces their evolution as they were applied in successive situations. But his teachings and experience, told here in his own words, are invaluable for all future students and participants in the struggle for social reform.

"Gandhi strove . . . to make religious faith re-enter the realm of politics. He endeavored to overcome the growing estrangement between politics and religion." — MARTIN BUBER

paper $1.95